African Indigenous Knowledge and the Disciplines

ANTI-COLONIAL EDUCATIONAL PERSPECTIVES FOR TRANSFORMATIVE CHANGE

Volume 2

Scope

Informed by an anti-colonial spirit of resistance to injustices, this book series examines the ways and the degree to which the legacy of colonialism continues to influence the content of school curriculum, shape teachers' teaching practices, and impact the outcome of the academic success of students, including students of color. Further, books published in this series illuminate the manner in which the legacy of colonialism remains one of the root causes of educational and socio-economic inequalities. This series also analyzes the ways and the extent to which such legacy has been responsible for many forms of classism that are race- and language-based. By so doing, this series illuminates the manner in which race intersects with class and language affecting the psychological, educational, cultural, and socio-economic conditions of historically and racially disenfranchised communities. All in all, this series highlights the ways and the degree to which the legacy of colonialism along with race-, language-, class- and gender-based discrimination continue to affect the existence of people, particularly people of color.

African Indigenous Knowledge and the Disciplines

Edited by

Gloria Emeagwali
Central Connecticut State University, USA

and

George J. Sefa Dei
University of Toronto, Canada

SENSE PUBLISHERS
ROTTERDAM / BOSTON / TAIPEI

A C.I.P. record for this book is available from the Library of Congress.

ISBN 978-94-6209-768-1 (paperback)
ISBN 978-94-6209-769-8 (hardback)
ISBN 978-94-6209-770-4 (e-book)

Published by: Sense Publishers,
P.O. Box 21858, 3001 AW Rotterdam, The Netherlands
https://www.sensepublishers.com/

Printed on acid-free paper

TABLE OF CONTENTS

ACKNOWLEDGEMENTS

In drawing inspiration for this project, one of us recalls two Western-trained Nigerian doctors who testified to the efficacy, brilliance, and even superiority in some cases of Indigenous African medical practice, but who were too terrified of their Western-trained instructors and peers to openly acknowledge their findings. They wanted to remain anonymous. They were afraid of being downgraded by their western-trained colleagues should their identity be known. We knew of the tyranny and viciousness of Eurocentric orthodoxy before coming into contact with these scholars; but that encounter strengthened a determination to pursue our interest in Indigenous Knowledge Systems and to make the case even stronger for the urgent decolonization of the academy – whether in terms of history, art, chemistry, agricultural science, mathematics, or, in this case, medicine. Eurocentric prejudice, intimidation, and disinformation must be challenged for Indigenous Studies and a decolonized academy to grow and blossom.

Gloria Emeagwali wishes to acknowledge Gumbo Mishack and M. Mosimege (South Africa); Ayele Bekerie (Ethiopia); Toyin Falola, Nurudeen Abubakar, M. Z. Zaruwa, Samuel Gwimbe, Okpeh Okpeh, CBN Ogbogbo, Olayemi Akinwumi (Nigeria); Paul Tarus (Kenya); Atia Apusigah (Ghana); Francis Gudyanga (Zimbabwe); Abdul Bangura (U.S and Sierra Leone); and Saba Saakana, Maureen Warner- Lewis (Trinidad & Tobago), who are among the special circle of scholars profoundly committed to Indigenous Studies, directly or indirectly, and with whom she has interacted over the years. They recognize that our enterprise is a noble one. We offer special thanks to all the contributors to this text for making this project possible. We also recognize the millions of local scientists and practitioners in various communities across Africa and its Diaspora, often unrecognized, but steadfast in their experimentation with the natural world and their environment, with very limited assistance from their respective neo-colonial governments, if any at all. Special thanks go to Ndidi Susan Emeagwali, former Managing Editor of *Techniques*, a publication of the Association for Career and Technical Education (ACTE). Her copy editing skills are superb.

George Dei would like to thank the students in his "African Development, Modernization and Development" and "Indigenous Knowledges and De-colonization" classes at the Ontario Institute for Studies in Education of the the University of Toronto (OISE/UT) for ideas shared with him over the years. These ideas have helped to shape his thinking on Indigenous knowledges in African Contexts. He also extends deep appreciation for his intellectual affiliation with faculty, staff, and students at the Centre For School and Community Science and Technology Studies (SACOST), University of Education, Winneba, Ghana, and the many local researchers of his Social Sciences and Humanities Research Council - sponsored project on African Indigenous Philosophies; they have been influential in his thinking and scholarly work.

ACKNOWLEDGEMENTS

Finally, we would both like to thank Sense Publishers for publishing this book, and particularly Michel Lokhorst, who has long been a champion in ensuring that the ideas of scholars in the Global South receive hearing in mainstream sources.

Gloria Emeagwali and George Dei

GLORIA EMEAGWALI AND GEORGE J. SEFA DEI

INTRODUCTION

The contribution of Africa to the development of the disciplines, particularly social science, has been well-noted (see Bates, Mudimbe, & O'Barr, 1993). Africa has been a rich source of data for the development of social science theories and paradigms. Academic scholarship has a duty to recognize these local cultural knowings as legitimate sources of knowledge for a number of reasons; foremost, to recognize African peoples as producers and creators of knowledge. Every society has its cultural knowledge system and it is on this basis that what is deemed scholarship rests. Africans have not been merely consumers of knowledge. Ancient African civilizations bore sophisticated knowledge systems deeply embedded in local culture and social politics. Local, indigenous knowledge resides in cultural memories. Through time, such forms of knowledge while transformed have not been abandoned by rural communities. Such knowledge has adapted to the times to serve pressing social issues and challenges. Such knowledge has not remained static, neither has it been confined to the shores of the African continent. Like all knowledge systems, such knowledges have diffused and interacted with other ways of knowing from other communities. In fact, many indigenous communities share knowledge systems in common with each other in terms of the principles, concepts, and ideas behind their knowledge. Unfortunately, rather than western science acknowledging the multiple, collaborative, and accumulative dimensions of knowledge, we see attempts to either dismiss, devalue, or negate indigenous knowledge as being not worthy of scholarly engagement. We have the sad situation where some uninformed, brainwashed African scholars themselves categorize their own indigenous ways of knowing as 'myths,' 'superstition,' and non-science. Rather than interrogate conventional understandings of science, what we have witnessed are attempts to work with narrow definitions of science and scholarship (see Asabere-Ameyaw, Dei, & Raheem, 2012). We need to reclaim Africa's indigenous ways of knowing to highlight her contributions and place in the global space of public knowledge production, and to challenge some of these questionable attitudes and forms of misinformation and prejudice.

Before proceeding any further, we would like to take up the question of whether the knowledge systems of Africa and Africans can be deemed 'Indigenous.' It is easy to quickly dismiss this question as being unworthy of our consideration, but we find it necessary to focus on this 'misguided' question given that the issue surfaces in some academic circles and conversations even today (see also Adefarakan, 2011). The *Indigenous* is contested for various reasons. For example, in North America, African *Indigeneity* is juxtaposed to Aboriginal *Indigeneity* in discourse of hierarchies or legitimacies. Our concern, of course, should not be confused with the legitimate expectation that African scholars who articulate

African *Indigeneity* must also acknowledge the case of the Indigenous and Aboriginal peoples in the Americas, and their struggle to reclaim land and self-autonomy. We come back to the question of African *Indigeneity* because as Dei (2008) has argued, to articulate an *Indigenous* discursive framework we must be duly informed by a complex knowledge base of the *Indigenous* in multiple and global contexts in Africa, Asia, North America, Europe, the Caribbean, and Latin America.

We must transcend the particular understanding of *Indigenous* informed by very restrictive Eurocentric definitions of *Indigeneity*. The understanding of the *Indigenous* and *Indigeneity* cannot be constructed within Western or Euro-American hegemonic conceptual schemes, and imposed on all groups across time and space. In other words, we assert that we must read the *Indigenous* in terms of an existence prior to European colonization of land in the various continents. However important Christopher Columbus and the *conquistadores* may appear to some, the world existed prior to the exploits of one group of European explorers, bandits, and pirates. Throughout Africa notwithstanding, inspite of ongoing colonizations and the continuing effects of globalization, there are people, particularly in rural communities, who still associate their existence to, and with, the land, and with their immediate socio-physical environments and surroundings. Land has been a source of *Indigenous* identity for Africans, in that through associations with the land, local cultures, spiritualities, politics, economics, and the relations of society to Nature are defined. There are knowledges associated with the land that continue to guide everyday existence. People continue to negotiate identities, cultures, and spiritualities with particular understandings of the place of the human in their environments. These phenomena constitute important dimensions of the knowledgebase, and such knowledge also informs everyday existence.

African *Indigeneity* must be read as both a process and a form of identity. It is an identity that defines who a people are at a particular point in time. But it is also a recognition that such identities are in a continual process of existence. The lesson here is that a peoples' *Indigeneity* and *Indigenousness* is not simply taken away from them simply because they encounter others on their homeland. The Eurocentric constructions of the *Indigenous* as primitive, culture-based, and static is a ploy to privilege European identity, and should be distinguished from what the people claim and assert of their own *Indigeniety* and *Indigenousness*. The latter is about the affirmation of self, community, history, culture, tradition, heritage, and ancestry. Eurocentric constructions are about establishing cultures of hierarchies as a way to accord privilege and power. This is how racism works and has worked in the past. To deny African peoples' their *Indigeneity* with the rationale that colonialism disrupted their self-defined and collectively actualized existence and their associations with the Land and their homeland, is itself racist and endorses the misguided and disingenuous insinuations of white supremacist ideology. We must ask why is it difficult to acknowledge African *Indigeneity* in contrast to the claim and assertion of others about their *Indigenous* existence, especially given the global reach of colonialism? What epistemological claims do we make in such disavowal?

If we begin to work seriously with the understanding that knowledge resides in people and in cultural memory, in accumulated techniques, skills, and strategies for survival, in epistemological frameworks and points of reference, in language and oral and written forms of documentation, in value systems and their diverse modes of explanation, in cosmology and various ways of understanding the universe we live in – inspite of European colonialism, we would recognize the meaning and significance of African *Indigeneity.*

We have written this book to contest knowledge, and particularly hegemonic knowledges that tend to masquerade as universal knowledges. Our learning objective has been to situate African Indigenous Knowledges in critical discussions about knowledge production in the academy. We examine the processes of interrogating, validating, and disseminating Indigenous African Knowledge Systems internally and globally and the various ways of knowing. This is no easy task. While we recognize the relevance of local and Indigenous African knowledges, we are also under no illusion as to the discriminatory tendencies discernible in the academy. Not all knowledges are given the same amount of capital in the academy. While some bodies of knowledge have been privileged and made dominant, other forms of knowledge are still being contested and are in the process of being delegitimized. Consequently, for us, this intellectual foray into African Indigenous Knowledge System has been a way to both politically and intellectually contest the denial of African ways of knowing, in science and scholarship. This book is thus a call for a paradigmatic shift in how we come to learn, teach, and study Africa in terms of content, subject matter, and overall curriculum. It is about an epistemic shift in Indigenous Knowledge Studies on Africa and the African Diaspora. African Indigenous Knowledge does not sit well with some scholars who feel threatened because of its critique of knowledge production in the academy and its challenge to the claims and assumptions of the exclusivity of western science. The anti-Indigenousness of the Western academy can be traced to the denial of African humanity dating back to the era of conquest, human trafficking, settler colonialism, and occupation. It is also linked to an obstinate reluctance to decolonize the academy. Because of the Eurocentric dismissal of Africa-centered knowledge systems, African scholars have been confronted with the task of arguing for their acceptability in the academy, on terms established by hegemonic forces. We must challenge this. African knowledge systems must be evaluated and taught on the principles established in local communities which serve to regulate knowledge production, validation, use and dissemination.

There are some questions that must be dealt with upfront as we embark on this intellectual journey to highlight, endorse, legitimize, validate and produce cultural knowledge systems on Africa's own terms. We need to follow and comprehend the epistemological, ontological, methodological, and axiological basis of Africa's Indigenous Knowledge Systems. What epistemological claims do we make in the various branches of knowledge? How can African scholars and Africanists posit and present African Indigenous Knowledge, and liberate, empower, and decolonize the field from Western domination in the process? We need to identify the epistemological foundations of indigenous knowledge and discover, evaluate, and understand how knowledge is created and disseminated in local communities. We need to understand and recognize the holistic, organic, and multidimensional interconnections of body, mind, soul, and spirit, as well as the interface of society, culture, and Nature. We need to establish the methodologies of studying African Indigenous Knowledges, including knowledge as co-created between producers, learners and users, and a methodological approach to knowledge inquiry that emphasizes principles of circularity, association with the Land and environments, and the integrative nature of social facts. There is also a need to deal with the political and ethical questions of African Indigenous Knowledges, as these relate to human survival and the pursuit of the causes of collectivity, community, and the common good.

This book sets out to identify aspects of Indigenous Knowledges that can be relevant to how we speak, teach, and learn about the academic disciplines. The various chapters have identified Indigenous Knowledges that can inform the teachings of these disciplines in our schools, colleges, and universities.

Gloria Emeagwali's opening chapter conceptualizes issues related to modernization, triumphalism, and neo-liberalism, to reconfirm the importance of Indigenous Knowledge Systems. She emphasizes the role of the historian in the retrieval and transmission of the corpus of strategies, practices, techniques, tools, intellectual resources, explanations, beliefs, and values that we associate with IKS. The point is made that history and the historian are crucial for the regeneration of Indigenous Knowledge Systems.

One of the under-researched areas of African Indigenous Knowledge Systems is chemistry. In the second, third, and fourth chapters of this text, Zaruwa, Barminas, Apampa, Ibok, and Kwaghe, scholars and professors at Adamawa State University, Nigeria, fill this gap and provide us with expert analyses of some of the underlying chemical processes historically generated by local indigenous scientists, in their brewing and tanning activities, with reference to Northeast Nigeria.

Samuel Barde Gwimbe follows with a scholarly discussion of ancient and contemporary terraces and the environmental and ecological techniques utilized in two Nigeria regions. His focus is on the Gwoza terraces, extended more than 40, 000 miles over mountainous terrain, in the Nigerian-Cameroonian area in the northeast, and the agricultural terraces of the Central Nigerian area. These five chapters highlight the ingenuity and skill of indigenous practitioners in the area of indigenous agricultural engineering and chemistry.

Professor Paulus Gerdes, President of the Commission for African Mathematics, AMUCHMA (Comissão da União Matemática Africana para a História da Matemática em África), 1986 to 2013, takes the discussion of IKS into the realm of Mathematics with a focus on endogenous experimentation and invention in southern Africa, more specifically, Mozambique. In his chapter, he explains that 'the richness of geometric ideas embedded and developed in a particular cultural practice' is illustrated through the example of Tonga basket weavers. He concludes by pointing out that the mastery of mathematical calculation in practical terms, as manifested in basketry, is unprecedented.

One of the core areas of African Knowledge Systems is Traditional Medicine. There are two chapters related to this subject, namely, chapters 8 & 9. Sarfo Nimoh and R.O Olaoye complement each other. Nimoh compares mainstream medicine with the Indigenous Medical Tradition, highlighting strengths and weaknesses, while Olaoye gives a glimpse into the training of practitioners, and the networking engaged in by practitioners, in terms of trade fairs and interpersonal contact.

The last four chapters are preoccupied with the curriculum. Obiokor reflects on art education; Fredua-Kwarteng and Ahia on Mathematics education; and Shizha on the curriculum in general. Obiokor, in chapter 10, discusses the relevance of Nigerian education to traditional society, and outlines the legacy of British colonial education in Nigeria. He explores the importance of local context in education and offers some insights on developing art programs that better serve indigenous and traditional value systems in the Nigerian case. Edward Shizha, in the chapter that follows, chapter eleven, discusses the benefits of indigenizing school curriculum in Africa and the role of indigenous knowledge or traditional ecological knowledge, in the indigenization process. Professor Shizha reminds us that 'pedagogy is crucial in determining success or failure in the schools' and that students learn best 'when the curriculum or knowledge is mediated' in a manner consistent with the methodologies they are used to. In the course of the chapter, he uses postcolonial discourse to analyze school curriculum in African schools. In chapter 12, Fredua-Kwarteng and Ahia draw mainly from their experiences as mathematics educators with a focus on the development of mathematical proficiency. Their underlying proposition is that in order to indigenize the curriculum, an appropriate local language of instruction must be used, and that there are unsavoury implications should one be denied one's mother tongue in the learning process.

The final chapter, authored by George Dei, is about infusing Indigenous Knowledges into the curricula of schools, colleges, and university. Dei sees this as a major obligatory challenge and so, too, the democratization and decolonization of the academy through an African-centred interpretation that would help local communities engage in meaningful problem-solving development and social change. Without such a process of indigenization, the curriculum would continue to be a source of alienation and dependency.

REFERENCES

Adefarakan, T. (2011). Reconceptualising the indigenous from anti-colonial and Black feminist perspectives: Living and imagining indigeneity differently. In *Indigenous Philosophies and Critical Education* (pp. 34-52). New York: Peter Lang.

Bates, R. H., Mudimbe, V. Y., & O'Barr, J. (1993). *African and the disciplines.* Chicago: University of Chicago Press.

Dei, G. J. S. (2008). Indigenous knowledge studies and the next generation: Pedagogical possibilities for anti-colonial education. *Australian Journal of Indigenous Education, 37,* Supplement, 5-13.

Emeagwali, G. (Ed.). (2006). *Africa and the academy: Challenging hegemonic discourses on Africa.* New Jersey: Africa World Press.

GLORIA EMEAGWALI

1. INTERSECTIONS BETWEEN AFRICA'S INDIGENOUS KNOWLEDGE SYSTEMS AND HISTORY

INTRODUCTION

In this chapter, we identify some of the issues related to the production, utilization, validation, transmission, and preservation of Indigenous Knowledge Systems (IK), in general, and Africa's Indigenous Knowledge Systems (AIK), in particular. We explore the rationale for research in this multidisciplinary field. In the course of discussion we make reference to selected primary sources that are of significance to historians in particular, and scholars of IK in general. Modernization, triumphalism, and neo-liberalism are also discussed in the course of the chapter to reconfirm the importance of alternative methodologies and local knowledge. The role of the historian in the retrieval, regeneration, and transmission of IK is explored and we conclude with recommendations for the enhancement of our professional capabilities as historians with respect to Indigenous Studies.

INDIGENOUS KNOWLEDGE AND ITS CRITICS

Indigenous Knowledge (IK) may be defined as the cumulative body of strategies, practices, techniques, tools, intellectual resources, explanations, beliefs, and values accumulated over time in a particular locality, without the interference and impositions of external hegemonic forces. Indigenous Knowledge Systems are not confined to the material sphere, but often interconnect with spiritual and non-material realms of existence. As pointed out by George Sefa Dei, however, Indigenous Knowledge is not static nor are we engaged in an exercise of romanticization (Dei, 2008). Nor is absolute insularity the objective. We simply refuse to devalue, ignore, underestimate, and marginalize indigenous forms of knowing, and alternative modes of discourse. We are also committed to highlighting African indigenous inventiveness for the awareness of ungrateful recipients and beneficiaries around the world. Edward Shizha has pointed out that the academy was 'the epicenter of colonial hegemony, indoctrination, and mental colonization,' and that the decolonization process entails a process of 'reclaiming, rethinking, reconstituting, rewriting, and validating' indigenous knowledge, and by implication, Africa's history (Shizha, 2010). Given the multi-layered structure of the Academy, the process is valid for primary, secondary, and tertiary education, and for students as well as educators, for whom education and knowledge meant the 'assimilation of eurocentric middle class habitus' (Shizha, 2010). A focus on

G. Emeagwali & G. J. S. Dei (eds.), African Indigenous Knowledge and the Disciplines, 1–17.

African cultural resource knowledge is a means of 'epistemological recuperation' and is 'counter-hegemonic' (Dei, 2008). The decolonization of the African Academy remains one of the biggest challenges not only in terms of the curriculum, teaching strategies, and textbooks, but also in terms of the democratization of knowledge and the regeneration, evaluation, and adaptation of old epistemologies to suit new post-colonial realities. Indigenous Knowledge provides a beacon of light within the tunnel of eurocentric dogma, misinformation, and untruths.

There are numerous critics of Indigenous Knowledge, among them exponents of the modernization school, and the neo-conservative ideologues associated with neoliberal thought and practice (Emeagwali, 2011, 2006). Modernization theorists and advocates are prone to view society with a rather simplistic *Rostovian* unilinearity, whereby positive societal change is conceived as a unidirectional movement toward a fixed and abstract goal called 'modernity:' a haven where, supposedly, all cultural and religious sensibilities are either numbed, or totally eradicated, and, where eurocentric values and norms reign supreme. The modernization theorists and advocates do not appreciate technological, cultural, and ethnic diversity, and define success in terms of slavish conformity and subordination to western norms and values. They differ slightly from their neoclassical and neoconservative counterparts, for whom the price mechanism and the market reign supreme, and over whom individualistic profit-seeking idols such as *the bull* and *the bear* preside. Whilst *the bull, the bear,* and *self-interest* are among the conceptual underpinnings of neoclassical and neoconservative thought, for the modernization theorists, narrow eurocentric-defined concepts labeled as *rationality* and *science* are seen as engines of progress and success. It is useful to note that philosophers of science, such as the late Feyerabend, cautioned against single-minded, simplistic definitions of what science was, and what it was not, since, for him, science and scientific methodology were as pluralistic, and diverse, as they were multidimensional (Feyerabend, 2010). Modernization theorists and their neo-liberal counterparts differ from scholars and practitioners of Indigenous Knowledge Systems in their views on equity, fairness, and access. For modernization advocates, rationality leads to progress, and progress to capacity-building and 'modernity.' But there is little discussion of the kinds of economic systems and distributive mechanisms inherent in the newly emerging 'modern' society envisioned by them. Not only do they fail to make a theoretical distinction between 'westernization' and the process they pontificate about, namely, 'modernity,' they also fail to confront the possibility that the society they try to construct may be considerably more dysfunctional and exploitative than the society they are at pains to replace. Very little attention is paid by modernization theorists to the nature of the distributive system they seek to create. In this mode, they differ from their neo-classical/neo-conservative ideologues who claim, from the start, that self-interest and greed are 'good' incentives to growth, and that wealth necessarily trickles down from the entrepreneurial and financial elite to the lower rungs of society, in a process that they acknowledge to be unfair. Greed is good, argue the neo-liberals, and profit-making, the price mechanism, individualism, privatization, and the commodification of everything on the planet, necessary pathways towards the promised land. Communitarianism and social benefit-sharing are anathemas to this mode of thinking. Modernization theorists, and those who envisage 'modernity' as the final destination, very often leave the issue of distribution hanging in the balance, and undefined. What is clear, though, is that for both schools of thought, Indigenous Knowledge is seen as being somewhat atavistic, primordial, and backward, and the quest for equity, dignity, respect, and accessibility, superfluous. In defense, scholars of IK have argued that no society or segment should be ostracized and relegated to a status of inferiority. They challenge arrogant, paternalistic, and overbearing ideologues, some of whom are complicit in marginalizing and devaluing systems of thought that do not fit within supremacist and racial exclusivity. They argue that IK must be part and parcel of the decolonization process and a challenge to modernization and neoconservative triumphalism, as well as to Western attempts at epistemological disenfranchisement of millions of people around the globe (Chilisa, 2012).

During the colonial era and in the post-colony, not only were the majority of scholars, at various levels, afraid to challenge the dominant eurocentered and eurocentric knowledge system and its values, they were also reluctant to admit, both to themselves and publicly, that their 'non-lettered' compatriots, shoved to the lower rungs of society, were indeed repositories of valuable primary knowledge. Some Western-trained doctors admitted privately the superiority of indigenous medical techniques in certain areas, but were too terrified to expand on this for fear of being ridiculed, and possibly 'demoted,' by their Western peers. Although they recognized the value of indigenous knowledge, they were forced to privilege only one epistemological and methodological tradition at the expense of all others. We must note also the tyranny of some religious systems in creating this atmosphere of fear, denial, and exclusion.

South Asian researchers of the defense laboratory in Assam, India, recently announced their intention to use the local chili pepper, 'bhut jolokia,' in the creation of non-toxic, environmentally friendly, aerosol sprays inspired by local knowledge. Meanwhile, researchers have identified frogs as useful earthquake predictors, given their ability to detect pre-seismic activity such as the release of gases and charged particles. Indigenous communities in several regions around the world have invariably proposed a connection between the behavior of animals and environmental activity such as earthquakes or tornadoes – additional testimony that local knowledge very often has a scientific basis.

Dei suggests in his discourse on the decolonization of knowledge, that there is indeed a direct relationship between Indigenous Knowledge and development. In his view, development relates to how people use 'their own creativity and resourcefulness' to respond 'to major economic and ecological stressors' (Dei, 2009). The suggestion is that development is more likely to be sustainable and sustained if driven by indigenous knowledge, growing as it were from local specificities.

AFRICAN INDIGENOUS KNOWLEDGE SYSTEMS

Africa's AIK includes a corpus of ideas and practices in various sectors such as medicine, agronomy, food processing, chemistry, textiles, architecture, biology, geography, and engineering, as well as history and literature. It is by definition multidisciplinary. For Sipho Seepe, AIK is also about 'reopening crucial files that were closed in the chaos and violence of colonialism' (Seepe, 2001). This accumulated knowledge is of relevance to self-esteem, sustained indigenous inventiveness, endogenous technological growth, and employment generation. Research into various endogenous resources of Africa is vital for decolonizing existing academies and research programs within and across institutions. Some questions remain. Should AIK blend old and new knowledge systems or should it integrate into the mainstream? Should it be dominated by a single scientific framework or should it move towards methodological pluralism rather than a single unified theory, so to speak? Should some of the interdisciplinary barriers be removed and if so how? These are issues yet to be resolved. But there is no doubt that historians, given their broad understanding of human society over time and space, and given their significant roles as custodians, narrators, documenters, and interpreters of the past, have a prominent role to play in AIK Studies.

Five waves of nationalists and liberators freed Africans from colonial and political domination, in what Onimode once referred to as 'flag independence.' The revolution took place in the 1950s and 1960s in several African countries, but the Portuguese colonies of Angola, Mozambique, and Guinea Bissau would follow a decade and a half later, in the mid-1970s. The hegemonic colonial edifice crumbled politically with the independence of Zimbabwe, in 1980, and Namibia and South Africa by the early 1990s (Falola, 2012; Khapoya, 2013; Gilbert et al., 2012). However, the decolonization of the African Academy remains one of the biggest challenges, not only in terms of the curriculum, teaching strategies, and textbooks, but also in terms of the democratization of knowledge, and the regeneration and adaptation of old epistemologies to suit new post-colonial realities. The Academy is indeed a site of struggle (Kovach, 2012).

Indigenous Knowledge Studies is crucial in this exercise, and history and the historian play vital roles. The African informal sector constituted at least 50% of economic activity in several of Africa's 53 nation states two decades ago (Baratt Brown). Soap makers, textile manufacturers, brewers of alcoholic beverages, producers of local pharmacological products, and manufacturers of a variety of tuber and cereal based flour, generated multiplier effects in the economy in the context of techniques and skills associated with indigenous knowledge. Actors within the informal sector also generated principles about business management and finance, and business etiquette was taken into consideration and improved upon in efforts to restructure and advance society in the context of self-reliance and sustainability.

The global financial meltdown of 2008 was a sober reminder to scholars, that, in the final analysis, unbridled free markets were not a panacea (Emeagwali, 2006, 2011; Stiglitz, 2010; Lewis, 2010; Skene, 2010; Roubini, 2010; Johnson & Kwak,

2010). Neither is overdependence on external financing and technical resources. The correct pathway to success apparently lies with the self-reliance of countries on their local primary resources and human capital, and the relentless, pragmatic, and judicious utilization of their indigenous and endogenous knowledge in people-centered structures that are inclusive, non-elitist and open to innovations and adaptations – a goal that would not be fully realized without historical memory and the historian's craft.

Ironically enough, transnational corporations are actively appropriating local knowledge simultaneous with contemporary attempts at erasing historical knowledge within local educational systems (Dei, 2009). That history is no longer taught at Nigerian primary and secondary schools, and is taught only at the tertiary level, is a case in point – even though this process is not irreversible – and the Historical Society of Nigeria must continue to challenge this policy.

SELECTED SOURCES RELEVANT TO AIK AND HISTORY IN VARIOUS REGIONS OF AFRICA

Among Africa's material artifacts and repositories are stone and bone tools; bronze, iron, copper, silver, and gold sculpture and jewelry; terracotta figurines; engineered structures such as pyramids, underground tombs, stelae, obelisks, temples, mosques, dams, and granaries; rock carvings, drawings, inscriptions and paintings; and agricultural terraces, fortifications and navigational devices. The sculptured temples of Lalibela and the 500 stelae and obelisks of Aksum, in Northern Ethiopia, are legendary – although more of the ancient sculptured churches lie a few miles from Axum in Mekelle, Northern Ethiopia, according to Professor Ayele Bekerie (Bekerie, 2010).

In terms of South African history, within the last decade, there have been several new additions to the historical record, among these, the artifacts found at Blombos Cave, South Africa, now dated approximately 100,000 years. The South African artifacts imply the making of jewelry and cosmetics. Most of all they imply inventiveness and creativity, logical thinking, and confirm that the ancient occupants of this region developed abstract symbols in the form of straight lines, intersected by the same number of diagonal and parallel lines and right angles (Henshilwood, 2009). The inhabitants of Blombos made good use of ochre as body paint, and fashioned perforated beads for decorative purposes (Henshilwood, D'errico, & Watts, 2009). Based on findings in 2011, we also know that the ancient South Africans also engaged in elementary chemistry and put together what is widely discerned as a paint factory (Henshilwood et al., 2011; Berna et al., 2011). Collectively, these findings point to a fascinating precocity on the part of the early Africans, in inventiveness and creative thinking. About 300 enclosures of Southern Africa, in countries such as Zimbabwe, Botswana, Mozambique, and South Africa, also constitute major resources for understanding Africa's past (Garlake, 2003; Asante, 2007).

Findings in West Africa have also been significant. In 2007, at Ounjougou, Mali, close to the Bandiagara Cliffs, Huysecom and his team excavated a ceramic assemblage dated from around 9400 BCE (Huysecom et al., 2009). These finds were no less important than those of Blombos, given the fact that they were among the oldest pots to be found in the continent, and were probably used to facilitate the use of wild cereal as food, given the grinding implements found in the vicinity. Huysecom points out that dozens of archeological sites, spread over 16 meters, have been associated with the region where these pots were found. The much celebrated Benin earthworks, ten thousand miles in length, are relatively more recent and go back to the 8th century AD – consisting of fortifications associated with Edo culture and the Benin Kingdom (Darling, 2009). Further west, in the Senegambian region, outside the village of Sine Ngayene, the largest group of megalithic complexes yet recorded anywhere, consisting of about 30,000 megaliths, obelisks and tumuli, have been located, leading to interesting but unanswered questions about their purpose (Fage, 1979). The above references are selected references of Africa's monumental architecture. This constitutes but a fraction of the collective legacy from the past, but should be of interest not only to researchers of AIK in general, but also to archeologists and historians. The raw materials used in these various constructions and structures; the timeframe and stylistic features embedded in them; the labor codes and work ethic associated with them; and issues related to urbanization, empire-building, elitism, labor mobilization, and the centralization of power – fall within the range of historical research. What epistemological and methodological frameworks informed these accomplishments, and how were these intellectual ideas reproduced regionally? What processes were crucial in the development of such creativity? Given the fundamental objectives of IK, namely, psychological discovery, restoration, retrieval of heritage, sustainability, respect and epistemological decolonization, these issues are of great significance as well. Indigenous Knowledge is about memory, culture, and various forms of knowledge-production and dissemination, and also includes the skills and expertise that communities developed to sustain their city states, kingdoms, empires, and general communities.

IK, HISTORY, AND THE MISAPPROPRIATED ARTIFACTS

The Battle of Magdala of 1868, led to a widespread confiscation of Ethiopian treasures, and set the stage for massive plunder of material artifacts from other parts of the continent. Carted off from the imperial Ethiopian treasury and the Ethiopian Church of the Saviour of the World, to the British Museum, were numerous items (Marcus, 1995). These included the following:
- 350 Ethiopian manuscripts, written in Amharic;
- 80 objects;
- A gold crown and gold chalice;
- 6 ecclesiastical manuscripts, deposited in Windsor castle, in the Victoria and Albert Museum, London;
- Nine engraved wooden tablets or tabots, representing the Ark of the Covenant.
In the case of Nubia and Egypt, while these regions were British colonies and protectorates, archaeologists such as Reisner, were given unprecedented access to

6

precious artifacts. From the Aksumite-Nubian-Egyptian complex of northeast Africa, numerous items were appropriated. A few were bought, illegally in some cases, and now constitute the basis of exhibits in various museums around the world.

Selected List of Plundered African Artifacts

Description of Artifact	Country of Origin	Present Location	Date of plunder and appropriation
Asante gold and silver jewelry, royal regalia, golden head of 20 cm, golden death mask	Ghana	Museum of Mankind; Wallace Collection; Pitt Rivers Museum, Oxford; Glasgow Museum and Art Gallery; Victoria and Albert Museum , London	1874 – Military expedition by the British against the Asante.
Manuscripts, royal regalia, engraved tablets and manuscripts	Ethiopia	Victoria and Albert Museum, London	1868 – Battle of Magdala
Benin Bronzes; ivory mask of Queen Mother Idia; Olokun bronze Head	Nigeria	British Museum, Museum of Mankind, Frankfurt Museum	1897 – Military Expedition and Conquest of Benin
Rosetta Stone, Bust of Nefertiti; Statue of Ramesses II	Egypt	British Museum, Museum of Turin	
Marble Statue of Apollo, Cyrene	Libya	British Museum	
Library of Umar Tall with countless manuscripts		Bibliotheque National, France	1890 – Conquest by the French

The various colonial powers carted away thousands of artifacts from Nigeria, Benin, Mali, Congo, and elsewhere in West and Central Africa, to their respective home countries. Twenty thousand Benin bronzes were among the numerous artifacts plundered from West Africa's Benin Empire. French colonial forces plundered and transferred the entire library of Umar Tall to the Bibliotheque National, in Paris, in 1890. Some Africans had to bury their manuscripts in the desert sand to avoid persecution and pillage. No compensation has been given so far for these stolen valuables. The loss of these valuable artifacts is particularly painful for researchers of all affiliations, including scholars working within the paradigm of Indigenous Knowledge Studies. Scholars of IK tend to pay a great deal of attention to oral sources of information to redress inherited imbalances (Kovach, 2012). It would be misguided and counter-productive, however, to completely ignore historical documents and other evidence of knowledge-production by indigenous thinkers.

REVISITING WRITTEN AND ORAL SOURCES

Documents written on papyrus and parchment, inscriptions on tombs, tombstones, walls and doorways, and graphic representations, show up in many parts of Africa. Some are in the form of pictographic or ideographic writing systems (Kreamer et al., 2007) and constitute part of the conventional sources. Ironically, though, not all writing systems were treated equally, and some were prioritized above others, for political purposes, and not necessarily for sound intellectual reasons. For example, the abstract Adinkra symbols of the Asante should be considered ideographic writing but the bulk of western scholars cast doubt on this classification. About a million Malian manuscripts became available over the last decades. Unfortunately, many of these were probably destroyed by Afghan and Pakistani invaders and refugees into Northern Mali a few years ago (Hunwick & Boye, 2008). We note the numerous documents written in Arabic in public and private libraries, in other parts of West Africa, such as Nigeria, Ghana, Niger, Senegal, Mauretania, and Cote d'Ivoire. African manuscripts, in museums such as the Ashmolean Museum, the British Museum, Oxford's Bodleian Library, and museums in other parts of Europe such as France, Germany, and Belgium, continue to be repositories of African primary sources of knowledge. So, too, the Vatican. Scrutiny of some of the documents strewn across European libraries and museums, is important for historical research and no less so for IK research, despite its emphasis on oral resources, as earlier mentioned. Many of these documents recount indigenous modes of existence in various dimensions even in cases where the scripts were externally derived. We make the point here that our preoccupation with orality and 'orature' should not lead to the exclusion of indigenous knowledge that has been documented in those writing systems that were externally derived.

Vital for IK are recollections of the past, inherited from earlier generations, and contemporaries, and transmitted in diverse forms of verbal testimonies – including oral narratives poetry, songs, legends, proverbs, interviews, and so on. The transmission process may have involved public performances (Johnson, 1997) or may have been embedded in popular culture. These orally transmitted recollections continue to supplement other historical sources of information. In some cases they have been more useful than written documents. The goal of these narrations may be the celebration of success and conquest of doubts, fears, and uncertainties; testimony about trials, tribulations and heroic deeds in the past, as well as the search for the ultimate truth. A major goal may be to provide answers about the historic role of various groups and personalities; develop pride in the nation; and assist in various forms of reconstruction. In the case of West Africa, the Oral Epics of Sundiata, Askia Mohammed, Son Jara, Bamana Segu, Almami Samori Toure, Wagadu, Lat Dior, and Njaajaan Njaay constitute a core of orally transmitted poetic histories, parallel to the central African narratives, such as the Mwindo Epic and the Epics of Kahindo and Mvet Moneblum (Belcher, 1999). These are among the classical models. Embedded within them are various values and historical truths. They embody common themes on human origins and the evolution of the world, virgin birth, journeys to the underworld, resurrection, life and death cycles, journeys from the land of the living to the world of the ancestors, the triumph of good over evil, and the saga of historic and fictional heroes of various identities in the context of indigenous explanations. Protagonists include Murile, the resurrected hero-god of Tanzania; Mwindo, the miracle child and later warrior king of Nyanga in the Congo; Lituolone, of virgin birth; Kwasi Benefo's grief and trauma over the death of his wives; and Uncama's journey into Mosima, the Underworld of the Dead, in the case of South Africa. Nobel Laureate Wangari Muta Maathai recounted an interesting tale of survival and naivete, *Konyeki Na Ithe*, in her memorable memoir, *Unbowed* (2006). In the final analysis, these fictional identities reveal a quest for the ultimate truth or destiny; give a blueprint for empowerment and survival over trials, tribulations, and uncertain challenges; and reveal profiles in courage and resistance relevant to the understanding of indigenous African values and philosophies.

Oral Epics and Narratives may collectively reveal local or family accounts or the past history of lineages; family privileges and inheritances; migration of specific extended families and closely related communities; inspirational tales to guide generations; popular cultural belief system; or local fauna, flora, and ecology. There are numerous gaps in the sources, and diverse cautionary strategies to be employed by researchers with respect to the specific names and detailed background information on many of the protagonists. What inspired the protagonists? How were they able to achieve their goals, and, precisely when? What instigated the moment of discovery, in the case of inventors? What specific changes and innovations occurred within the specific time period? These are some of the questions that we sometimes have difficulty with but proceed to grapple with.

There are numerous points of interaction and interconnection between the historian of Africa and the AIK researcher coming from various disciplines. Oral history, whether through formalized epics or through less structured orally transmitted narratives, is central to AIK in general and historians in particular. In the context of indigenous research, however, there seems to be greater emphasis on the spiritual and the ceremonial, and portals of knowing inclusive of ceremonies, visions and dreams. IK tends to be more holistic in its epistemology, with a greater tendency towards a holistic understanding. (Kapoor & Shiza, 2010). With IK there is also greater reliance on narrative and a recognition that ' story as methodology is decolonizing research' (Kovach, 2012). Kovach also implies that IK research is relational and built on collective responsibility with greater sensitivity to intellectual property rights, benefit sharing, and non-exploitative methods of research. We shall now reflect briefly on aspects of African Indigenous Knowledge that underscores its intellectual viability. We focus on biotherapy, cupping, and the intellectual knowledge and efficacy surrounding natural products.

AFRICAN INDIGENOUS KNOWLEDGE: BIOTHERAPY, CUPPING, AND AFRICAN TRADITIONAL MEDICINE (ATM)

We define ATM as an accumulated corpus of diagnostic procedure, preventive and curative techniques and interventions, associated with healing and wellness. As observed from various sources, diagnostic procedure includes observation, case history, observation of urine, and clinical examination of body temperature as well as divination. Preventive and curative methodologies over time have included a wide range of techniques, including biotherapy and cupping, spinal manipulation, bone setting, inoculation, quarantine, fumigation and steam inhalation. Surgery, inclusive of scarification, circumcision, the removal of inflamed tonsils, the incision of abscesses and guinea worm extraction is also central to medical intervention in the case of ATM (Sofowora, 1984; Emeagwali, 2007). Although biotherapy and cupping are not the only interventions by traditional medical practitioners, we focus on the latter in this discussion, to highlight the current transformation taking place in medical institutions, most of which fifteen years ago were hostile, not only to live medical techniques, but also to many of the underlying principles utilized by indigenous practitioners of ATM.

Over the last decade, the large-scale adoption of 'live medical techniques' associated with maggots and leeches, in German, British, and Australian medical institutions, has revolutionized medical practice. Biotherapy is a field that has been known in Africa, in the ancient Aksumite-Nubian-Egyptian complex, since around 1500 BCE, although not necessarily by that name (Allen, 2007). We now have numerous recent narratives of the successful usage of leeches and maggots in treating infected wounds, and in post-surgical blood removal. It is now openly admitted that maggots successfully remove dead tissue, kill harmful bacteria in various wounds, and are of particular significance in reconstructive surgery. In the case of the leech, its saliva apparently contains an anti-coagulant, a blood thinner that prevents blood clots, and restores blood flow (Thearle, 2008). The FDA of the United States classified maggots and leeches as 'medical devices' in 2004, approving an application from Ricarimpex SAS to market leeches for medical purposes. One of the more celebrated cases is that of a diabetic patient in the United States who chose to experiment with the use of maggots rather than undergo amputation to cure a post surgical infected wound that resisted antibiotics and every other form of therapy. Maggot therapy ultimately preempted amputation by liquefying dead tissue, killing bacteria, and stimulating healing. Until a decade ago, the methodology was viewed with unbridled scepticism, and even scorn, by western-trained practitioners and patients.

Other techniques utilized by African traditional practitioners in addition to biotherapy, include cupping, heat therapy, hydrotherapy, and spinal manipulation. Unlike leech and maggot therapy, which have proven to be effective in dead tissue removal, and the healing of wounds, cupping therapy involves the creation of a vacuum and localized pressure that ultimately facilitates suction. Some practitioners propose that cupping also leads to the release of harmful toxins. In 2009, Andreas Michalsen and co-researchers, supported by a grant from the Karl and Veronica Carstens Foundation, Germany, concluded that cupping therapy was effective in the treatment of Carpal Tunnel Syndrome (CTS), after a random trial (Michalsen et al., 2009). They noted that the severity of symptoms in patients was substantially reduced after cupping, and that the treatment was 'safe and well-tolerated.' Their conclusions correlate with the view of African traditional medical practitioners, who for generations have used this technique of cupping largely for pain relief, although not exclusively so.

INDIGENOUS KNOWLEDGE AND AFRICAN NATURAL PRODUCTS

In African Traditional Medicine (ATM), plants are at the center of therapeutic healing, being used as anesthetics, antidotes, and antibiotics. Medicinal plants have been associated with dermatological preparations and gastrointestinal care. Plants have also been used in hypertensive care and to control spasms and fevers. Pharmaceutical companies have been known to tap into the knowledge of indigenous practitioners to identify plants of therapeutic value. Having copied the molecular structure of the various plants identified, they synthesize them in the laboratory and make huge profits from the final product. The compensation for the knowledge acquired from local practitioners continues to be inadequate, as discussed by Paul Kipkosgei Tarus in a recent interview (2012). A major handicap for laboratory research and the isolation of active medicinal ingredients is the high cost of instrumentation; but even so, tremendous gains have been made in various laboratories around the world in identifying useful products. This is a clear example of how laboratory expertise can be used to evaluate the medicinal composition of plants traditionally held in high esteem by local experts. This enhances the verification processes. Traditional practitioners have relied exclusively on popular collective testimony on the efficacy of natural products; given the excessively high cost of the various types of spectrometers used in laboratory research, traditional methodologies would continue to prevail.

Laboratory analysis has endorsed much of the traditional medicinal claims for the baobab, *Andansonia digitata,* a plant cherished by generations of Africans. De Caluwe et al. pointed out that the fruit pulp of a baobab has ten times the Vitamic C (ascorbic acid) content of an orange, and one of the highest levels of ascorbic acid to be found in a fruit. The leaves contain high quantities of Vitamin A and all the essential amino acids, and high quantities of iron and calcium. The bark is high in calcium, copper, iron, and zinc, as well as anti-malarial ingredients and anti-oxidants useful for coping with cardiovascular disease, cancer, and age-related illnesses (De Caluwe et al., 2009).

P. O. Ogunyale's herbal medication for sickle cell disease, *Nicosan,* consisting of *Piper guineense* (Black pepper), *Pterocarpus osun* (camwood), *Eugenia caryophyllum* (clove), and *Sorghum bicolor* (sorghum), traditionally used to cure anemia, is now recognized as an effective treatment for sickle cell disease (Patent 5800819) (Nathan, Tripathi, Wu, & Belanger, 2009). It is heartening to note that the National Institute for Pharmaceutical Research and Development (NIPRD), in Abuja, Nigeria, was instrumental in the evaluation of the efficacy of the product.

In their discussion of Nigerian plants with anti-diabetic properties, Steve Ogbonnia and Chimezie Anyakora identified about 75 different plants used by Nigerian traditional doctors (2009), including *aloe vera,* another promising plant for the treatment of diabetes. A similar endeavor has been undertaken by Mohammed Sayed Aly Mohammed in terms of malaria (2009). Oluwole Amusan, at the Swaziland Institute for Research in Traditional Medicine, identified *Euclea natalensis, Clausena anisata,* and *Aloe marlothii* as effective plants in the treatment of diseases of the cardiovascular system. *Cheilanthus calomendos, Dioscorea dregeana,* and *Pellaea calomelanos* have been recognized as useful in mental disorder (Rodolfo Juliani et al., 2009). (That we have apparently lost the taxonomic battle with respect to the naming of these plants is indeed regrettable.) ATM practitioners in these regions concur and claim that this information is not new to them. They knew this all along, having discovered this from ancestral and community research.

African medical traditions are holistic. The mind and body are viewed as interconnected. Supernatural-centered explanations coexist with naturalistic, empirical, behavioral accounts. African traditional medical practitioners have been accused of undue secrecy and a general reluctance to fully disclose the active ingredients in their elixirs, infusions, and poultices, as well as a tendency to individualize rather than standardize their prescriptions. One may counter these accusations by pointing to the elaborate veil of secrecy that envelops most contemporary inventions and processes elsewhere; one could argue that African traditional medical practitioners have been shrewd in attempting to safeguard their intellectual property rights, an issue that is central to any discourse on local knowledge systems (Mazonde & Thomas, 2007). The one-size-fits-all prescriptive tendencies in western medical institutions may not necessarily be the best way of treatment, and a more personalized way of dispensation takes into consideration age, weight, dietary, genetic, and other differentials, according to interviewees. It is interesting to note that the most recent trend in Western medicine is to use genetic data with the aim of the personalization of medicaments and treatment.

INDIGENOUS CHEMISTRY

Two recent discoveries have revolutionized our thinking about indigenous chemistry in Ancient Africa. The first is the discovery in Wonderwerk Cave, South Africa, in April 2012, that ancient Africans made fire about a million years ago. Inhabitants at Zhoukoudian, about fifty kilometers off Beijing, did so about 800,000 years ago and were previously thought to be the earliest documented group to do so. The use of fire meant that elementary forms of matter, including raw meat, would now be transformed into a new state.

The second significant discovery was the discovery of an ancient paint factory, in the vicinity of Blombos cave, about two hundred miles from Cape Town, South Africa. There ancient Africans created ochre by grinding iron oxide to a powder, and blending this with animal fat and charcoal that they then stirred with a bone spatula. The mixture was then poured into shells. The paint factory and processing workshop, found in 2008 by Henshilwood and a multinational team of researchers, was 100,000 years old. As explained by Professor Henshilwood, "a liquefied ochre-rich mixture was produced and stored in two Haliotis midae (abalone) shells" and charcoal, grindstones, hammerstones, bone and ochre were among the artifacts utilized to make the paint. This action has been described as 'a benchmark in the evolution of human cognition.' It is also the earliest and best-documented evidence we have of early chemistry.

Traditional knowledge about the tanning of leather reflected a high degree of knowledge about chemistry. According to Zaruwa and Kwaghe, in parts of Northeast Nigeria, the tanning of leather from animal hides and skins involved the addition of calcium powder obtained from incinerated cattle bones and also potash, followed by bird droppings, to soaked skin, in a process that had proven scientific credentials, namely, 'the denaturation of proteinous materials' (Zaruwa et al.). By adding bird droppings to the hides, they were actually adding uric acid, made of carbon, nitrogen, oxygen, and hydrogen and set in motion an endothermic reaction with water molecules. The tanners usually concluded the process by applying vegetable oil from the seeds of *Kaya senegalensis*, a preservative, also known to possess antimicrobial properties.

Zaruwa points out that in the production of *Argi,* a local gin, several scientific principles are utilized. *Argi is* essentially a distillate, a purified liquid, vaporized and collected in the form of condensed alcohol. In the first instance, the practitioners use fermented sorghum, in a locally constructed steamer pot, placed below another vessel, the condenser, filled with cold water. The condensate cooler is usually located within the steamer pot. The process involves the fermentation of sorghum in the first instance. Fermentation occurs with the introduction of microbial contaminants into the mash, and this helps in the breakdown of carbohydrates from larger particles into smaller ones (Zaruwa et al.). At the heart of the process is experimentation with local grain, in this case sorghum, and the creation of devices that facilitated the scientific process of distillation.

CONCLUDING REMARKS AND RECOMMENDATIONS

It has been suggested that the decolonization process has five phases, namely, the process of recovery of identity, artifacts, language, and cultural information; a process of mourning for what is being lost; dreaming, reformulation, and invocation of other possibilities for research; commitment to including silenced voices; and action that includes strategies for social transformation (Poka Laenui, 2000). Transformation at the level of the academy and in the context of IK implies change, not only in the curriculum, but also in instructional strategies, so that a more interactive mode of teaching and learning complements the teacher-centered approach.

Colonial and neo-colonial strategies of disinformation, systematically aimed at belittling and marginalizing Africa and Africans, both within and outside of the academy, should be constantly challenged and replaced by a narrative which properly situates Africa's history at the center of the learning process, in the context of sound, intellectual activity, and activist community-based research (Emeagwali, 1992a, 1992b, 1993, 2003, 2006). Dynamic, participatory praxiological encounters with the community could facilitate the rediscovery of indigenous epistemologies, and undermine discriminatory allocations of teaching and learning resources. Democratic forms of knowledge production could also enhance the process of political democratization by empowering participants, and negating processes of 'inferiorization' initiated during the period of colonial occupation (Dei, 2008). This in turn has the positive role of deepening the appreciation of local natural products for contemporary usage in all relevant spheres of activity.

In the past, Africans formulated hypotheses about their environment, made use of local resources and created innumerable inventions using what was locally available, whether 100,000 years ago at Blombos, 9,000 years ago in Mali, in the case of pottery, or 6,000 years ago at Dufuna, Nigeria.

There is no room for arrogance, paternalism, and condescension in capacity-building and innovation, nor should individualism and self-interest be necessarily placed on a pedestal, above a communitarian mode, and a more holistic cosmology. In the journey towards Africa-centered research, methodological clarity, and a truly decolonized academy, the historian should play a significant role – preferably within the paradigm of Indigenous Knowledge, given its explicit adoption, so far, of a transformative paradigm.

There is urgent need for digital libraries comprising databases of indigenous knowledge, in various fields, along the lines of the Indian Digital Library of Traditional Knowledge, and following the guidelines of the World Intellectual Property Organization. With the passage of time, we are losing not only human resources but a great deal of fauna and flora. Monsanto, and other U.S.-based companies engaged in genetic engineering, are accelerating the process of ecological and environmental degradation on a daily basis. To recoup the losses, we also need multiple Green Belt Movements and seed banks throughout the continent, all guided by multidisciplinary teams of Indigenous Knowledge specialists devoted to the retrieval, preservation, and dissemination of indigenous knowledge across the continent. History and historians have a crucial role to play in the creation of epistemological and methodological options, a movement that Professor Dike initiated in 1959 with his revolutionary work on Trade and Politics in the Niger Delta and in whose honor we humbly give this lecture.

REFERENCES

Akinwumi, O. et al. (2007). *African indigenous science and knowledge systems – Triumphs and tribulations – Essays in honour of Gloria Thomas Emeagwali.* Abuja: Roots.

Amusan, A. (2009). Herbal medicine in Swaziland. In H. Rodolfo Juliani et al. (Eds.), *African natural plant products: New discoveries and challenges in chemistry and quality.* Washington D.C: American Chemical Society.

Beaumont et al. (2012). Early evidence of San material culture represented by organic artifacts from Border Cave, South Africa. *Proceedings of the National Academy of Sciences of the United States of America, 109*(33) (August 14).

Bekerie, A. (2010). Interview held at Mekelle University, Mekelle, Ethiopia.

Barratt Brown, A. (1997). *Africa's choices after thirty years of the World Bank*.

Belcher, S. (1999). *Epic traditions in Africa*. Bloomington: Indiana University Press.

Carlson, T. et al. (2001). Case study of medicinal plant research in Guinea. *Econ Botany*, *55*, 4.

Chilisa, B. (2012). *Indigenous research methodologies*.

Darling, P. (1998). Legacy in earth – Ancient Benin and Ishan, Southern Nigeria. In K. Wesler (Ed.), *Historical archaeology in Nigeria*. Trenton, NJ: Africa World Press.

De Caluwe, E. et al. (2009). Baobab (Adansonia digitata L.). A review of traditional uses in phytochemistry and pharmacology. In H. Rodolfo Juliani et al. (Eds.), *African natural plant products: New discoveries and challenges in chemistry and quality*. Washington D.C: American Chemical Society.

Dei, G., & Simmons, M. (2009). The indigenous as a site on decolonizing knowledge for conventional development and the link with education: The African case. In J. Langdon (Ed.), *Indigenous knowledges, development and education*. Rotterdam: Sense.

Dike, O. (1959). *Trade and politics in the Niger Delta. 1830-1885: An introduction to the economic and political history of Nigeria*. Oxford, UK.

Dirar, H. (1993). *The indigenous fermented foods of the Sudan: A study in African food and nutrition*. CAB International.

Ehret, C. (2002). *The civilizations of Africa*. Charlottesville: University of Virginia Press.

Emeagwali, G. (2011). The neo-liberal agenda and the IMF/World Bank structural adjustment programs with reference to Africa. In D. Kapoor (Ed.), *Critical perspectives on neo-liberal globalization, development and education in Africa and Asia*. Rotterdam: Sense Publishers.

Emeagwali, G. (Ed.). (1993a). *Historical development of science and technology in Nigeria*. Lewiston, NY: Edwin Mellen.

Emeagwali, G. (Ed.). (1993b). *African systems of science, technology and art*. London: Karnak.

Emeagwali, G. (Ed.). (1992). *Science and technology in African history*. Lewiston, NY: Edwin Mellen.

Emeagwali, G. (Ed.). (1995). *Women pay the price*. NJ: Africa World Press.

Emeagwali, G. (Ed.). (2006a). *Africa and the academy. Challenging hegemonic discourses on Africa*. NJ: AWP

Emeagwali, G. (Ed.). (2006b). *The African experience: Past, present and future*. New York: Whittier.

Fage, J. D. (2001). *A history of Africa*. New York: Taylor and Francis.

Falola, T. (2009). *Colonialism and violence in Nigeria*. Indiana University Press.

Garlake, P. (2002). *Early art and architecture of Africa*. Oxford University Press.

Gilbert, E., & Reynolds, J. T. (Eds.). (2012). *Africa in world history*. Pearson.

Gillow, J. (2009). *African textile – Color and creation across a continent*.

Henshilwood, C. S., D'Errico, F., & Watts, I. (2009). Engraved ochres from the Middle Stone Age levels at Blombos Cave, South Africa. *Journal of Human Evolution*, 31 May.

Henshilwood, C. S., d'Errico, F., van Niekerk, K. L., Coquinot, Y., Jacobs, Z., Lauritzen, S.-E., Menu, M., & García-Moreno, R. (2011). 100,000-year-old ochre-processing workshop at Blombos Cave, South Africa. *Science, 334*, 219.

Hopper, C. (Ed.). (2002). *Indigenous knowledge and the integration of knowledge systems*. Claaremont, South Africa: New Africa Books.

Hunwick, A., & Boye, J. (2008). *The hidden treasures of Timbuktu: Rediscovering Africa's literary culture*. London: Thames & Hudson.

Huysecom et al. (2009). Antiquity. The emergence of pottery in Africa during the tenth millennium BC: New evidence from Ounjougou (Mali). *A Quarterly Review of World Archeology*, *83*(322), 905-917.

Johnson, J. et al. (1997). *Oral epics from Africa*. Bloomington: Indiana University Press.

Johnson, S., & Kwak, J. (2010). *13 bankers, the Wall Street takeover and the next financial meltdown*. New York: Pantheon Books.

Kapoor, D. (Ed.). (2011). *Critical perspectives on neo-liberal globalization, development and education in Africa and Asia*. Rotterdam: Sense Publishers.

15

Kapoor, D., & Shiza, E. (2010). *Indigenous knowledge and learning in Asia/Pacific and Africa.* New York: Palgrave Macmillan.

Khapoya, V. (2013). *The African experience.* New York: Pearson.

Kreamer et al. (2007). *Inscribing meaning: Writing and graphic systems in African art.* Washington DC: Smithsonian National Museum of Art.

Kovach, M. (2012). *Indigenous methodologies: Characteristics, conversations and contexts.* Toronto: University of Toronto Press.

Laenui, P. (2000). Processes of decolonization. In M. Battiste (Ed.), *Reclaiming indigenous voice and vision.* Toronto: UBC Press.

Langdon, J. (Ed.). (2009). *Indigenous knowledges, development and education.* Rotterdam: Sense.

Lost Crops of Africa. (2006). Washington DC: National Academy of Science.

Maathai, W. (2006). *Unbowed, A memoir.* New York: Anchor.

Mazonde, I., & Thomas, P. (Eds.). (2007). *Indigenous knowledge systems and intellectual property in the twenty-first century.* Dakar: Codesria.

Michalsen, A. et al. (2009). Effects of traditional cupping therapy in patients with carpal tunnel syndrome: A randomized controlled trial. *J Pain, 10*(6), June, 601-608. (Epub 2009 Apr 19)

Mohammed, S. A. M. (2009). Traditional medicinal plants and malaria in Africa. In H. Rodolfo Juliani et al. (Eds.), *African natural plant products: New discoveries and challenges in chemistry and quality.* Washington D.C: American Chemical Society.

Ogbonnia, S., & Anyakora, C. (2009). Chemistry and biological evaluations of Nigerian plants with anti-diabetic properties. In H. Rodolfo Juliani et al. (Eds.), *African natural plant products: New discoveries and challenges in chemistry and quality.* Washington D.C: American Chemical Society.

Rodolfo Juliani, H. et al. (2010). *African natural plant products: New discoveries and challenges in chemistry and quality.* UK: Oxford University Press.

Rostow, W. W. (1960). *The stages of economic growth: A non-communist manifesto.* Cambridge: Cambridge University Press.

Roubini, N. (2010). *Crisis economics: A crash course in the future of finance.* New York: Penguin.

Sofowora, A. (1984). *Medicinal plants and traditional medicine in Africa.* John Wiley and Sons.

Shiva,V. (1997). *Biopiracy: The plunder of nature and knowledge.* Boston: Southend Press.

Shizha, E. (2010). Rethinking and reconstituting indigenous knowledge and voices in the Academy in Zimbabwe: A decolonization process. In D. Kapoor & E. Shiza (Eds.), *Indigenous knowledge and learning in Asia/Pacific and Africa.* New York: Palgrave Macmillan.

Seepe, S. (2001). IKS can benefit everyone. *Daily Mail,* October 19.

Stiglitz, J. (2002). *Globalization and its discontents.* London: Penguin.

Stiglitz, J. (2009). Capitalist fools. *Vanity Fair,* January.

Stiglitz, J. (2010). *Freefall – America, free markets and the sinking of the world economy.* New York: N. W Norton.

Swami, N., Prema, T., Wu, Q., & Belanger, F. C. (2009). Nicosan: Phytomedicinal treatment for SickleCell disease. In H. Rodolfo Juliani et al. (Eds.), *African natural plant products: New discoveries and challenges in chemistry and quality.* Washington D.C: American Chemical Society.

Tarus, P. (2012). Reflections on research in African traditional medicine. Gloria Emeagwali Productions; 16 min., 2 secs.; MPEG. http://vimeo.com/49120175

Thearle, J. (2008). Leeches in medicine. *ANZ Journal of Surgery. Royal Australasian College of Surgeons, 68*(4), 292-295.

The humble leech's medical magic. (2004). news.bbc.co.uk/2hi/health/3858087.stm. Friday, 2 July.

Wilford, J. (2011). African cave yields evidence of a prehistoric paint factory. *The New York Times,* October 13. See http://www.nytimes.com/2011/10/14/science/14paint.html

Zaruwa, M., & Kwaghe, Z. E. (2014). Traditional tannery and dyeing (Yirie) methods: A science par excellence in Northeastern Nigeria. In G. Emeagwali & G. J. S. Dei (Eds.), *African indigenous knowledge and the disciplines.* Rotterdam: Sense Publishers (this volume, chapter 4).

Zaruwa, M., Barminas, J. T., & Apampa, R. O. (2014). Indigenous distillation in northeastern Nigeria and the production of Argi. See chapter two. In G. Emeagwali & G. J. S. Dei (Eds.), *African indigenous knowledge and the disciplines*. Rotterdam: Sense Publishers (this volume, chapter 2).

M. Z. ZARUWA, J. T. BARMINAS AND R. O. APAMPA

2. INDIGENOUS DISTILLATION IN NORTHEASTERN NIGERIA AND THE PRODUCTION OF *ARGI*

INTRODUCTION

The production of various beverages differs in methodology depending on what is desired, and this varies from one community to the other. The production of alcoholic beverages may vary slightly, but the principle is similar if well investigated. In Midwestern and Southeastern Nigeria, the production of the so-called African whisky, *ogogoro*, is widely spread and the gin itself has become one of the peoples' cultural beverages. Today *ogogoro* is produced in grades depending on its alcoholic content. It is used as beverage and in the manufacture of other beverages, in traditional medicine and in cosmetics and sprays.

The nearest equivalent to *ogogoro* that is found in the northeastern part of Nigeria amazes many beholders because of the simplicity of its production and the principle behind it.

ARGI AN AFRICAN DISTILLATE

Argi pronounced "arrghi" is a distillate (condensed steam) from a fermented mash, mainly from a carbohydrate source. The word Argi is believed to be of *Higgi/Marghi* language, language of the descendant of the Sukur kingdom of old. Some individuals spoken to, especially the aged, responded that the word itself could have originated from their Chadian or Cameroonian cousins meaning the Higgi on the Cameroonian side of the border or the so called Godogodo community on the Chadian side. Irrespective of where Argi comes from, the liquor is consumed widely among the various communities in northeastern Nigeria. Preliminary studies on Argi showed that it contains between 10 to 35% alcohol depending on the maker and the constituents of the primary raw material. The amazing thing about Argi is the method employed in its production. In basic sciences, the term distillation is simply defined as the purification of liquid by vaporizing it with heat, condensing it within a cold environment, and then collecting the purified liquid called the distillate. Ordinarily, distillation is the method employed in the production of gin (whisky) and spirits that are consumed as beverages, or used industrially in the production of other substances, such as petrol and kerosene.

G. Emeagwali & G. J. S. Dei (eds.), African Indigenous Knowledge and the Disciplines, 19–21.

THE PRODUCTION OF ARGI

The raw materials for the production of Argi are mainly leftovers of prepared sorghum flour (tuwon dawa) and a traditional brew (burukutu) that is also consumed as beer. The former is normally crushed into bits and mixed with water to form a liquid mash. This is allowed to stand for three or more days during which time a fermentation process would have occurred. The earliest documented similarity to Argi is from ancient China. The methods of production of both the Chinese alcohol and Argi are very similar. The creation process involves the following:

1. A container – used to produce steam by heating water in it.
2. A steamer – in which fermented grain mash is placed at the bottom of the screen.
3. The condenser – which was named "top pot" in ancient times, and was placed on the top of the steamer and filled with cold water in such a way that spirit vapor reached to its wall at the bottom, then condensed.
4. A condensate collector – usually inside the steamer, at the bottom of the cooler.

The process of fermentation occurs as a result of the presence of microbial contaminants within the mash, or those introduced into it from the environment. In fermentation, microbes secrete proteinous substances called enzymes, which help in the breakdown of carbohydrates from larger particles into smaller particles; in the process, alcohol is formed. This process occurs very well in closed or airtight containers. The production of Argi follows a similar pattern in ancient and modern distilleries. The central concept and principle is that a fermented mash is heated and the vaporized alcoholic content is condensed and collected as alcohol (spirit).

Traditionally, earthen wares and bamboo sticks were used. The bamboo sticks were perforated at the joints to make a pipe. At present, however, modern metallic pipes have replaced the bamboo sticks. The earthen ware is used as a traditional condenser. This is normally filled with cold water so that the pipe that passes through it can be cooled to effect condensation of the vaporized alcohol. The pipe is made to pass through the condensing earthen ware, after which it is sealed with mud at any possible outlet. The fermenting and heating chamber are all made up of earthen wares. The cover is made up of similar material. When in use the fermenting chamber is sealed with freshly prepared mud. When the broth is poured into the fermenting chamber, care is taken to ensure that the maximum level does not exceed the three-quarter limit of the pot, so that when it boils, it would have no contact with the pipe, which serves as a delivery tube (within the condenser). Naturally, the vapor emanating from the boiling broth would go through the only available opening, the delivery tube. It is when it finds itself within the pipe that the vapor condenses as a result of the cooling effect of the water within the condenser.

During the collection of the condensed alcohol, it comes in drops and the entire distillate appears milky or whitish. This, however, changes with time, probably as a result of maturity.

CONCLUSION

The production of Argi points to the ingenuity of the ancestors of the communities that have since settled within this region, northeastern Nigeria. Many questions remain unanswered. but we can only conclude that, Argi belongs to the people of the old Sukur kingdom, namely, the Higgi, Marghi and others within that axis. There was no evidence whatsoever that it had any foreign contribution in the ingenuity of its production.

M. Z. ZARUWA, N. U. IBOK AND I. U. IBOK

3. TRADITIONAL BREWING TECHNIQUE IN NORTHERN NIGERIA

An Indigenous Approach to the Exploitation of Enzymes (Tsiro)

INTRODUCTION

Beer and other similar drinks are the most consumed beverages in the world after water (Okambawa, 2002). Studies show that the earliest available records of brewing is that of the Egyptians (Hemeket or Zythum or Zythus) and ancient Sumerians of Iraq, said to be over five thousands years ago. The ancient Egyptians held their traditional beer in high esteem. The ancient Egyptians added flavour with herbs and spices and regarded it as medicine. Its level of significance was such that it was buried along with the Pharaohs (Guash et al., 2006), and also used as offering to the gods. Perhaps what may have been responsible for these exceptional attitudes towards beer was the wisdom behind its method of production (brewing).

In contemporary times, brewing has become one of the most successful major industries worldwide. In the United States alone, 18,000 brewers produced more than 175 million barrels of beer in 2002. Each American would be assumed to consume about 83 litres (22 gallons) of beer (Azulay, 2002).

Looking at Northeastern Nigeria, the traditional method of brewing is as old as the communities found in this area. While the word "beer" sounds foreign to inhabitants of this area, the common name used, presumed to be in Hausa or a 'pidgin' of some evolved language, is 'giya' (alcohol) generally referred to as 'burukutu.' At the heart of the traditional brewing process is the exploitation and use of enzymes.

An enzyme is a biological catalyst (Rodelez, 2012). In chemistry, the word catalyst is defined as any substance that hastens a chemical reaction, but remains unchanged at the end of the reaction. Enzymes identified by conventional science number up to 800. Their presence has been confirmed in plants as well as animals and their activities range from production to preservation through catalysis. The primary role of enzymes in brewing is to aid the breakdown or conversion of sugars into alcohol (Patzsch, 2012).

In association with catalysis is a vast array of traditional food preparation methods that involve steps that lower their toxicity levels and improve their nutritional properties, thus rendering them safe for consumption. Yeast decreases the levels of tannins, a stomach irritating chemical and protein denaturer, but increases the levels of B vitamins and essential amino acid (Zoecklein et al., 1999). Fermentation is a biochemical process in which sugars are converted into alcohol by enzymes produced from yeast cells or sprouted grains called 'tsiro' in Hausa. In

G. Emeagwali & G. J. S. Dei (eds.), African Indigenous Knowledge and the Disciplines, 23–28.

biochemical terms, fermentation is better explained in phases or stages, which are mainly three in number. The process is aided by yeast cells which are either obtained artificially or exist naturally in the atmosphere. The process is a continuous one. This is why beer (and wine) improves with age, thereby improving its alcoholic content and other organoleptic properties as long as enzymes are present (Blasco et al., 2011).

TSIRO: THE SOURCE OF ENZYMES

The word Tsiro means sprouted grains. The communities located around the Northeastern part of Nigeria have various uses and names for the sprouted grains in various languages, for example, in Lunguda – 'Bwaha'; Marghi – 'Thlam'; Kamuwe – 'Zarabalha'; Bura – 'Thali'; Fali – 'Brunan'; Nzany – 'Tsibote'; Bachama – 'Murozume'; Kilba – 'Thlam' and so on. Nutritional scientists and those of similar discipline claim that sprouts are the most complete and nutritionally stable of all foods tested. They contain vitamins, minerals, proteins, and enzymes (Takana, 2004). Sprouts are defined to be predigested foods which have a higher biological efficiency value than whole seeds, raw or cooked. The sprouting process was previously observed under the influence of light to create chlorophyll, thus making it very effective in overcoming protein deficiency anemia (Mathewson, 1980). It is claimed by the same experts that the sprout prevents depletion and early disappearance of sexual energy as a result of its high vitamin E content (Duruibe et al., 1980).

In the wheat grain for example, vitamin B12 quadruples. Other B vitamins increase 3 to 12 times their normal values. Vitamin E content triples during sprouting. It was also observed that the fiber content increases three- to fourfold, that of the whole wheat bread (Larry, 2007). Sprout grains were also reported to be rich in vitamin C, which are mainly of fruit origin. Carotenoids A and some vitamin B were observed to be present in sprout grains in significant proportions (www.sproutgrain.com).

Scientific studies have proven that sprouting makes food safer for consumption. This is because it helps to remove anti-nutritional factors such as enzyme inhibitors, including tannins, phytates, and others (Soetan & Oyewole, 2009). The merits of sprouts are recorded by experts and its benefits may have been recognized by traditional African brewers. The main constitute of sprouts is its high enzyme content, which is exploited for both protein and carbohydrate digestion (Peary & Warren, 2006). Basic nutritional science teaches that while the high enzyme content of sprouts can be destroyed in the presence of high temperatures, its presence within food or drink surely enriches it (Kent, 2009). The nutritional content of the traditional African brew can therefore be said to be high.

Another interesting phenomenon about 'tsiro' is that modern science attributes anti-aging properties to alcoholic beverages (Blasco et al., 2011). This is because its rich enzyme content is said to help the body in several metabolic processes since aging is caused by enzyme depletion within the cells. How African communities in the early times came across this knowledge is unknown. While there are doubts about the details, however, it is worthy to note that African indigenous knowledge encompassed a rich tradition, culture, and spiritual life. In the Michika and neigbouring communities, the transfer of the knowledge about traditional brewing is known to be mainly from mother to daughter. The traditional brewing in itself is a unique art among these communities that spread across the Northeastern states of Nigeria.

DRAWBACKS IN MODERN BREWING PROCESS

Though brewing has evolved over a very long time, the introduction of modern scientific techniques has made it one of the largest industries in the world. This however has a few drawbacks, mainly as a result of the fact that the process is hastened in order to maximize profit.

The conversion of sugars to alcohol can be accomplished either by the use of enzyme extracts constrained in the sprouted grains, or malt as the case may be. On a very large scale, starch or complex sugar is treated with synthetic or mineral acids, in what is referred to as acid hydrolysis (Taherzadeh, 2007). The heating and conversion of the starch takes place simultaneously. The added acid is neutralized with the addition of another chemical, calcium hydroxide (Lime), or some other base before it is subjected to fermentation. This process is allowed only on a large-scale basis because heating and fermentation times are shortened, and its neutralization renders the nutrients contained in the grains unavailable because it denatures them.

'TSIRO' IN THE BREWING PROCESS

The brewing process among African communities in Northeastern Nigeria is very similar. In these parts, brewing is predominantly done by women, but the largest percentage of what is brewed is mainly consumed by the men. In the communities studied, a man is supposed to have a pot of brewed beer at all times, either for him or because of guests who traditionally come unannounced. Women are not exempted from the consumption of the brewed liquor. In the past, the consumption of this brew was considered a thing done by all except the very young. The adulteration of the traditional method of preparation has in some ways justified the call for abstinence. This is because of the use of metallic containers such as drums (instead of the earthen wares), found to be responsible for some disease conditions (tetanus and metalo-toxic) among the consumers of the local brews (Duruibe et al., 2007).

Though grains such as sorghum, millet, and rice, and sometimes a blend with maize, are used for brewing traditional beer, sorghum is the main raw material that is used. The 'tsiro,' on the other hand, is made from any of the aforementioned grains. Sometimes a blend may be used as well. This process is called malting. To malt cereals, one-tenth or less of the grain to be used for the brewing process is washed with cold water and kept in a humid place for about three to four days to trigger partial germination. The sprouting process releases enzyme inhibitors enabling the production of enzymes to commence. The enzyme activity turns the grains into simple predigested state. It turns fats and carbohydrates into simple sugars and proteins into amino acids and peptones. The sprouted grains are lower in calories and carbohydrates than the original (Takano, 2004). Some vitamins are known to increase by as much as 500% during sprouting (Kent, 2010; Dale, 2006).

This batch is then brought out to be dried in the open. The sprouted grains are often stored over a long period of time to the extent that moulds are observed to grow on them. These moulds, users claim, add catalytic efficacy to the sprout. The drying of the grains in the sun stalemates the enzyme activity within it. During sprouting, the enzyme levels are improved by about 300% of what is normal. All of it is trapped within the grain when it dries up. This is the reason behind the pulverization of the grain before use. When asked how their forefathers came about this method of malting, some of the respondents speculated that it was by trial and error (Personal Contact, 2013). This practice could not be traced to any period or a particular era, but says a lot about the wisdom of the ancient settlers of these areas.

THE TRADITIONAL BREWING PROCESSES

Some quantity of sorghum is cleaned by sorting out foreign particles, washing the sorghum, submerging it in water for a day or two, and milling it. This will enable the farinaceous part of the grain to dissolve with ease when it is milled. The water is usually more than the milled grain, so as to attain total submersion of the flour in the water. The container is left open and allowed to stand for three days. To the local brewer, the forces of nature are allowed to act on the opened jar. This enables atmospheric yeast cells to contaminate the mixture and commence the fermentation process. The water is poured out after three days. At this stage the paste is properly soaked and oozes out a strong somewhat pleasant smell. The container is placed on fire and continuously stirred with a wooden rod to ensure a uniform gelatinization of the starch. The container is brought down from the fire after it is observed that the paste has completely gelatinized.

The container is removed from the heat and the content is allowed to cool for about 3 to 4 hours. The hard cooled dough is then spread on a flat surface and broken into pieces, thus creating the wide surface area for aeration and cooling. The cooling of the dough and exposure creates an additional avenue for further microbial activity.

The dough is transferred back into a container in small amounts, while at the same time being mixed with the 'tsiro' flour (no water is added). The whole content of the container is stirred constantly with a wooden rod as a stirrer. As a result of the effect of the enzyme on the starch and the continuous stirring, the entire content of the pot is liquefied. At this point, mash is partially sweetened due to the action of the enzyme on starch. This process is scientifically referred to as enzymatic hydrolysis (Taherzadeh, 2007) of the starch. It is the chemical breakdown of molecules (macromolecules) into simpler molecules or glucose.

The mash is allowed to stand for at least three days, during which it would enable further breakdown (fermentation/hydrolysis) of the starch by the enzymes, aided by the yeasts cells which were introduced earlier. During this period, sugars or carbohydrates are converted into alcohol. This is followed by the emancipation of a pleasant flavour from the mash.

The entire mash is stirred thoroughly using a rod to expel the bubbles formed within and to ensure a thorough mix. It is left for another 4 to 6 hours so that the enzymatic activity can proceed further. A sack cloth is used in the sieving process. The filtrate is collected in a basin leaving the residue within the sack. A little amount of water is added into the sack cloth to press out the remaining product from within. The principle is that fine particles of the mash pass through the sack cloth leaving the coarse particles trapped in the sack. The filtrate containing the brew still contains active enzymes and some microbial cells. This is heated for the following reasons, namely (i). to sterilize the beer, (ii). to deactivate the enzymes, and (iii). to add warmth to it while it is being spiced with traditional spices or flavours, the most prominent being alligator paper. The brew will be ready for consumption after it is removed from the heat and allowed to cool slightly.

CONCLUSION

The end product of this procedure is an alcoholic beverage brewed with a technique that none could point to in terms of its earliest starting point. A comparison of modern brewing methods with the traditional type as practiced in northeastern Nigeria shows that the basic principles are similar and, to a large extent, healthier since no toxic substances are added to it. This is as a result of the extra nutrients formed in the enzyme, and the yeast or microbial cells having been destroyed by simple sterilization.

REFERENCES

Azulay sol. (2002). *Earth Times*. News release, San Diego.

Blasco, L., Vinas, M., & Villa, T. G. (2011). Protein influencing foam formation in wine and beer: The role of yeast. *International Microbiology*, 14, 61-71.

Dale, K. (2006). Superoxide dismutase boosting the body's primary anti-oxidant defense. *Biochem. Soc. Trans. 31*(6), 1305-1307.

Duruibe, J. O., Ogwuegbu, M. O. C., & Egwurugwu, J. N. (2007). Heavy metal pollution and biotoxic effects. *International Journal of Physics Sciences*, 2(5), 112-118.

Guash-Jane, M. R., Lacueva, C. A., Jauregui, O., & Lamuel-Reventos, R. M. (2006). First evidence of white wine in ancient Egypt from Tutankhamun's tomb. *Journal of Archeological Science, 33*(8), 1075-1080.

Interview with resident, Mubi, Nigeria, January 2013.

Kent, L. T. (2010). *List of enzymes in sprouting seeds*. www.livestrong.com/article/217438-list-of-enzymes-in-sprouting-seeds/

Larry, C. (2007). *Food for life*. www.food.com, www.sproutedgrains.com

Mathewson, S. W. (1980). *The manual for the home and farm production of alcohol fuel* (pp. 23-30). USA: Ted Speed Press.

Okambawa, R. (2002). *Shakparo: A traditional West African sorghum beer*.

Patzsch, I. K. (2002). *Multi-talented enzyme produced on large scale*. Research news. Fraunhofer Center for Chemical-Biotechnological Processes CBP. Germany

Peary, S. W., & Warren, P. (2006). *Super nutrition gardening*. Avery Publishing Co.

Rodelez, Y. (2012). Competition for catalytic resources alters biological network dynamics. *Physics Review Letters, 108*(1), 018102.

Soetan, K. O., & Oyewole, E. O. (2009). The need for adequate processing to reduce the anti-nutrition factors in plants used as human foods and animal feeds: A review. *African Journal of Food Science, 3*(9), 223-232.

Taherzadeh, M. J., & Karimi, K. (2007). Acid-based hydrolysis processes for ethanol from Lignocellulosic materials: A review. *Bioethanol. Rev. BioResources, 2*(3), 472-499.

Takano, J. (2004). *Sprouts, why do they call it wonder food? Part 1.* www.pyroenergen.com/articles 07/sprouts_health_benefits.htm

Zoecklein, B., Fugelsang, K., Gump, B., & Nury, F. (1999). *Wine analysis and production* (pp. 97-114). New York: Kluwer Academic Publishers.

M. Z. ZARUWA AND Z. E. KWAGHE

4. TRADITIONAL TANNERY AND DYEING (YIRIE) METHODS

A Science Par Excellence in Northeastern Nigeria

TRADITIONAL LEATHER TANNING IN NORTHEASTERN NIGERIA

This study takes a critical look at the ingenuity behind traditional African tannery and dyeing methods in some parts of Northeastern Nigeria, in Adamawa State. It points to the basic concepts and the science involved in traditional tannery and dyeing using locally sourced materials.

Northeastern Nigeria has a long history of traditional leather tanning. The various ethnic communities that now inhabit this part of Nigeria share many things in common in terms of finished leather products from animal hides and skin, and to a large extent the traditional methods involved in the process.

Several sites visited and individuals questioned, all of whom come from the different parts covering the six geopolitical zones of Northeastern Nigeria, pointed out that the process of tanning hides in the various regions appears to carry very similar features. It is worthy of note that tanning as an occupation has almost disappeared from communities where it was once practiced. All that is left now are half buried vats and sites abandoned by former owners to domestic animals or converted to other uses. This is the same case with the dyeing process.

In Michika Local Government Area of Adamawa State, the only operational tanning facility was operated by a 74-year-old man who died in 2011; a gentleman (a relative of the owner) in his forties who served as manager is in charge at present. This tanning site is the only one within the northern axis of Adamawa State that still uses traditional techniques with minor modifications. Like most traditions, the tanner said he served as an apprentice to the original owner of the site some 51 years ago, and he has been there since the owner of the site passed away. In his view, tanning is a tradition that was passed on to his generation. Due to the strenuous nature of the process, the younger generation does not show any interest in the process, hence its gradual disappearance (Murungan et al., 2006).

TANNING METHOD

In the tanning method of Michika locality, hides or skin are soaked in water for a whole day. This is to aid the softening of the material. The soaking and all other treatments are carried out in vats, which are dug into the ground, or plastered on the inside with cement. In the past, big earthen wares were half buried into the ground. The tanners used forms of calcium powder gotten from incinerated cattle

G. Emeagwali & G. J. S. Dei (eds.), African Indigenous Knowledge and the Disciplines, 29–33.

bones and potash. These substances are added to the soaked hide or skin. It is measured proportionately according to the number of hides or skin in the vats and allowed to stay for a day.

The scientific basis for this is similar to the explanation given by the tanner. The hide or skin is made up of a protein fiber that is very strong in tensile strength; the best way of rendering it susceptible to the desired texture is by the denaturation process. This is achieved by exposing it to high salinity and a salty environment. This procedure would loosen the adhesion of the hair to the skin and would render it stretchable. The skin is removed and placed on what looks like a work stone or table. Here a double-handled and blunt-edged knife is used to remove the hairs on it. This could take up to 30 to 45 minutes if goat or ram skin is used and depending on the size. Into a second vat already half-filled with water, a cup of quelea bird dropping is added. The hides are allowed to remain in this for another day. The droppings of birds are rich in ammonia (or rather uric acid). Like ammonia, it is an organic acid made up of carbon, nitrogen, oxygen, and hydrogen. This is a very important material in the tanning industry in this part of northeastern Nigeria. Other animal droppings such as those of pigeon, peacock, and chicken were said to be used in other parts such as Northern Cameroon and Southern parts of Niger and Chad. The tanner stressed that quelea droppings give the best results in the final removal of hairs on the hides (Interview, 2013).

The part played by the quelea birds' dropping seems to be underestimated by the traditional tanner. Other people confirmed that the droppings help to eliminate the strong stench, and that it speeds up the cleaning of the material. These reasons are supported scientifically. Ammonia is a raw material used in the manufacturing of products like hair conditioners, facial cleaners, bath oils, and lotions, as an odour or dirt remover. It creates what is referred to as an endothermic reaction with water molecules (Chido et al., 2003), hence it can be said to enhance the removal of water molecules from the hides and skin during drying.

The traditional art of tannery and dyeing of animal hide has scientific complexities that may fascinate the average observer. This is seen with the choice of plant (Acacia nilotica) used in the process. Acacia nilotica is a tree indigenous to Nigeria (Quattrocchi, 2000; Sheik, 1989). The seeds of this Acacia nilotica, which are long finger-like and brownish, are called 'gabaruwa' in Hausa language or 'kejelevwa' in the Kamuwe language of Michika. The seeds are milled or pounded in mortars, after which a measure is soaked in hot water. The hide or skin is soaked again in this new mixture for a whole day. This is done while the mixture is still hot because it adds to the aesthetic characteristic of the leather and gives it a unique toughness. These reasons are also supported by modern science both in the tanning industry and elsewhere. The Acacia nilotica seeds, like the mother tree, are rich in tannin or tannic acid (Malviya et al., 2011), which is used in contemporary tanning as a final addition before waxing. However in traditional tanning methods, the use of the tannic acid from plant parts is repeated twice, and at two different stages. Going by the effect of tannin or tannic acid on proteinous tissue, it can be assumed that the first stage of using the tannic acid is to denature the protein to remove the gummy fleshy tissues from the hides and skin, using the same double-handle knife that was used to scrape off the hairs.

The skin is soaked for a second time in the tannous solution for a whole day. This serves as the final stage of converting hide and skin into leather before it is sprayed and dried on ropes, or sometimes it is nailed to a flat surface using pegs. A second use of the tannin or tannic acid is to enhance extensibility of the skin to enable water loss during the drying process. The tanner affirmed that the tannic acid may or may not be used for a second time depending on what the leather is to be used for. In other words, whenever the local tanner is producing leather for specific uses such as shoes or matchet or knife sheaths, he will have different textures.

The final process of the tanning is the oiling. This involves the application of vegetable oil or oil from the seeds of Kaya senegalensis. The oil serves as a preservative, though it is known scientifically to possess antimicrobial properties (Audu-Peter et al., 2006); it also enhances the flexibility of the leather. The oiled leather would finally be placed or spread under the sun to dry while the heat enhances the thorough percolation of the oil micelles into the hide. The aesthetic properties such as colouring and other forms of decoration of the hide are therefore added from this stage. The finished leather may not always be oiled before the dye stuff is applied. However, the tradition in Michika involves the application of oil (vegetable oil) on the leather. It is rubbed on the surface of the leather until the tanner is satisfied that the oil has been absorbed considerably into the leather. The dried and oiled leather is then soaked in water for about three hours; this serves to loosen the fiber contained in the leather so as to enhance penetration of the dye into it. The leather is then transferred into a hot water vessel while still being heated.

To another vessel of hot water is added a desired quantity of the dyestuff. The dyestuff depends on the desired colour, whether red, black, yellow, or blue. The various dyestuffs have different methods of preparation. Presently, imported dyestuff has replaced the traditional types primarily because the process of its preparation is cumbersome and probably expensive.

The leather from one vat of hot water is transferred into another with the dyestuff and allowed to stay for between 45 minutes to one hour, during which a wooden rod is used to turn the whole mixture. The leather is then removed from the vessel containing the dye and spread on fine sand to dry. The tanner sometimes employs apprentices who wear specially made footwear that are worn for massaging the dye into the leather. Previously, the shoes were made from animal leather, but now they are replaced with rubber. The leather is left in the sun after this process, and when it is dried enough, neatly folded into desired shapes, and pressed using the same shoes.

MANUFACTURE OF LOCAL DYESTUFF FOR USE ON LEATHER

Black Dye

The manufacture of local dyestuffs involves the use of iron fillings which are collected from the blacksmith's workshop in early times, but today the filling can be obtained from places where other forms of metal works are carried out. The fillings are mixed with sugarcane, extracts, or sugar (Zumeriye & Alper, 2007), and the Acacia nilotica seed powder in the desired proportion in hot water. The mixture is left to stand for a whole day. This is used on the leather if black-coloured finished product is desired and left for an hour before it is spread to dry. It should be noted that what actually introduces the black colour in this mixture is the iron fillings. Whether the discovery of this method is accidental or by experiment is undetermined.

Blue-black Dye (Yirie)

The blue-black dye is made from leaves, in what can simply be referred to as organic or vegetable dye (Cardon, 2007). It is the most popular of all traditional dyestuffs used in northeastern Nigeria. The plant from which this dye is made is called 'yirie' in the Kamuwe language. The plant is said to have other uses other than as a colouring agent. It is known to possess several pharmacological properties (Unader, 1991) in addition to it being used in the tanning and dyeing industry. Botanists refer to the plant as phyllanthus amarus (Schum and Thonn), from the family Euphorbiacea. This plant grows widely in the said part of Nigeria as weeds. It grows up to 80cm high with many branches and numerous small leaves on lateral branches. Its leaves are about 5-10 mm long and 3-4 mm wide and its flowers are greenish and small, up to 1.5 mm in diameter. The fruit of phyllanthus amarus is round, brownish and 1.5-2 mm wide. Each capsule contains six small seeds. 'Yirie' is harvested and spread under a roof to dry, after which it is pounded and mixed with hot water and potash, and stirred thoroughly to ensure a total dissolution of the potash. While the mixture is still hot, the dried leather is immersed in the mixture and allowed to stay for at least an hour with occasional turning using a rod. The 'yirie' dye and its equivalent are widely used from the northeast to the central part of Nigeria on clothing and other ornamental paraphernalia.

Red Dye

Prior to the coming of 'garula' (imported dyes), red coloured dyes were made from sorghum stalks. The stalks were chosen meticulously after harvest and chopped into small pieces with a knife. Experts claim that the redness of the stalks could be as a result of fungal infection (Mutegi, 2010), or some genetic abnormality in the crop. The red stalk pieces are left to dry in the sun and later crushed into powder in traditionally carved mortar. The red powder is mixed with potash powder in an earthen ware that has hot water up to the middle, while it is continuously stirred with a wooden rod. This mixture is used to dye dried leather to the desired taste. It should be noted that the waste products that are produced during this whole process was and is still considered a very rich garden manure.

CONCLUSION

The traditional methods of tanning and dyeing in northeastern Nigeria anticipate and reflect to a large extent the fundamental basis of contemporary tanning and dyeing. These principles were neither linked to spirits nor magic but trial and error experimentation as well as accidental discovery. It therefore points to the fact that at some point, our ancestors had the effrontery to carry out trials that involved testing the efficacy of one substance over another, which we in contemporary times associate with scientific research.

REFERENCES

Audu-Peter, J. D., Olorunfemi, P. O., & Njoku, N. (2006). Antimicrobial and pharmaceutical properties of Khaya senegalensis seed oil. *Journal of Pharmacy and Bioresources, 3*(1), 19-24.

Cardon, D. (2007). *Natural dyes: Sources, tradition, technology and science.* Archetype Publications.

Chido, S., Kondakova, O., Micheini, M. C., Russo, N., & Sillicia, E. (2003). Reaction of bare VO+ and FeO+ with ammoia. *Inorganic Chemistry, 42*(26), 8773-8782.

Interviews. (2013). Selected interviews in Mubi with Emmanuel Agbo, Gambo Ahmed, and Clement Wadawasina and others individuals – 2006 and 2007.

Maviya, S., Rawat, S., Kharia, A., & Verma, M. (2011). Medicinal attributes of Acacia nilotica Linn. A comprehensive review on ethnopharmcological claims. *International Journal of Pharmacology and Life Science (IJPLS), 2*(6), 830-837.

Murungan, K., Saravababu, S., & Arunachalam, P. (2006). Screening of tannins acyl hydrolase's producing tannery effluent fungal isolates using simple agar plate and Smf process. *BioResources Online.*

Mutegi, E. et al. (2010). Ecogeographical distribution of wild, weedy and cultivated Sorghum bicolor (L.) Moench in Kenya: Implications for conservation and crop-to-wild gene flow. *Genetic Resources and Crop Evolution, 57*(2), 243-253.

Quattrocchi, U. (2000). *CRC world dictionary of plant names* (p. 6). 1 A-C. CRC Press.

Sheik, M. I. (1989). Acacia nilotica (L). *Its production, management, and utilization. Pakistan regional wood energy development programme in Asia* (p. 45). GCP/111/NET Field document No. 20, F.A.D Bangkok 10200, and Thailand.

Unader, D. W. (1991). Callus induction in Phyllanthus species and inhibition of viral DNA polymerase and reverse transcription by callus extracts. *Biomedical and Life Sciences Technology, 98*(4), 946-949.

Wilfred, P. (2006) *Directory of microbicides for the protection of materials and processes.* Berlin: Springer.

Zumeriye, A., & Alper, I. (2007). Uses of dried sugar pulp for binary biosorption of Gemazol Turquoise blue-G-reactive dye and copper (II) ions. *Chemical Engineering Journal, 127*, 1-3.

SAMUEL BARDE GWIMBE

5. TERRACING AND AGRICULTURE IN CENTRAL NIGERIA WITH A FOCUS ON YIL NGAS

INTRODUCTION

Yil Ngas is located on the south-eastern escarpment of the Jos Plateau, Nigeria. It stretches down from the rather rugged edge of the plateau to its foothills, covering an area of about 2,000 square kilometers. It lies between latitudes 9° to 10° North and longitudes 9° to 10° East. The indigenous inhabitants called it Yil Ngas, which literally denotes 'Ngas country,' or 'Ngas land.' Until 1906, when British colonial encroachment began, Yil Ngas was largely characterized by independent and politically non-centralized societies or polities.

Various Ngas traditions of origin and migration often tend to retrace the routes of migration of their ancestors from the Chad Basin to Yil Ngas or from the Chad Basin through Kwararafa in the lower Benue Valley to Yil Ngas. Some lineages claim being autochthonous. Their language belongs in the Chadic branch of the Afro-Asiatic family of languages. By the end of the nineteenth and beginning of the twentieth century, the Ngas lived in several politically non-centralized communities but had culturally been transformed into a cohesive society with a measure of concrete, internal historical development. Several British colonial invaders in the first decade of the twentieth century, described Ngas communities as thickly populated. This chapter broaches on their pre-colonial techniques of soil and water conservation, especially the building of terraces in agriculture.

THE PHYSIOGRAPHY

Captain Renny, a British colonial officer who first led colonial soldiers to commence the conquest of Yil Ngas in 1906, gave this on-the-spot report to his superior military officers.

"The Angass inhabit a large tract of rough mountainous country ... inside the area inhabited by the tribe there are practically no roads or even tracks, the whole country being a vast mountain range extremely rough and rocky and intersected in every direction by deep ravines that would render marching impossible for a column during the rains."[1]

Renny visited more of the outcrop highland territory presently shared between Pankshin, Wokkos, and Ampang-East Districts of today than elsewhere in Yil Ngas. Renny's description implies that Yil Ngas as an environment was practically uncultivable. That was not, and is not, the case. In such a hilly environment, factors of erosion existed. Its impact on the landscape of Yil Ngas, however, did not demand such exaggerated qualifications. Dimka, a recent observer of the

G. Emeagwali & G. J. S. Dei (eds.), African Indigenous Knowledge and the Disciplines, 35–43.

geography of Yil Ngas, said with particular reference to its hills, that: "Most of these hills have been badly eroded by swift rivers giving rise to a very rugged topography with interlocking spurs."[2] Yet cultivation of crops is a continuing reality in the area.

Here and there, inselbergs and other rock-masses could be seen today, in Yil Ngas, astride outcrops, hills and hillocks which are in turn either perching atop mountain ranges or scattered on the valleys and the vast downlands extending from the foothills; the very ground itself is strewn with sandstones, gravels, plutons, mica, feldspars, granites and so on. This is a blunt testimony to persistent denudation processes. The major forces of denudation in Yil Ngas are water and fire. We focus here mainly on how man contained the eroding power of water through terrace-building especially on farms.

The hydraulic denudation fostering the erosion of Yil Ngas over the centuries, however, is not of great magnitude in its carrying content, being that the land has long been a watershed country, often characterized by steep slopes and swift streams. Between the rock-masses, hillocks and hills, sometimes wet-crevices, gorges, ravines, and rivulets, features of a watershed country, are found, whose waters, especially during the wet season wantonly furrow the land-surface and flow into bigger streams and rivers. The Taman drains the western and southern areas into the Shimankar, which in turn empties into the River Benue. The Gyangyang, in conjunction with the Nyinang (Yinang) drain the northern and eastern areas of Yil Ngas, into the Wase, which in turn empties into the River Benue. The Lere stream flows partially out of Yil Ngas northwards until it eventually goes into the Gongola, which in turn, empties into the Benue. All of these waters do eventually drain into the River Benue.

Yil Ngas suffers from an annual dry season's water shortage. By the beginning of the twentieth century, the present trend of seasonal scarcity of drinkable water already existed in Yil Ngas. It was not peculiar to the communities on the hills; those on the broken foothills were not exempted. Because of the slopes, most of the streams usually flood their banks during the rainy or wet-seasons. Great velocities, especially after the torrents between the months of June and August, usually characterize the streams and rivulets. The case seems to be with some merit that there were greater water resources in Yil Ngas by the beginning than by the end of the twentieth century. Inter-spaced along the broad dry sandy streambeds of Yil Ngas during the earlier decades of the twentieth century, were several ponds, good for swimming, fishing, drinking, especially by livestock and so on.[3]

From the rock-crevices or highland valleys, good, cool and clear water flowed out perennially. Such springs still exist: B'utjei-mwa (b'utjei, in the singular) or gushing springs erupted once in a while and were dreaded because of their destructiveness. Today, some streams have changed their courses, and most riverbeds have not only widened but are deeper with steep banks in the downlands. In the hills, the streams are swifter and 'valleys' are marked with deep canyons and gorges.

By the end of the nineteenth century, there were some vast plains, largely uncultivated, that have now, today, been subjected to cultivation.[4] Most hills and hillsides were, however, cultivated, in spite of soil erosion by running water. Dimka again observed, that:

> From the source, the rivers are swift, cutting deep into the mountainsides, creating V-shaped valleys with a few falls. At the foot of the escarpment, much of the gradient is reduced and most of the rivers have characteristics of mature rivers depositing silt over a distance of about 300-360 meters on either side of the banks.[5] That kind of transference of silt still continues, so long as the land remains sloppy.

By the end of the nineteenth century, there existed cultivated techniques of containing the process in Yil Ngas otherwise it should have rendered the highlands totally uncultivable, therefore uninhabitable, to farmers, by now. Captain Foulkes, a military colonialist and ethnographer, after being in contact with Yil Ngas for about a year, in 1907, took a personal interest in documenting what he called the 'customs of the Angass.' With reference to their agriculture, he noted with astonishment that: "The soil is exceedingly fertile ...."[6] An astonishing revelation about Yil Ngas, in spite of its notorious stoniness, which the travelling spies or 'Survey Party' in 1904 had frighteningly appreciated as a full obstacle to crop-cultivation.[7] Foulkes further described the features of Yil Ngas soil using soil types which his fellow British colonial readers were familiar with:

> The formation is sandstone and, for the most part, red sandstone, the latter on the high ground showing the rich colouring of Devonshire fields. In the plain Angass the sandstone is not much in evidence, the surface being strewn with granite rocks and the detritus there from.[8]

Recently, Dimka has maintained that:

> ... most soils range from gravely to sandy loam. Laboratory tests have revealed PH6.7. Shallow soils are underlain by hard lateritic pan, some few centimetres below the surface. In rocky hollows, soils are deep, and rich, enriched through weathering of soil nutrients from the rocks. Poorest soils are found at the foot of the escarpment far away the foot of the plateau due to over-cultivation and exposure by soil erosion.[9]

The rugged physiography of Yil Ngas, its characteristic mountains, hills, streams and soils, therefore, have remained seemingly the same since the beginning of the twentieth century, save for the intensity of soil erosion and the dessication of water resources, leading to the emergence of poorer and poorer soils 'far away from the foot' of the Jos Plateau and drier river-beds in the dry seasons.

PRE-COLONIAL AGRICULTURE AND TERRACES IN YIL NGAS

Their whole social and religious fabric is founded on an agricultural basis.
They are essentially agriculturists and judging from results, admirable ones.
(Foulkes, 1907)[10]

Agriculture was the principal economic activity practised by Ngas people by the
beginning of the twentieth century. Foulkes made a correct assessment of the
whole basis of their life in 1907, when he said they were essentially admirable
agriculturists. Yet, in the next breadth, blinded by his colonialist mentality which
saw no good thing as coming from Yil Ngas, or Africa for that matter, Foulkes
scandalized them: "Their [agricultural] system appears too good for their own
intelligence to have evolved." And, if the Ngas did not evolve it, how did they
come by it? Foulkes' opinion was that "they must have been taught it," and
agriculture "being mainly a mechanical process there was little to forget," after
they must have been taught.[11] Foulkes did not, however, suggest who might have
taught agriculture to the Ngas to make his false assertion seem true.

Like his predecessors the British spies, who three years before were in Yil Ngas,
Foulkes narrated what he saw in 1907 regarding their use of every available space,
their intense expenditure of labour and dogged commitment to the building and
maintenance of terraces, especially on hilly farm sites: "In the hills [Hill Angas
area] every little scrap of ground is utilized, and whole mountain-sides are terraced
up at an enormous expenditure of labor. On the steeper slopes the terraces may be
3ft [three feet] high, built up of rocks and stones, and frequently only a few inches
wide, just enough room for one row of guinea corn."[12] That shows how meticulous
they were about making terraces in order to get as much of the soil as possible.

Practising agriculture in a geographic environment characterized with the kind
of topography that Yil Ngas had and still has, must have, no doubt, been labor
intensive. But Foulkes failed to give the credit of knowing how to overcome such a
tough environment, through terrace-building, to the Ngas people. Had he done so,
his rationale for constraining the Ngas to submit to the British regime, which he
represented, would have been undermined. Colonial whims and caprices made it
such that the colonialists sometimes portrayed the colonised as"warlike" and
healthy, but at other times, as "lazy" and "unintelligent," though they always
exploited their labor. Thus, Foulkes labored to suggest in 1907 that the Ngas were
hard-working and had daringly subjected most of their 'tough' area to cultivation,
yet he also thought they were "low in intelligence."

Foulkes did not realise, as it were, that when the going got tough, the Ngas
people being tough, got going. They had embraced shifting cultivation, which
incidentally he knew nothing about, and developed an attractive method of terrace-
building on their farms, yet to him they were just pedantic laborers! That was not
the case. They approached agriculture creatively. Throughout Yil Ngas, in addition
to terrace-building, techniques of shifting cultivation were utilized in the farm
sector on the one hand, and intensive cultivation largely blended with mixed-
cropping, especially in the homestead farm sector. Whether it was the Ngas

communities on the highland hills or those on the broken and hilly plains, they generally cultivated the hilltops and hillsides as well as the plains and valleys, employing the techniques of building and or repairing of terraces and cultivating the beds created as a result of terracing.

The comparative size of Ngas settlements vis-à-vis those of their lowland neighbors by the end of the nineteenth century, to an extent, indicated the large size of Ngas labor-forces at the time. Ngas settlements were large, but pitched on mountain ranges, hills, hillsides and plains. Emerging from Tarokland to the southeast of Yil Ngas in 1904, the Survey Party of British Geographic Society comparatively observed that: "From now onwards, instead of scattered hamlets the people usually live in large villages without stockades."[13] Doubtless, the use of stockades to surround settlement premises was a feature of the lowland peoples, which included, among others, the Jukun, Goemai, Yom, Gerka, Tel and Tarok, whose settlements spies had visited before getting into the Ngas country. Capt. Renny, who got to Yil Ngas two years later, reported that Ngas settlements were "very thickly populated and the population of the whole tribe must be at least 250,000." Furthermore: "All the [Ngas] towns are built in separate compounds (holding 20 to 80 people) scattered as a rule over several square miles in the hills, some of them constructed on the highest peaks which are well-nigh inaccessible."[14] Let us infer from that, that by the beginning of the twentieth century, the Ngas settlements, said to be large in area, constructed mostly on peaks, with separately built compounds, had on average 50 folks per compound, indicative of a large workforce.

From the way their houses were built, settlements were patterned, sites were selected, the Ngas did not only demonstrate that they understood, and had mastered, their environment to a great extent, but were a people with experience and principles in dealing with nature; by the beginning of the twentieth century, they had already recorded various victories in that regard. The Foulkeses of this world could not successfully deny those victories to distort their history. One such victory was terrace-building on especially rocky hillside farms.

The Ngas developed a system of terracing, which was viewed by the colonialists as one of the best in Africa. Terracing was probably the most amazing phenomenon the early colonialists saw in Yil Ngas. Some thought that white-skinned people possibly from the north must have brought it into Yil Ngas.[15] Others thought of the utter difficulty of tilling such a stony terrain, and simply wondered how and from where the Ngas borrowed the technique of building terraces. Thus, Boyd Alexander, leader of the Survey Party of spies, observed with reference to what he saw and initially thought in the first week of July 1904, that there was very little grass, and few bushes, and it must have been very difficult to grow crops in such a stony soil.[16] Before reporting on how terraces were built in pre-colonial times in Yil Ngas, let us briefly examine terrace-building in some parts of the world.

In conducting a survey of four terracing-building societies, Critchley and Brommer have suggested that the most ancient terraces are in the foothills of the Himalayas in the State of Uttaranchal in India; those terraces are well over a thousand years old.[17] They further state that in the said Himalayan foothills, "the terrace walls or 'risers' are sometimes stone-faced – when stone is available – but more often they are earth structures."[18] This is exactly what was and is still to an extent practised in Yil Ngas, where, in most cases, stones are available on most farms, except in valleys and on banks of streams where either or both of two earth structure types are usually raised. The smaller earth structure in Yil Ngas is known as gung while the bigger is known as *mbanki*, more or less a dike. A stone-built terrace in Yil Ngas is known as *pang or pang'gang*.

Another situation cited by Crithley and Brommer, which in our reckoning is similar to what was observed in Yil Ngas by the beginning of the twentienth century, and to an extent still remains today, is the case of the area around Yogyakarta city in south-central Java, where "using terraces like stepping-stones" farmers cultivated the hillsides. "The result is a landscape of bench terraces that have a slight backslope, allowing excess runoff to drain away."[19] But unlike the Java situation, the antiquity of terrace-building in Yil Ngas should, in our opinion, date earlier than the nineteenth century. At present that remains a subject of a separate research.

Regarding the two African examples of terrace-building farming communities cited by Crithley and Brommer, namely, Kabale District in south-west Uganda and Venda area of Limpopo Province of South Africa, the former was stimulated and acquired the practice during the 1940s through colonial ordinances, thus it is of recent origin. In Venda, however, "a tradition of building houses and terrace walls with stone has existed for generations," very reminiscent of what was accomplished in Yil Ngas in pre-colonial times. "Most of the terraces have stone-faced walls (mitsheto) that have been constructed with pride and considerable masonry skill."[20] That is reminiscent of what was accomplished in Yil Ngas in pre-colonial times, as the next paragraph purports to show.

The Survey Party of the British Geographic Society, whose initial decision was that it was difficult to cultivate crops in Yil Ngas, did not conceal their deference for the ingenuity of the Ngas people in terracing their entire country, which they marveled at in 1904:

> The whole land was mapped out into little terraces sometimes only a foot or two broad, built to hold up the rain as it ran down the hill, and prevent the soil from being washed away. In places no longer cultivated, only the dilapidated terrace walls remained, through the rents of which in course of time the soil had been blown or washed down. In this case one saw only low walls encircling a hill, and I cannot but think, though with deference ... that a similar cause may have led to the erection of the extraordinary systems of concentric walls, which exist in Rhodesia [Zimbabwe] ....[21]

Furthermore, Boyd Alexander, who compiled their 1907 published report, did not conceal his sense of wonderment about the terracing when he testified to the fact that every available space on the Ngas people's farms was already cultivated:

Dugurh [Dungung] stands at the foot of Mt. Ampang [Zwal Pang], which is over 4,000 ft high. We climbed this and found a large plateau at the top covered with populous villages. It was wonderful to see the way in which every inch of the ground was cultivated. Even spaces not more than a square foot in area, where a little soil had been collected, had been planted with millet or guinea corn, which is the ordinary food of the people throughout the country.[22]

The difference between the initial impression of the colonial spies and what they later saw was the employment of appropriate 'technology.' The technique of terracing was employed at all altitudes, in the foothills and in the hills. Valleys, swamps, plains, hilltops and hillsides were mostly cultivated, except when they were left to fallow.

Their tools, which were designed to face the hardest grounds, were therefore very strong. They included the chen sak (chen gon) or big hoe, the chen kos or small hoe, the sep or ax, the hammer, the kyeang, the nuk, and the mbamji, a pestle-like digger with a flat-bladed metal head and a wooden handle. These tools were of different sizes, for different services. With their aid, man appeared to have subjected every inch of available ground in Yil Ngas to cultivation up to the beginning of the twentieth century. With large communities, it was necessary that adequate, and possibly surplus, food supply was guaranteed, which in such a terrain, apart from enough man-power, required the use of appropriate tools and technical ideas, such as *kak kh pang'gang (or kak kh pang)*, which literally means building or repairing of terraces. Once built, stone-faced terraces were repaired from time to time or at every stage of the cultivation process, especially during clearing, weeding, and mulching in a given planting year, as long as there were breaches on them. In order to preserve the neat arrangement of terraces on farms, cattle-herders were sometimes forbidden from grazing their animals on leftover stalks of harvested corn. Earth terraces were also subject to repair either to conserve moisture or prevent flooding of farms by water.

By the beginning of the twentieth century, stones or rock pieces were being used in various other important ways as h'k nchwa'lang or sling stones, *h'k char'char* or hand-thrown stones, h'k shin'gwak and *h'k sar shin,* which are grinding or mill stones, *h'k t'r'ng, h'k pang-dyer, h'k gh'zj'ok, h'k pii-bwir* and so on. Stones were used as *h'k dyik lu* or building blocks, thus the Ngas, by the turn of century in question, built mostly stonewalled huts. *H'k shii-lu* were stones used for constructing foundations of dwellings and other buildings in place. For granary or corn-bin walls and ceilings, however, refined clay mixed with mud and brittle grasses to produce a type of mortar, was artfully (or ceramically) used as plaster and/or embroidery.

In every big ancestral compound, there was a *nefur*, an arena or dance theatre, circumscribed by a *pang* (this is its second meaning) or a lowly-built circle, or semi circle, of stones, neatly arranged up to two or three feet high and about two feet wide. Hence the term *pang nefur* is sometimes used to describe a nefur. The frontage of every house where there was no nefur had a po pang, which means a smaller place than a nefur, where some stones were put for people to sit on, during moments of rest, grief, brief consultations or, joy, especially as spectators during song and dance presentations.

The raising of bare stone walls without using any mortar or clay, in the historical development of the Ngas people, up to AD 1900, was probably an epitome or a relic of their pre iron-smelting and-working period. Among them, the po pang was lower than the *pang nefur* which was, in turn, lower but wider than the *bong n'ng*, or cattle kraal. A *bong n'ng's* height is about the same as that of a lu tap, the small, bare stone-walled, thatch-roofed watchshed. A lu tap smacks of how Ngas pre-colonial ancestors simply took advantage of their rocky terrain to meet their watch-shelter and farm-recreational needs. It seems tenable to suppose that in earlier times the initial home was a lu tap, an advanced alternative to cave-dwelling.[23]

Using mortar or clay in buildings must have been developed or acquired later, when perhaps the Ngas had already attained the iron-working stage and could take advantage of iron-headed tools not only to dig up much clay, but also to mix mortar. When clay was discovered and used in pre-colonial Yil Ngas is an archeological unknown. But Ngas pottery and other clay articles (dated 1900) made of very good clay have survived not only as vessels of an age, but unique works of art.

Today, the situation has greatly changed. The large settlements in Yil Ngas by the beginning of the twentieth century are no longer a big deal. Places which were more or less large collections of labor-power, which naturally translated into a generally sound scope of production, have dwindled a lot due to emigration. All capable folks (whether males or females, children or the aged, the visually-handicapped or the lame, rulers or the ruled) participated in food production within the pre-colonial economy of Yil Ngas; today such attitude to work is merely a historical referent. There were practically no idlers, beggars, or other forms of lumpen population; today there are.

CONCLUSION

The inhabitants of Yil Ngas by AD 1900 had fashioned out the means, techniques, and tools appropriate for sustaining their struggle for existence in a natural environment, especially through building and maintaining terraces on hill, hillside, and valley farms.

By the beginning of the twentieth century, most neighbourhoods in Yil Ngas, where farms were usually operated, had terrace features of being cultivated or having been cultivated before. Explorers and colonialists saw contour lines or dilapidated walls of age-old terraces in the bushes, apart from the maintained terraces seen in farm-plots still being cultivated. Therefore, by the end of the nineteenth and the beginning of the twentieth century, the problem of Ngas agriculturists was not that of a too difficult, intractable natural environment, as of that of threats to peace which the soon-coming colonial regime constituted. Their environment as maintained and sustained was resourceful enough to meet their various needs of food, shelter, clothing, tools, water, and so on.

Today, terrace-building and the repairing of terraces are still being done. But most farmers would prefer to cultivate less troublesome locations to reduce the labor demands of terraced locations. It has become fashionable now to farm the valleys and plains and to neglect the hilltops and sides. This gradual 'shift' of preference for the valleys over the cultivation of the hillsides has had a negative impact on the relationship with the environment in Yil Ngas, especially as it concerns soil and moisture conservation.

NOTES

[1] L. F. Renny (Captain), 'Report on Angass Expedition: From O. C. Troops, Bauchi, Brigade Major, N.N.R.' in: SNP 6, C140/1907, Bauchi Province – Patrols and Expeditions (Confidential), National Archives, Kaduna.

[2] Adini S. Dimka, 'The Geography of Pankshin' in his: *The Impact of Universal Primary Education Rural Farm Labour and the Economy of Pankshin Local Government Area of Plateau State* (BA Dissertation, Ahmadu Bello University, Zaria, 1983), 11.

[3] Samuel Barde Gwimbe, *Roots of Rural Poverty in Yil Ngas of Plateau State: A Political Economy of Colonial Exploitation and Social Deprivation* (MA Thesis, Ahmadu Bello University, Zaria, 2001), 43.

[4] Gwimbe, *Roots of Rural Poverty in Yil Ngas of Plateau State*, 44.

[5] Dimka, 'The Geography of Pankshin' in his: *The Impact of Universal Primary Education Rural Farm Labour and the Economy of Pankshin Local Government Area of Plateau State*, 11.

[6] H. D. Foulkes (Captain), *Some Preliminary Notes on the Angass*, 1907, SNP 379/1910, National Archives, Kaduna.

[7] Boyd Alexander, *From the Niger to the Nile, Volume 1* (London, Edward Arnold, 1907), 11.

[8] Foulkes, *Some Preliminary Notes on the Angass*.

[9] Dimka, 'The Geography of Pankshin' in his: *The Impact of Universal Primary Education Rural Farm Labour and the Economy of Pankshin Local Government Area of Plateau State*, 11.

[10] Foulkes, *Some Preliminary Notes on the Angass*.

[11] Foulkes, *Some Preliminary Notes on the Angass*.

[12] Foulkes, *Some Preliminary Notes on the Angass*.

[13] Alexander, *From the Niger to the Nile*, 95.

[14] Renny, 'Report on Angass Expedition.'

[15] Foulkes, *Some Preliminary Notes on the Angass*.

[16] Alexander, *From the Niger to the Nile*, 11.

[17] William Critchley and Marit Brommer, 'Understanding Traditional Terracing,' in *LEISA*, (December 2003), 14.

[18] Critchley and Brommer, 'Understanding Traditional Terracing' *LEISA*, 14.

[19] Critchley and Brommer, 'Understanding Traditional Terracing,' *LEISA*, 14.

[20] Critchley and Brommer, 'Understanding Traditional Terracing,' *LEISA*, 14.

[21] Alexander, *From the Niger to the Nile*, 97.

[22] Alexander, *From the Niger to the Nile*, 97.

[23] Gwimbe, *Roots of Rural Poverty in Yil Ngas of Plateau State*, 61.

SAMUEL BARDE GWIMBE

6. ANCIENT TERRACES ON HIGHLAND FRINGES SOUTH OF THE CHAD BASIN

The Case of Gwoza and Yil Ngas

INTRODUCTION

Location and Traditions

'Yil Ngas'[1] is an indigenous place - name meaning 'Ngasland' or 'territory of the Ngas', an ethnic nationality in central Nigeria. It is located on the southeast escarpment of the Jos Plateau, stretching down from the hilly and spacious edge of the plateau to its equally spacious foothills, stretching further into the borders of Bauchi State to the north and northeast, and rolling sloppily towards the Benue valley to the southeast. However for the purposes of this chapter, we are concerned with the whole of Kanke Local Government Area and Pankshin (North and Central State-Legislative Constituencies of Pankshin) Local Government Area of Plateau State only. Migrant Kanuri, Hausa, and Fulani had begun to settle in the area during the nineteenth century, especially in some parts of what is now Kanke Local Government Area.[2] Until 1906, when British colonial encroachment into Yil Ngas began, the whole area was largely characterized by independent and politically non-centralized communities, which reportedly were thickly populated.[3] It was not until 1919 that forces of British colonial encroachment finally took total command of Yil Ngas.

'Gwoza' on the other hand, is a place-name referring to the pre-colonial homeland of some twelve smaller but related ethnic nationalities,[4] which contains many towns and villages and it roughly lies between latitudes 10 and 11° North, as well as between longitudes 13 and 14° East, as could be seen on any appropriate atlas of the area. Gwoza is pitched on the southeastern edge of Borno State, hinged on the Cameroun border, occupying what in some historical works are known as the Mandara Mountains (or Hills) and their surrounding foothills. Its eleven pre-colonial ethnic nationalities spoke languages in the Laamang-cluster of the Chadic branch of the Afro-Asiatic Family of Languages, though others have settled in the area, especially in the twentieth century. Gwoza is a vast mountainous area with several towns and villages, but the area's main town is also known as 'Gwoza.' In this chapter, the term is used with reference to the general area in question, not just its main town. There are fourteen ethnic nationalities inhabiting the Gwoza area presently, which comprise the Dughwede, Zagwada (also known as Gudupe, and

G. Emeagwali & G. J. S. Dei (eds.), African Indigenous Knowledge and the Disciplines, 45–62.

Guduf), Mafa, Gavva, Chikide, Zalidivah, Waha, Cinene, Gamargu, Guvuko, Mandara, Glavda, Marghi, and migrant Kanuri, Fulani, and Hausa.[5] According to an informant, the name 'Gwoza' derives from 'ngu ze', a Dughwede expression meaning 'let's go to the farm'. Over the course of time, the pronunciation was unjustifiably corrupted to what it is now.[6] Between 1902 and 1913, Gwoza fell to the colonial encroachment of the Germans, who had militarily invaded the area from the Cameroun side, and finally took possession of the land and made it part of colonial Cameroun. Gwoza was largely characterized by long-embattled, hill-based, reportedly densely populated communities that had held their turf for centuries against different shades of invaders and enemies.[7] In 1919, however, following the Treaty of Versailles in the aftermath of the First World War, Gwoza changed hands ceasing to be part of German Cameroun and became part of British Cameroons, included under colonial Nigeria, as a mandated territory.

It is amazing to notice that several Gwoza and Ngas traditions of origin virtually point to the same area: the Chad Basin, particularly to Borno. Some Gwoza traditions would even add Ngazargamu.[8] At the same time, there are also traditions that claim some autochthonous historical belonging in the areas or vicinities of the areas they inhabit today. It is difficult now to totally accept the Chad-Basin-pointing-tradition type and reject the local-vicinity-pointing-tradition type of traditions of origin either in the Gwoza or Ngas accounts. Possibilities of truth tend to exist in either regard. Thus, it is safer to accommodate the two sets of traditions. As Abdullahi Smith has rightly advanced, the areas in question, which more or less fall in the Guinea Savanna zone, if not in the Middle Belt, was hitherto a centuries-long buffer zone bringing Chadic and earlier Benue-Congo language communities mainly into peaceful contact; but thereafter, they sometimes interfused, assimilated, and pressured each other, leading either to changes in language (thus of cultural identity) or local migrations within the region.[9]

Both Gwoza and Yil Ngas are situated somewhat immediately south, and basically outside, of the Chad Basin. Yil Ngas, being part of the Jos Plateau massif and its southeast foothills, is situated on the Chad Basin's southwest fringes while Gwoza is directly on its south-central fringes.[10] The analysis of current historical linguistic evidence actually classifies Shhk Ngas, or the Ngas Language, as well as the main Gwoza languages known as the Laamang group (excluding in this regard, the Kanuri and Fulani language, in their vicinity), within the Chadic Branch of the Afro-Asiatic Family of Languages.[11]

To an extent, this contention which places locations of Gwoza and Yil Ngas in the same bracket as it were, as both lying immediately outside, as well as lying to the south of the Chad Basin, supports, or tends to support, claims that southward migrations of peoples from the Chad Basin must have occurred in the long pre-colonial past. Thanks to unforgotten Chad Basin-pointing traditions of origin, such peoples must have metamorphosed, among others, into the present Ngas and Gwoza peoples, that is, into the communities whose farm terraces are comparatively surveyed here, claims of authochtoneity in some quarters of both areas, notwithstanding. Palmer in the 1920s had advanced the view that the Ngas were cognate with groups such as the Bade, Bole, Ngizim, Ngasar, and Ngijim,[12] who are still in the Chad Basin and therefore are geo-political neighbors of the peoples of Gwoza. For the Gwoza peoples, Connah holds the view that they migrated from the north down, not from across the Cameroun border immediately to the south up to their present place.[13] Thus a scenic picture of gradual process(es) of southerly (for Gwoza nationalities) and south-westerly (for the Ngas and kin nationalities') dispersion from the Bornoan mainland and shores, or west-bank of Lake Chad, that is, inside the Chad Basin itself, must have taken place, to areas lying immediately to the south along the fringes of the basin. It is absurd for Robert McNetting to consider Ngas traditions of Bornoan origin as somehow meaningless.[14] The fact that Gwoza and Yil Ngas belong together in the Guinea Savanna zone is an important issue; the relative difference of Gwoza lying in the Northern Guinea Savanna while Yil Ngas lies in the Southern Guinea Savanna belt, or sub-zone, is equally significant.[15]

Available evidence indicates more or less that located along the same southern fringes of the Chad Basin are other terrace-building peoples and communities such as the Kulere, Kofyar, and Berom of Hoss in Plateau State and Burra of Biu and Higgi of Minchika in Borno and Adamawa States.[16] Hence our general concern with highland communities lying along the southern fringes of the Chad Basin, and our specific and primary concern with Gwoza and Yil Ngas, both of which the title of this chapter betray. It is hoped that in the future, other terrace-building communities situated along the southern fringes of the Chad Basin, and/or elsewhere, shall further be studied or at least surveyed to gain a more inclusive picture of this subject in the history of Africa.

SOME TERRACE HISTORIOGRAPHY ISSUES

Simply put, terraces may be defined as deliberately constructed contour banks that are effective in safeguarding against erosion on a given farm side, especially on a sloppy landscape. According to Kowal and Kassam, "Experience indicates that well-constructed contour banks are an effective safeguard against major erosion and probably the most practical means of controlling run-off and erosion in the Savanna environment."[17] Thus, Gwoza and Yil Ngas, among other historical communities known to have developed the terracing technique, deserve to be applauded for possessing the knowledge and maintaining the usage of an effective erosion-controlling technology in the Guinea Savanna. Their derision, as featured in some writings, is unwarranted. Commenting in the 1950s on contemporary Nigerian communities known for building terraces in agriculture, which were mostly indicative of continuities from the pre-colonial past, Buchanan and Pugh maintained: "Skilful and well-developed farms of terrace agriculture are to be found among the pagan peoples ...."[18] That derogatory category of 'pagan peoples' fortunately or unfortunately included all the communities of Gwoza and Yil Ngas, as well as numerous other communities situated in the Nigerian Middle Belt, or in the wider Guinea Savanna, who practised African indigenous religions and had at the time neither embraced Islam, spread from the North, nor Christianity, spread from the South, to any significant dimension.

As if such negative reportage about the so-called 'pagan' peoples, though skilful developers of farm terraces(!), was not enough, Buchanan and Pugh further suggested that in view of the supposedly sad historical past that the skilful but 'pagan' developers of terraces must have had, they willy-nilly had to build the terraces. In their own words, the communities were "invariably associated with a defensive hill-top concentration of settlement, and represent a natural adjustment to the difficulties of an upland environment."[19] A careful reader may notice the critical concepts 'invariably' and 'natural adjustment' as saying the people acted by either instinct, sheer constraint or conditioning, or weight of necessity, rather than by any sense of ingenuity or innovation, in building and maintaining the terraces! Such reconstruction is both false and unfair. Terraces were built because of a need to utilize the available resources in a difficult environment to develop a food supply. Furthermore, if possession of the technique was a natural adjustment to the challenges of a difficult, upland environment, then it ought to stand in evidence that all mountainous communities naturally possessed the technique of building admirable terraces on their farms, to suit Buchanan and Pugh's suggestion; unfortunately, that is not the case.[20]

Neither could we accept the hypothesis that wherever the technique of building terraces obtained in pre-colonial Nigeria or Africa at large, it was invariably and always an indication of a defensive hilltop concentration of settlement, which Buchanan and Pugh purport to suggest. In Gwoza, however, that position, or hypothesis of a defensive hilltop concentration of settlements, may seem tenable given the fact that the best examples of terraces in Gwoza today are up, astride the mountains, and hardly in the foothills, even though intense downhill migration appears to have taken place in the last 100 years. Though covered with some vegetation, the more or less sandy, stoneless appearance of the soils in the foothills of Gwoza on the one hand, and the practice of cultivating farms without the aid of ridges in Gwoza in the mountains and foothills on the other, however, might have functioned to give a sharp contrast between the foothills where there are really no significant terraces, and the mountaintops (and, especially in the south, hillsides) of Gwoza where there are well-preserved and visibly well-built dry-stone terraces; this betrays the impression of a terrain of hitherto defensive hilltop concentration of settlements. It is dangerously inadequate to build and advocate a general theory based on the experience and evidence of Gwoza as a homogenous community, alone, and superimpose it on the explanation of a host of other terrace-building communities in Nigeria, such as Buchanan and Pugh have willy-nilly done. Such reductionism is untenable. In Yil Ngas, evidence of terraces are visible in both the mountain-based and in the foothill and downland communities, built with equal ability and circumspection. Differences between rates of downhill and uphill migration in Yil Ngas, in the last hundred years, might have virtually been very small given the fact that greater commercial and urban development, especially with the choice and development of Pankshin town since 1909 as a regional headquarters, have occurred in the more hilly edge of the Jos Plateau, where Pankshin town is situated, than in the foothills; unlike the case in Gwoza, where its major urban and commercial developments in the last hundred years have been in the foothills, where Gwoza town is situated. Furthermore, it is difficult to postulate any differences between hill and plains Ngas settlements to the extent of suggesting that either area was characteristic of a foothill or hilltop 'concentration of settlement' by the beginning of the twentieth century. If anything, early European travelers simply stated that Ngas settlements, when compared with those of their neighbors in the Benue valley, were large, populated and unstockaded.[21] For Gwoza, however, it has been suggested that in past centuries their mainly mountain-based settlements, on the Gwoza peninsula, were characterized by high population densities; further substantiating the tenability of the hypothesis of a defensive hilltop concentration of settlement, in that regard.[22]

The salient impression, attributable to Buchanan and Pugh, which ultimately suggests that hill-dwelling communities happened to have built terraces due to the practice of a defense economy (being as it were surrounded or kept under siege by their invading enemies!) rather than out of sheer concern to conquer the environment and ensure food production, also leaves something to be desired. While commenting on Gwoza, Buchanan and Pugh, said, "This highly specialised agricultural economy developed in response to special historical circumstances, viz. past insecurity due slave-raiding ...."[23] Furthermore:

> The whole area was in the past subject to continual raiding by the neighbouring Fulani, Kanuri and Mandara [supposedly of Mora, situated on the plains], and it was in response to the insecurity created by these raids that the present pattern of hill settlement evolved.[24]

Stanhope White, writing in 1941 on Gwoza, also maintains that:

> Until the British occupation in 1919 the people were confined almost exclusively to the hills, and the neighbouring plains were cultivated only to a small extent by the farmers from villages on the slopes above ... anyone venturing on to the plains was liable to capture by small slave-raiding parties on the look out for such prey, whilst corn crops were liable to destruction or pillage at any time.[25]

On a general note, it would be difficult to deny that the quest for security and defense, though varying in strategy and situation, has been (and still is) the vogue of all human societies whether on the hills or plains, hence Gwoza communities could not be an exception. The foregoing impression of air-tight separation between erstwhile inhabitants of Gwoza peninsula and their neighbors in the surrounding plains up to 1919 due to intense "slave-raiding" seems exaggerated. There must have been moments of war and tension, no doubt, but moments of peace and great diplomacy between Gwoza communities and their neighbors on the plains both far and near, could not be totally gainsaid. The old belief that due to invasions, entire populations in Africa were constrained to either emigrate or, as it were, to totally isolate themselves from others is being held with scepticism in some quarters nowadays.[26] If anything, the practice of a defense economy must have been complemented with efforts at diplomacy. Be that as it may. Suffice it simply to recognize the ingenuity of hill inhabitants in managing their environments, especially in building terraces in agriculture, appreciating their meaningful contribution, which ironically Buchanan and Pugh have also tried to do (as shown in endnote 30) – but not without contempt, as shown in the foregoing.

In the same article in 1941, Stanhope White reported that the then contemporary inhabitants of Gwoza, settlers as they were, did not perceive themselves as descendants of the forebears who constructed the dry-stone terraces on the peninsula, but simply maintained and utilized what they found: "The present inhabitants all say that their forebears found the present system of terraces on entering the area, and it is obvious that it must have taken centuries of work to bring the system to its present state of perfection."[27] As a result, it is difficult to determine how old the terrace-building practice or system in Gwoza is, until some archeological investigation is done.[28] Stanhope White reports further that during his research, he found a late Paleolithic or early Neolithic artifact, whose details he did not disclose, on one of the spurs of the Gwoza Mountains; this is quite suggestive of the antiquity of man on the peninsula.[29] On the other hand, and to the best of the present author's knowledge, the Ngas have never attributed the development of their terrace-building practice to forebears of unknown identity other than to their own ancestors.

Given the supposedly ancient antiquity of the Gwoza terraces, it is possible that, before the emigration of various ancestral lineages that later metamorphosed into the present Ngas and other related groups from the Chad Basin, they had known, practised and maintained the terrace-building technology. Pushing far this hypothesis would not be safe since it seems clear that the present Ngas themselves are partly descendants of emigrants from the Chad Basin and partly descendants of authochtonous lineages, who possess only the memory of having been in Yil Ngas for a long time. Conducting a wider field research alongside archaeological investigation might engender antidotes to the pending questions regarding the dates or antiquity of terrace-building technologies in either Gwoza or Yil Ngas. For the time-being, we would be content to state that both are quite old, probably ancient, not later than the first half of the second millennium AD.

COMPARABLE PROPOSITIONS

One great advantage of this comparative survey is the opportunity granted to not only look at two distinct scenarios through the present author's eyes, but also to bring into critical limelight the comparable analyses and propositions of several scholars and authors, written often exclusively about either Gwoza or Yil Ngas, often desirous of stating that either the Gwoza or Ngas scenario which they know represents the best example of terraces in Africa at any bargain. Describing the terraces of Gwoza in specific terms, Buchanan and Pugh assert:

> It is a tribute to the ingenuity and labour of the pagan farmer that the rocky hillsides and grudging soils of the area were able to support a population whose density, as at the beginning of British occupation in 1919, has been estimated at over 130 per square mile ....

Except where topographic conditions make it quite impossible, the hill slopes are girdled with an elaborate system of drystone terraces. ...On gentler slopes less elaborate systems of erosion control are used, notably lines of fascines held in place by boulders or small mounds of earth thrown up by hoes; this latter represents a rudimentary form of contour banking.[30]

Let us compare that with the following reference on terraces in Yil Ngas, which Elizabeth Isichei wrote in 1982, and in the process, quoted Captain Foulkes who lived in the area as a colonial administrator between 1908 and 1911:

the peoples of the area showed a very high degree of mastery of its contrasting environments ... the precipitous slopes of the southern escarpment; the homeland of the Hill Ngas, where generations have contained the soil by elaborate dry-stone walling... One early visitor to Ngasland claimed that the people's agricultural techniques were so elaborate that they must have learnt them from elsewhere! ...

All early European visitors were profoundly impressed by the great skill of the area's agriculturalists .... Other observers commented on the Ngas dry-stone walling, the work of generations, which contained the thin soil, prevented erosion and cleared the stones from the rocky fields: '... whole mountain sides are terraced up at enormous expenditure of labour. On the steeper slopes the terraces may be 3 ft high, built of rocks and stones, and frequently only a few inches wide, just room for one row of guinea corn.'[31]

In the same article written in 1941, Stanhope White (on whom Buchanan and Pugh, as far as the terraces in Gwoza were concerned, basically depend) maintains:

It is a remarkable sight to see the miles of terraces in the south of the area, following every valley and spur for miles and extending vertically for some 2,500 feet. Tops of the hills have been surrounded by the top-most wall of the terraces, and the space then infilled to give flat expanses of varying size. Where the slope is gentle, the terraces are very wide, but the vast majority of the order of 4 feet high, 5 to 10 feet wide; some terraces, however, are simply a few inches wide, and allow one line of corn only to be sown thereon .... These terrace-walls have been carefully built up after the fashion of the dry-stone walls of northern England, and the work is in no way inferior to that of the latter.[32]

Let us compare White's views above with those of Boyd Alexander and his colleagues, who visited Yil Ngas in 1904 as a Survey Party of The British Geographic Society, expressing similar astonishment with Ngas terraces and agriculture:

It was wonderful to see the way in which every inch of ground was cultivated .... The whole land was mapped out into little terraces sometimes only a foot or two broad, built up to the rain as it ran down the hill and prevent the soil from being washed away. In places no longer cultivated, only the dilapidated terrace walls remained, through the rents of which in course of time the soil had been blown or washed down. In this case one saw only low walls encircling a hill, and I cannot but think, though with deference ... that a similar cause may have led to the erection of the extraordinary systems of concentric walls ... in Rhodesia [Zimbabwe].[33]

In January 2007, the following reference on agriculture in Gwoza, indicating the difference between the hill-based terrace farming and plains farming, was made:

> The people of Gwoza are predominantly subsistence farmers, composed of the plain land/terrace farmers. The mountain hill dwellers practice terrace farming which involves a lot of skills in soil management techniques. Due to the limited availability of vast plain land to plant crops, the few which are between the terraces are traditionally managed by supplementing the planting of different crops every two years.[34]

Then let us compare that position on Gwoza with, though working on the Kofyar, congeners of the Ngas as he calls them, Robert McNettings' noticeable comment for the terraces in Yil Ngas, in the process of which he cited a statement of Fairbairn written in 1943:

> The example of practical engineering in building of terraces and the adaptation of different ridging techniques to varying conditions is striking. One expert [Fairbairn] after describing the more modest terraces and ridges of the neighboring Angas called them 'a perfect demonstration of theoretical anti-erosion measures carried out on a wide and successful scale over a period of centuries.'[35]

Thus, here we are, confronted with the 'remarkable to see,' ingenious, very extensive terraces built like 'the dry-stone walls of northern England,' as claimed with reference to terraces of Gwoza; and the 'wonderful to see,' with 'a very high degree of mastery,' or a 'striking example of practical engineering,' or 'a perfect demonstration of success,' 'built like the concentric walls of Zimbabwe,' as claimed with reference to the terraces of Yil Ngas. These were claimed by different sets of scholars who, apparently, as this is very obvious from their works, did not show any knowledge (or if they knew something, did not exhibit any awareness) of either Gwoza or Yil Ngas when advocating the merits of its counterpart which they wrote about. Hence each set of scholars spoke with superlative phraseology, being fortunately (or unfortunately) fully satisfied with their findings.

There is no gainsaying the fact that the claim that the Ngas were taught the technique of terracing by foreigners is not tenable, as shown elsewhere.[36] What could be conceded thus far as a possibility in the cosmogonies of Gwoza and Yil Nags, is that terrace-building technology seems to be a relic of a pre-Kanuri Chadic civilization that flourished in the Bornoan area, in which hypothetical case, alongside the ancient constructors of Gwoza terraces in the southern uplands of Borno; the Ngas ancestors possessed the knowledge and the practice before migrating to their present place of abode on the Jos Plateau. On the other hand, however, the technology could also have been developed when the Chad Basin emigrants came into contact with the authochtons in Yil Ngas. It remains a pointer that the technology has remained indigenous to Yil Ngas. But for the peoples of Gwoza, as White reported in 1941, the technology might be very old; so old as to have been abandoned by its original developers, given the waves of human migration, displacement and relocation drifting away from the Chad Basin to its immediate north and later found and acquired; which partially explains why it has not been significantly translated, if at all, to suit the plains cultivation in the foothills of Gwoza peninsula. Until wider research is done, these positions would be only educated guesses, however.

FIELD REPORT

In October 2007, the present author went on a one-person field trip to Gwoza, a location he had not visited before. With his knowledge of Yil Ngas, his homeland, which he had visited several times, a brief comparative eyewitness account of the two scenarios is attempted here. The field report is presented on the basis of similarities and dissimilarities; hoping that by means of that format, readers would gain a deeper understanding of the issues broached. Let us now proceed with the similarities and dissimilarities, upholding each consideration, simultaneously:

Dry Stone Terraces

The appearance, size, length, height and general structure of dry-stone terraces in Gwoza and Yil Ngas are very similar. The author could not see any differences. Pictures taken from Gwoza and Yil Ngas, for instance, if not indicated have striking resemblances that could confuse anyone. When the author showed pictures taken in Yil Ngas at Gwoza, informants and/or contacts began to make educated guesses as to where in Gwoza those pictures were supposedly taken, but were visibly stunned when they were told the pictures were actually taken at Yil Ngas in far away Plateau State.

The terrace-stone types, with diameters of 3 inches to 1 foot, on the terraces in Gwoza at locations high on the top of the mountains, are mostly brown and polished granites, and a few quartz, smooth as though packed from the dry bed of a mighty river; whereas the terrace-stone types on the terraces in Yil Ngas, of similar diameters, are mostly greyish granites. Interlaced here and there, however, though in very rare supply on Ngas farms, are white, brown, and reddish feldspars that are hardly smooth. Smooth feldspars in Yil Ngas are mostly found on dry-stream beds, not on the mountains. To the present author, the evidence of smooth granites astride the Gwoza Mountains is nothing but blatant evidence supporting the view that in past millennia, the shores of the Mega Chad, a formerly very wide presentiment of Lake Chad, had actually been at the Gwoza peninsula.[37]

Earth Terraces

Since pre-colonial times, both the dry stone-laid and the raised-earth terraces have been, and still are, constructed in Gwoza and Yil Ngas today. Earth terraces, in particular, are being built and presently maintained with equal circumspection in both areas. They are intermittently constructed alongside the dry-stone terraces on most farm sides, depending on the absence of stones on such farm sides, serving the same purpose of conserving water and soil nutrients from easily running down the slopes. In both Gwoza and Yil Ngas, there are low and high terraces depending on the gradients on a given farm side. Oftentimes, high terraces are of dry-stone formation, while low terraces are of raised-earth formation, that is, especially in Yil Ngas. In Gwoza, on the other hand, low terraces, though usually covered with earth on the surface, like all typical earth terraces, are underneath, laid with "lines of fascines held in place by boulders or small mounds of earth thrown up by hoes; this latter represents a rudimentary form of contour banking."[38] Sharing his experience and sudden amazement in Gwoza in 1992, Keith Hess maintains:

> It may be a bit of an exaggeration but if sustainable agriculture is your goal, their way of farming rates high.

Even around the base of the mountain, there is a hint of something different. Stalks, branches and stones form contour lines across some of the fields. Though an effective method of soil and water conservation, this technique is little practiced elsewhere in Nigeria. But it is in ascending the stair-step mountain trails that one really becomes impressed. All of a sudden there are stone-walled terraces everywhere![39]

The sudden appearance of dry-stone and earth terraces at the top of the Gwoza Mountains, as well as the use of fascines on low terraces, also astonished the present author because he was seeing earth terraces under-laid with fascines for the first time. Earth terraces in Gwoza are under-laid with dry stalks of sorghum or millet, sometimes with 'wait-a-bit' thorn-bush sticks, which are sometimes tied together: these are the fascines. These are used especially where there are no stones due, supposedly, to the sandy nature of their soils. Over the stalks and sticks some earth or soil was put as a covering on the top-side of terraces, but any observer could see juttings, if not complete features of the fascines, on the step-side of the terraces. If, as Buchanan and Pugh suggest, this fascines-using practice in Gwoza is rudimentary, then the distinctly different practice in Yil Ngas, which involves the raising of pure-earth contour banks, or terraces, may be an indication of attainment of a more advanced agricultural level. Earth terraces in Yil Ngas can hold back water without the aid of such stalks due partly to the loamy nature of their type of soil, and the use of other technologies.

Due to the usefulness of the *wait-a-bit thornbushes* in Gwoza, to use Stanhope White's name for it again, they are neither cut nor cleared out of the farm premises, but left alone or preserved for any necessary use; this indicates another sharp contrast with the practice on farms in Yil Ngas, where all shrubs are cleared out, especially thorns and thornbushes. Extracted branches from the *wait-a-bit thornbushes* in Gwoza are often at places spread across beds of low crops and legumes such as groundnuts, beans, bambara nuts, tiger nuts and so on, to keep monkeys and baboons from ravaging them when they are ripe before harvest.[40] On the other hand, it does not seem wrong to assert that due to hunting, deforestation, unsanctioned bush burning, and other negating activities such as swidden agriculture, the ape population in Yil Ngas has dwindled to a low point, at least in the last 50 years. Even so, the Ngas often utilize the age-old facility of the *lu tap*, the walled, thatch-roofed circular domains permanently constructed and maintained on their farm premises, as a watch-shed to stay in order to drive off ape and bird pests.[41] The dry-stone walls often betray a hard-not-to-notice symmetry with the surrounding dry-stone terrace walls on a given farm side.

Length of Terrace Contours

In Gwoza as well as Yil Ngas, terrace walls or lines are laid in such a manner that allows them to connect, interlap, and sometimes criss-cross, and are hardly unraveled or constructed in a continuous manner of parallel contours, for more than 20 meters at a stretch. In as much as Stanhope White roughly guessed the aggregate or total mileage of all the terrace lines or contours, if joined one to another in one unbroken continuum, to be in the order of 20,000 miles in Gwoza,[42] he did not wish readers to think that there were any single terraces of that length and dimension in Gwoza! In Yil Ngas, terraces were built not only on the edges and foothills of the Jos Plateau massif, that is, in what colonialists called Hill Angas, but also in the downlands, a wide area stretching away from the foothills, which the colonialists called Plains Angas. Hence the aggregate mileage of the terrace lines or contours in Yil Ngas would be far higher, probably in the order of 40,000 miles, given the fact that the whole pre-colonial area of Yil Ngas is spread into four local government areas today; this includes the indigenous, though smaller, Ngas communities in Tafawa Balewa and Bogoro Local Government Areas of Bauchi State, not part of the area of study in this chapter.

Terrace agriculture was and is still practised by the Ngas in the entire area. As the 1904 Survey Party reported about the Yil Ngas, the whole land was mapped out into terraces, with only sacred plots and shrines exempted. The case in Gwoza, is quite unlike that of Yil Ngas: evidence of terraces and/or terrace farming were and still are relegated to the foothills and hilltop premises of the Gwoza peninsula; there are none on the plain farms. The terrace beds in Gwoza, especially where the gradient is gentler, are wider; indeed they are bound to be wider than those in Yil Ngas, for reasons treated in 'Toolkit of Terrace-Farmers' below.

Spread of Terraced Landscapes

The best known terraces in Gwoza are astride the hills, where the settlements are of older antiquity neither on the plains nor in the foothills. Hence a curious researcher climbs up to the top of the hills. The present author had an arduous several hours climb from Plain Guduf to Hill Guduf to examine some terraces and take pictures.

Very good-looking (whether stone-laid or earth) terraces in Yil Ngas, on the other hand, can virtually be found everywhere, whether on the hills or on the plains. A brief look into the pre-colonial past of Gwoza when, at some times, they had to contend with Jihadists and other invaders for centuries may, to an extent, help us understand why the evidence of terraces lies mainly on the hills not in their foothills. The Ngas, on the other hand, managed to defend and retain comparatively greater political freedom from external encroachment and containment; and thus tilled the hilltops, hillsides, foothills of their land, both far and near with ingenuity, for a long time.

The Gwoza terrain exhibits a sharp contrast between the hills; that is, the Gwoza Hills jutt up into the air with escarpments that are mostly rocky, except around Limankara area, or entire southern parts where the hillsides are gentler and more cultivable being less rocky than at other places. The surrounding foothills of Gwoza are virtually plains and more or less stand at the same level all around, especially with the firki fadamas[43] lying to the north towards Bama. Yil Ngas, on the other hand, exhibits the roving intercourse between the edge of the Jos Plateau, characterized by many hills, and their foothills, also characterized by many hills or hillocks. Hence some scholars have described the area as a geographical shatterbelt.[44] The whole Yil Ngas area, whether on the Jos Plateau edge or in the downlands, is characterized with rolling hills, ridges, and scattered hillocks, valleys, and similar formations. The main point here is differences in political experiences, which functioned to either hinder the building of terraces on the plains, as was probably the case in Gwoza, or permit the free spread and wide development of the technique, as was basically the case in Yil Ngas.

Toolkit of Terrace-Farmers

The implements of peasant farm-labour in Gwoza exclude the big hoe. In Yil Ngas, the big-hoe is very necessary for tilling the ground. Terraced beds in Gwoza are without any ridges. Coming into contact with these realities were surprising discoveries for the present author. In Yil Ngas, Ngas-made large spade-blade hoes are loaded with a lot of iron material, making the blades usually quite heavy,[45] partly to easily pierce their stony farm grounds, and partly, and probably unconsciously, to bear testimony to the great availability of iron ore in the area. The chenkom was a very large big hoe blade made and used as a form of currency in pre-colonial Yil Ngas, indicative of the great significance of the big hoe in their political economy. Being on the edge of the Chadian *firki,* and actually practising *firki* farming on their plains, Gwoza farmers, on the other hand, appear to have contented themselves over the centuries with tool-types common to the *firki* environment, tools bearing reminiscences of ancient Sahara dwellers. To follow Graham Connah, "It is not surprising therefore that the tool-kit of the earliest settlers on the Chadian firki ... include the implements typical of the Saharan Neolithic namely, polished stone axes and others which reflect the lacustrine environment namely plain bone points and bone harpoons."[46] It actually seems that the present tool-kit of the Gwoza peasant farmer, which basically include only the small hoe, ax, knife and a digging stick (which may have or not have an iron-head), is an improved pedigree of the one Connah mentions. On the other hand, the Ngas peasant farmer has at his or her disposal the big hoe, the small hoe, the *kyeang* (designed to be used both as a big hoe and a small-hoe), the ax and an iron-headed digging stick. In the absence of the big hoe, it would be an uphill task to make ridges, but they are not made on the terraced beds of Gwoza.

As already stated, ridges are not made in Gwoza before cultivation of crops is done, regardless of whether it is on the hill-top or hillside terraced beds or on the plain farms. As a result, their terrace beds are generally wider than those in Yil Ngas, where ridges are made on the terraced beds. Through the technique of ridging, smaller earth terraces are sometimes made within the area of wider dry-stone terraces. According to McNetting, *"Terracing alone is not the final solution to problems of conservation and water control. A characteristic African solution to the problem of keeping crops above the standing water resulting from heavy rains is to create ridges and mounds."*[47] Located in the southern Guinea Savanna belt, distinct from Gwoza, which is in the northern Guinea Savanna belt in Yil Ngas, farmers had long ago gone the extra mile to practice ridging, due probably to its heavier rainfall. Other problems become elicited by that position. It does not follow, for instance, that other communities in the northern Guinea Savanna, like Gwoza, do not practice ridging. Neither does it follow that all communities in the southern Guinea Savanna, like Yil Ngas, practice ridging.

The Taroh, immediate neighbours of the Ngas to the south, and main inhabitants of Langtang North and Langtang South Local Government Areas of Plateau State, are somehow like the peoples of Gwoza who do not have the big hoe nor make ridges before planting their cereal crops. It is usually during mulching that the Taroh use their small hoes to build ridges around their sorghum or millet crops on plain cleared grounds. In their hilly areas, the Taroh make simple ridges and gather stones to control erosion, but not as elaborately as the terraces in Gwoza or neighboring Yil Ngas.[48] The soils in Langtang, being on the fringes of the Benue valley, and Gwoza are also very similar: sharp-sandy and soft. While the Laamang languages in Gwoza are Chadic, the Taroh language is Benue-Congo.[49] Thus, there is no obvious evidence of old relationships between the two communities, as far as historical linguistics is concerned. Therefore, we are left with one of two options to resolve the dilemma; first, that Gwoza and Langtang were not quite stimulated to develop or adopt the big hoe and/or make ridges due to the softness of their grounds, and, second, that due to lack of iron ore to make the big hoe, they had to make do with what they could afford. The present author prefers the second option. But apart from the mentioned differences and obvious similarities between the manufactured toolkit of the terrace-farmers of Yil Ngas and Gwoza, the major tool in building and repairing of dry-stone terraces remains the two hands of peasant homo-sapiens. Whether in Gwoza or Yil Ngas, peasant farmers have often made sure that their farm terraces are well kept to leave the grounds or beds clear for crop cultivation, through the use of their bare hands and other implements such as small hoes, which both communities had.

CONCLUSION

Terraces in Gwoza and Yil Ngas are both of great antiquity. It is difficult to state the ages in which the terrace-building technology was first developed either in Gwoza or Yil Ngas. The Gwoza communities, who reportedly once denied having any knowledge of or connections with the original builders of their terraces albeit they have owned, kept, maintained and used them well enough, are now apparently revisiting that initial position.[50] The Ngas perceive themselves as direct descendants of the original builders of their terraces. They too have kept and maintained their terraces well enough. The probable uniting explanation considered here is that terrace-building technologies in Gwoza and Yil Ngas are, or might have been, relics of a pre-Kanuri Chadic civilization in the Borno area, from which some elements must have migrated to the present places under review.

It is now a non-issue to state whether the dry-stone terraces in Gwoza are better built than those in Yil Ngas or the other way round. The structure, neatness, sizes and purposes of the terraces are basically the same. Until wider surveys are done, we could only maintain, for the time-being, that the dry-stone terraces in Gwoza and Yil Ngas are virtually among the oldest and best in Africa. In the area of earth terraces, however, the practice in Yil Ngas, who utilize the big hoe and the ridging technique to build different assortments of earth terraces, is probably more advanced than the one in Gwoza. Yil Ngas, whose population (as shown in endnote 4) was likely to be higher than that of Gwoza, might also have evinced a higher aggregate mileage of terraces; moreover, unlike the practice at Gwoza, the whole pre-colonial landscape of Yil Ngas was and still is largely marked by terrace contours everywhere. The toolkit utilized in Yil Ngas also appears to have been wider than that of Gwoza. Hence, while the origins and antiquity of terrace-building technologies in Gwoza and Yil Ngas may trace back to the pre-Kanuri era in the Chad Basin, it may be correctly stated that in view of the variables considered in this paper, the level of the terrace practice appears to have advanced slightly higher in Yil Ngas than in Gwoza. Even so, the practice in Gwoza, in its own right, is of excellent standard. This comparative survey, among other things, has valuably helped us to carefully examine the two systems of terracing and to subsequently present the basic conclusion of our findings; they are both of excellent standard and reflect outstanding engineering skills and ingenuity.

NOTES

[1] The area inhabits many Ngas towns and villages, and it roughly lies between latitudes 9 and 10° North, as well as between longitudes 9 and 10° East, as could be seen on any appropriate atlas of the area.

[2] Samuel Barde Gwimbe, *Roots of Rural Poverty in Yil Ngas of Plateau State, AD 1902-1952: A Political Economy of Colonial Exploitation and Social Deprivation* (MA Thesis, Ahmadu Bello University, Zaria, 2001), 109.

[3] Gwimbe, *Roots of Rural Poverty in Yil Ngas of Plateau State*, 62.

[4] Stanhope White, 'Agricultural Economy of the Hill Pagans of Dikwa Emirate, Cameroons (British Mandate),' *Farm and Forest* (Vol V, December 1944; Reprinted from: *The Empire Journal of Experimental Agriculture*, Vol. IX No. 35 – January 1941), 130. At the time, Stanhope White found

only eight ethnic nationalities, which he calls clans, including, with their estimated populations: Wakara (roughly 12, 900 strong), Hidkala (7,200), Azgavana (9,400), Kuvoko (1,700), Matakum (1,600), Buhe (9,200), Chikkide (4,600), and Glebda (5,700). A total of 58,100 persons therefore stands as the projected population of Gwoza in the early 1940s, which as shown in White's paper, might have grown in density to 170 per square mile, higher than the suggested 130 per square mile, during the late nineteenth century. On the other hand, the poplation of the Ngas was estimated in 1919 to be 76,089, which, if projected to have increased in the early 1940s, it would be somewhere in the upwards of 100,000. For details of that 1919 estimate, See: F B Gall, Gazetteer of Bauchi Province, London, Waterlow & Sons, 1920, 18. Yil Ngas at the time was placed under Bauchi Province.

5 This both implies that Kanuri, Fulani and Hausa elements moved into the Gwoza area only in the twentieth century, on the one hand, and that White's 1941 list is lacking in certain details, on the other. However some peoples often called ethnic nationalities may just be dialect-based groups forming parts of bigger ethnic groups.

6 Personal Interview: Nathan Habila, 41, Civil Servant: Local Government Works Engineer, Dughwede ethnic-Nigerian, interviewed at Gwoza, 20th October 2007. He also said the name 'Gwoza' could also mean 'land area.' Interviews with local inhabitants of the area, March 2013.

7 Khapoya, V. The African Experience (NY: Pearson, 2013). Philips, J. (Ed.), Writing African History (University of Rochester Press, 2005); K. M. Buchanan and J. C. Pugh, Land and People in Nigeria: The Human Geography of Nigeria and its Environmental Background (London, University of London Press, 1955).

8 See Gwimbe, Building Terraces in Agriculture, 1-2, regarding the Ngas side of the issue. During a group interview – with Musa Wahe, 55, Teacher, a Guduf (Gwoza) ethnic-Nigerian; Habila Kulkwe, 62, Civil Servant/Farmer, also a Guduf (Gwoza) ethnic-Nigerian; and, Emmanuel Mbitsa, 55, Carpenter/Farmer, another Guduf (Gwoza) ethnic-Nigerian, at New Guduf, in the foothills of Gwoza peninsula, on 21st October 2007 – it was stated that the Zwagwada (or Guduf) people were said to have moved from Ngazargamu in the north, into the Camerounian area, in the south, before relocating to their present area on the Gwoza peninsula.

9 Abdullahi Smith, A Little New Light: Selected Historical Writings of Professor Abdullahi Smith (Zaria: The Abdullahi Smith Centre for Historical Research, 1987), 83.

10 The southwest shores of the Mega Chad, whose limits define the borders of the Chad Basin, rested more or less directly on the northern edge of the Jos Plateau, around Jos, thus only slightly away from the borders of Yil Ngas lying to the southeast, thus, the latter lies quite within its southern fringes. In defining the limits of the Chad Basin, Graham Connah gives this narration: "The Chad Basin, bounded by Air, Hoggar, Tibesti, Ennedi, Marra, Adamawa, Mandara highlands [Gwoza], and the Jos Plateau covers an area of about two million square kilometres." See: Graham Connah, 'Some Contributions of Archaeology to the Study of the History of Borno,' in Bala Usman and Nur Alkali (Eds.), Studies in the History of Pre-Colonial Borno (Zaria: Northern Nigeria Publishing Company, 1983), 5.

11 Babawale et al. Teaching and propagating African and Diaspora History and Culture (Lagos: Centre for Black and African Arts and Civilization, 2009); Keir Hansford, John Bendor-Samuel and Ron Stanford, Studies in Nigerian Languages, No. 5 An Index of Nigerian Languages (Accra: Summer Institute of Linguistics, Ghana, 1976), 118.

12 This was later put in printed form in C. G. Ames, Gazetteer of Plateau Province (London: Frank Cass, 1934), 22.

13 See Connah, African Civilizations: An Archaeological Perspective (Cambridge University Press, 2002). Graham Connah, Three Thousand Years in Africa: Man and His Environment in the Lake Chad Region of Nigeria (Cambridge: Cambridge University Press, 1979), 18. Stanhope White maintains that: "The peoples now dominant all affirm that they came from the south at some distant period ... " without mentioning specifically and categorically which peoples he was referring to (see his 'Agricultural Economy of the Hill Pagans of Dikwa Emirate,' Farm and Forest, 130). However, it seems probable that due to the agency of local intra-Gwoza peninsula movements or migrations,

including the movements following the colonial change of mandate in 1919, as it were, which removed Gwoza from the German Cameroun more or less to the south, and added it to the British Nigeria, more or less to the north, could, in the course of time, partially have engendered a south-pointing tradition of migration. But the Gwoza peoples' languages are predominantly Laamang-Chadic, a fact which corroborates the north-pointing traditions of migration.

[14] Robert McCNetting, *Hill Farmers of Nigeria: Cultural Ecology of the Kofyar of the Jos Plateau* (Seattle: University of Washington Press, 1970), 44.

[15] J. M. Kowal and A. H. Kassam, *Agricultural Ecology of Savanna: A Study of West Africa* (Oxford: Clarendon Press, 1978), 31.

[16] Buchanan and Pugh, *Land and People in Nigeria*, 110; and J. H. Mackay, 'Perspective in Land Planning: Part 2,' *Farm and Forest* (Vol. V, December 1944), 106.

[17] Kowal and Kassam, *Agricultural Ecology of Savanna*, 174.

[18] Buchanan and Pugh, *Land and People in Nigeria*, 109.

[19] Buchanan and Pugh, *Land and People in Nigeria*, 109.

[20] I have seen hillside farms of the Eggon, Mada, Mwaghavul, Pyem, Taroh and so on, where elaborate, if any, terraces are not in evidence.

[21] Gwimbe, *Roots of Rural Poverty in Yil Ngas of Plateau State*, 38.

[22] White, 'Agricultural Economy of the Hill Pagans of Dikwa Emirate,' *Farm and Forest*, 131. It should be noted that the figures suggested in the article are guessed, not based on research.

[23] Buchanan and Pugh, *Land and People in Nigeria*, 111.

[24] Buchanan and Pugh, *Land and People in Nigeria*, 110.

[25] White, 'Agricultural Economy of the Hill Pagans of Dikwa Emirate,' *Farm and Forest*, 130.

[26] Connah, *Three Thousand Years in Africa*, 38.

[27] White, 'Agricultural Economy of the Hill Pagans of Dikwa Emirate,' *Farm and Forest*, 131.

[28] During my research-visit to Gwoza, I learnt that one anthropologist by the name of Gerhard Kosack had visited and stayed for a while in Gwoza , on research, from London, shortly before I got there. A time would come when hopefully the Gwoza peninsula would eventually witness archaeological investigations.

[29] White, 'Agricultural Economy of the Hill Pagans of Dikwa Emirate,' *Farm and Forest*, 131.

[30] Buchanan and Pugh, *Land and People in Nigeria*, 110.

[31] Elizabeth Isichei (Ed.), *Studies in the History of Plateau State, Nigeria* (London: Macmillan Press, 1982), 31-32.

[32] White, 'Agricultural Economy of the Hill Pagans of Dikwa Emirate,' *Farm and Forest*, 131.

[33] Boyd Alexander, *From the Niger to the Nile* (Vol I, London, Edward Anold, 1907), 97.

[34] 'Agriculture: Plain Land and Terrace Farming,' in *Rural Voices* (A Rural Highlights Publication, January 2007), 8.

[35] McCNetting, *Hill Farmers of Nigeria*, 61.

[36] Gwimbe, *Roots of Rural Poverty in Yil Ngas of Plateau State*, 75-77.

[37] White, 'Agricultural Economy of the Hill Pagans of Dikwa Emirate,' *Farm and Forest*, 130. White also noticed and reports the surprising smoothness of the stones on the terraces and rocky hillsides of Gwoza.

[38] Buchanan and Pugh, *Land and People in Nigeria*, 110.

[39] Keith Eugene Hess, 'The Most Advanced Agriculture in Nigeria,' in Keith Eugene Hess (Ed.), *MCC West Africa's Environmental & Food Concerns Newsletter*, No 9, April 1992, 10. Regarding the article's surprising title, the author says in its opening sentence: "That was my immediate response to the question, 'What do you think of Gwoza?' It may be a bit of an exaggeration …" which simply paved the way, as shown in the citation, in the text of this note, for his personal opinion. In other words, the title was a product of a spur-of-the-moment response, not his candid personal opinion, nor the product of a research.

[40] Personal Interview: Ishaya Haske, 23, photographer, my escort, in Gwoza and a young Mafa (Gwoza) ethnic-Nigerian, at Guduf hills, 21st October 2007.

[41] Gwimbe, *Roots of Rural Poverty in Yil Ngas of Plateau State*, 60-61; Gwimbe, *Building Terraces in Agriculture*, 12.

[42] White, 'Agricultural Economy of the Hill Pagans of Dikwa Emirate,' *Farm and Forest*, 131.

[43] Connah defines firki as "the clay plains to the west, south and east of the present lake," meaning Lake Chad. See Connah, 'Some Contributions of Archaeology to the Study of the History of Borno,' in Usman and Alkali, *Studies in the History of Pre-Colonial Borno*, 6. Firki agriculture involves the transplanting of seedlings of the masokawa sorghum species between September and November. It flourishes only on reserved underground moisture not on any rains (which by then have normally ceased), then is harvested in either December or January. It is practised to an extent in the foothills and plains of Gwoza, though mostly practised in the Chadian firki fadamas, and was to me an unimaginable, unanticipated, discovery. It seems to be a form of agricultural production with the least effort. Once the crops, with the aid of their shaft-like digging sticks, have already been transplanted in holes on the plain ground, the plots having hitherto been cleared by bush burning, the farmers would simply wait for harvest!

[44] Ames, *Gazetteer of Plateau Province*, 9.

[45] Isichei, *Studies in the History of Plateau State, Nigeria*, 33-34. Isichei further maintains that: "The kenti or Kyang obtained by the lowland Ngas from the Bauchi Kantana [who partially inhabit Kanam local Government Area of Plateau State, lying to the south-east of Yil Ngas] was five inches long and three and a half inches wide. The chen [or big hoe] made by the hill Ngas was much larger and spade-shaped." Neighbors of the Ngas were and are sometimes surprised with the size of Ngas hoes.

[46] Connah, 'Some Contributions of Archaeology to the Study of the History of Borno,' in Usman and Alkali, *Studies in the History of Pre-Colonial Borno*, 7.

[47] McCNetting, *Hill Farmers of Nigeria*, 58.

[48] Personal phone Interview: Peter Yilkur Daji, 50, Civil Servant: History Academic, of Taroh ethnicity on 22nd October 2007.

[49] Hansford, Bendor-Samuel and Stanford, *Studies in Nigerian Languages*, 153.

[50] Generally speaking, all the consulted informants in Gwoza, between 17th and 21st October 2007 and 2013 – including, among others, Rev. Daniel Gula, 68, Retired Personage, a Glavda; Mrs Ruth Kathlene Gula, 67, Briton/Missionary, Married/Resident in Gwoza for more than 35 years; Nathan Habila, 41, Civil Servant: Local Government Works Engineer, a Dughwede; Ishaya Haske, 23, my Photographer/Gwoza Escort, a Mafa; Musa Wahe, 55, Teacher, a Guduf; Habila Kulkwe, 62, Civil Servant/Farmer, a Guduf; Emmanuel Mbitsa, 55, Carpenter/Farmer, a Guduf; Umar Abba, 23, Applicant/Inn-keeper, a Dughwede – presented the common position that the current inhabitants in Gwoza were/are the descendants of the erstwhile/original terrace-builders. In 1992, the position was not quite different from that of 1941 but, was most possessive: "The people seem to think they have always lived on the mountain and that they always built terraces!" See Hess, 'The Most Advanced Agriculture in Nigeria,' in Hess, *MCC West Africa's Environmental & Food Concerns Newsletter*, 10.

PAULUS GERDES

7. CREATIVE GEOMETRIC THOUGHT AND ENDOGENOUS KNOWLEDGE PRODUCTION

Example of Experimentation and Invention Among Tonga Women in Southeast Mozambique

INTRODUCTION: GEOMETRY IN AFRICA

The peoples of Africa south of the Sahara desert constitute a vibrant cultural mosaic, extremely rich in its diversity. Among the peoples of the sub-Saharan region, interest in imagining, creating and exploring forms and shapes has blossomed in diverse cultural and social contexts with such an intensity that with reason, it may be said that "Africa geometrizes" (Gerdes, 1999, p. xiii; cf. Zaslavsky, 1973). The books *Geometry from Africa* (Gerdes, 1999), *African Fractals, Modern Computing and Indigenous Design* (Eglash, 1998), *Women, Art and Geometry in Southern Africa* (Gerdes, 1995, 1998), and *African Basketry: A Gallery of Twill-Plaited Designs and Patterns* (Gerdes, 2007) present regional and thematic overviews of geometrical ideas and practices in African cultures.

Case studies of geometrical exploration in specific African cultures are presented in the books *Sona Geometry from Angola: Mathematics of an African Tradition* (Gerdes, 1994, 2006), *Sipatsi: Basketry and Geometry in the Tonga Culture of Inhambane (Mozambique, Africa)* (Gerdes, 2009), *Otthava: Making Baskets and Doing Geometry in the Makhuwa Culture in the Northeast of Mozambique* (Gerdes, 2010a), and *Tinhlèlò, Interweaving Art and Mathematics: Colorful Circular Basket Trays from the South of Mozambique* (Gerdes, 2010b). For an annotated bibliography of and overview of research on mathematical ideas in African cultures and history, see Gerdes and Djebbar (2007, 2011).

In the following, the richness of geometric ideas embedded and developed in a particular cultural practice will be illustrated through the example of female Tonga basket weavers.

TONGA BASKET WEAVERS

The Vatonga, that is the 'people of Tonga origin,' inhabit predominantly the region surrounding the Bay of Inhambane, in the Southeast of Mozambique, at a distance of about 450 km from the capital Maputo. The language they speak is called Gitonga. The principal neighboring ethnic groups are the Vatshwa and the Vacopi. Traditionally, the Vatonga are a patrilinear and patrilocal group: a married woman lives with her husband and is rather isolated from her own lineage group. Besides

G. Emeagwali & G. J. S. Dei (eds.), African Indigenous Knowledge and the Disciplines, 63–82.

basket weaving and pottery, almost no other income and prestige-generating activities have been allowed to women. For their daily survival, the Vatonga depend mostly on agriculture and fishing. There are "several types of Vatonga, from those who still strongly maintain the so-called 'traditional' practices (which are not frozen) to those who have embraced diverse influences, of which Christianity, Islam, and Westernized forms of education may be predominant." (Gregório Firmino in Gerdes, 2009, pp. 411-412). Basket weaving is the sphere of activity in which Tonga women excel.

The woven handbags are called *gipatsi* (singular) and *sipatsi* (plural) in Gitonga. Because of their utility and beauty they have been among the most widely appreciated products of Mozambican craft nationally as well as by visitors from abroad.

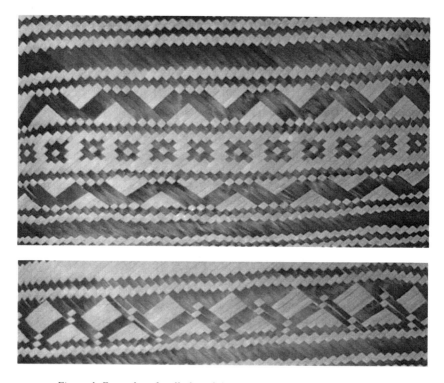

Figure 1. Examples of twill plaited decorative bands on sipatsi handbags

Shortly after the Independence of Mozambique in 1975, I started to acquire Tonga handbags and I have taken *sipatsi* with me on my travels abroad as gifts for colleagues and friends. I have observed the great interest that *sipatsi* generated and how they are admired for their ornamentation (see the examples in Figure 1). At various talks, I have spoken about mathematical aspects related to the production of *sipatsi*. From the mid 1980s onwards, I have systematically collected *sipatsi*. The collection that I had established, until 1993, showed the existence of about 100 motifs, which reveals the power of the imagination, the force of the conceptualisation, and the artistic and geometric creativity of the women and men who weave *sipatsi*. Figure 2 presents a basket weaver at work. With my student, Gildo Bulafo, I published a first book in 1994 on the Tonga handbags (Gerdes & Bulafo, 1994); the book explained how these handbags are produced, presented a catalogue of strip patterns, and showed how they may be explored in the mathematics classroom and, in particular, in mathematics teacher education.

Figure 2. The basket weaver Luísa Office at work (1993)

Knowledge Production

The science and creativity of the Tonga basket weavers knows no limits ...

The first edition of the *Sipatsi*-book (Gerdes & Bulafo, 1994) was realized shortly after the end of the war in Mozambique in 1992. Whereas during the war some men were drawn into the activity of *sipatsi* weaving, after the war this activity became once more exclusively an occupation of Tonga women, as it had originally been.

The post-war period has witnessed an explosion of female creativity. Peace seems to have contributed to the liberation of the creativity and inventiveness of the women basket weavers. Since the end of the war, hundreds of new patterns have been invented, as attested in the second (Gerdes, 2003) and third edition (Gerdes, 2009) of the *Sipatsi*-book.

Throughout this period, the seven theoretically possible symmetry classes of strip patterns are observable in the *sipatsi* I have collected. Over time, a relative stability of the preference for symmetry, and for specific symmetry classes may be noted.

In the last fifteen years, several new phenomena have been observed, ranging from color transformation, introduction of plane patterns, to decoration of a new type of objects, like hats, and the implicit use of codes.

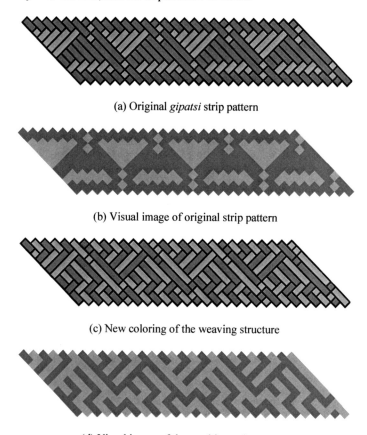

(a) Original *gipatsi* strip pattern

(b) Visual image of original strip pattern

(c) New coloring of the weaving structure

(d) Visual image of the resulting strip pattern

Figure 3. Example of a color transformation of s woven strip pattern

Tonga women have invented a color transformation of plaited strip patterns whereby they use alternating colors in both weaving directions (see the example in Figure 3). Weaving such a strip demands a lot from the basket weaver: almost 'closing her eyes,' she has to think and work in the manner of the original strip pattern in order to achieve the new pattern; thinking only in terms of the new pattern would complicate the execution of the weaving.

Tonga women have also invented a class of plane patterns. Recently, they have made twill-plaited baskets, where groups of artificially dyed strands alternate with groups of natural-colored strands in both weaving directions. Taking all the variables and symmetries into account, the basket weavers have discovered and invented all possible mathematical 'solutions.' Sometimes, when there are two solutions, the basket weaver interweaves the two corresponding different plane patterns into the same bag, thus teaching the observer that there are two patterns belonging to the same class: a clear example of 'cultural didactics' (see the example in Figure 4).

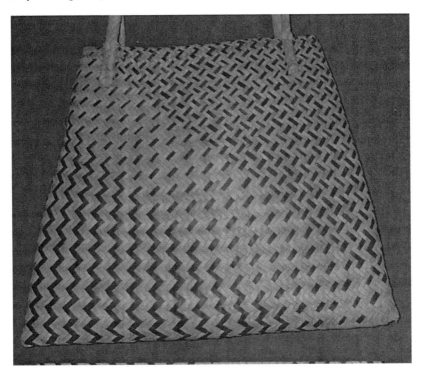

Figure 4. Large handbag displaying two designs that correspond to three-over-three weaving, whereby, in both weaving directions, each time a group of two naturally colored strands alternates with one dyed strand.

The cultural phenomenon of Tonga handbag production presents a concrete example of how tradition and innovation may be interwoven. Experimentation, exploring possibilities and systematic variation are characteristics of the *sipatsi* mathematic-artistic weaving activity. The weavers themselves say that they 'weave music' into their designs and patterns.

Frequently, studies of decoration, designs and patterns, and basketry present us with a 'snapshot,' which captures a fragment, an instant, in a cultural process. The expanded, third edition of the *Sipatsi*-book, resulting from over thirty years of enquiring, collecting and observing, is exceptional. It presents a series of 'snapshots,' which collectively constitute a short film, that records an unfolding exploration of personal and collective memory, of combinations of color and pattern, and of variations of order and logic to create new designs.

The book presents several ephemeral phenomena: new ideas that appear, are implemented, and are then overtaken by still newer ideas .... For instance, in Chapter 8 it presents the example of a creative woman, a *sipatsi* weaver, who, in a very short timespan, invented and wove all possible plane patterns of culturally acceptable dimensions. In effect, like a professional researcher, she 'wrote' her research 'paper' and 'published' it by making baskets with all the possible patterns, and thereafter, went on to explore further dimensions of the initial study. But, her 'research paper' would not have been 'read' nor 'cited,' had it not been observed by an 'outsider,' in this case, an interested *ethnomathematician*. The invention itself of the plane patterns responds, however, to the intellectual, geometric and artistic capacities of their creator(s), revealing, demonstrating and underscoring the mathematical inventiveness of the female Tonga basket weavers.

This longitudinal study contributes to the collective Tonga and national memory and prevents the permanent loss of several original, creative ideas and their resulting patterns. By publishing the analysis and the catalogues of Tonga patterns and ideas, the *Sipatsi*-book may contribute to a cultural pyramid of personal and communal memory, intellectual capacity and creative innovation.

In the following, parts of Chapter 18 of the *Sipatsi* book are reproduced to give an idea of experimentation and invention in the basket-weaving practice of Tonga women.

Experimentation and Invention

As I was nearing completion of the expanded, third edition of the *Sipatsi*-book, I went for a last visit to the Central Market of Maputo on May 15, 2008. A final, and unexpected surprise was waiting for me: there I found three *sipatsi* handbags with handles, and a completely new design, all made by the same woman from the peninsula of Linga-Linga, according to Rosalina Langa, the basket seller.

The first two purses have the same size and proportions, and their covers display exactly the same design, albeit the colors of the dyed strands are different, dark brown and purple, respectively. Figures 5 and 6 present both twill-plaited purses.

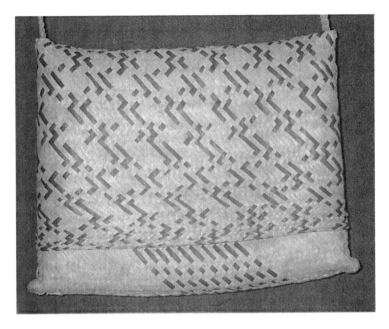

Figure 5. The first purse

Figure 6. The second purse

The weaving structure is as follows: regular 'over-two-under-two' (2/2) twill-plaited bands of three rows are alternated with jumps of five strands as illustrated in Figure 7. At the top there are regular 2/2 twill-plaited bands of six rows, and at the bottom, of eight rows, instead of three rows as elsewhere.

The basket weaver has selected a special coloring for her purses. In the first weaving direction, she has introduced naturally colored strands (hereinafter denoted by 0) and artificially dyed strands (hereinafter denoted by 1) in groups of eight, according to the *code* 10100000, that is, from the left to the right as in Figure 8, first one dyed strand (1), then one naturally colored strand (0), then another dyed strand (1), followed by five naturally colored strands (00000).

Figure 7. The weaving structure

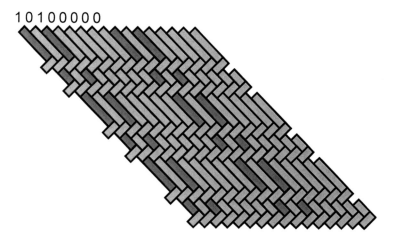

Figure 8. Using the 10100000 code in the first weaving direction

In the second weaving direction, she has used the same code 10100000, as is illustrated in Figure 9.

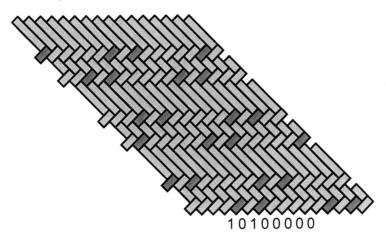

10100000

Figure 9. Using the 10100000 code in the second weaving direction

Figure 10 presents the corresponding part of the pattern of the colored design that results from using the same code in both weaving directions.

10100000

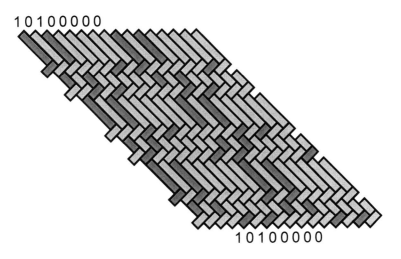

10100000

Figure 10. This demonstrates the way in which the basket weaver has used the 10100000 code in both weaving directions.

Figure 11 presents the visual impression of the design.

10100000

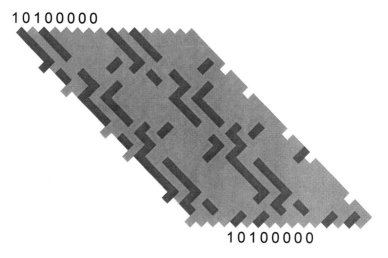

10100000

Figure 11. Visual image

In the case of both baskets, the artisan has broken her own code and period 8 once, on the right bottom side, by introducing ten strands instead of eight and using the code 1010100000. As a consequence, the two faces of each purse have different visual images. Figure 12 presents part of the coloring of the weaving pattern of the opposite face of these two *gipatsi* purses.

10100000

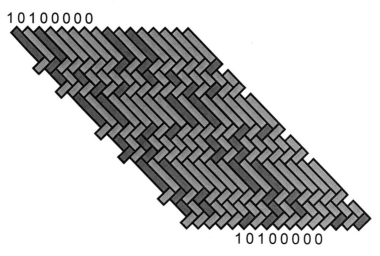

10100000

Figure 12. Part of the opposite face

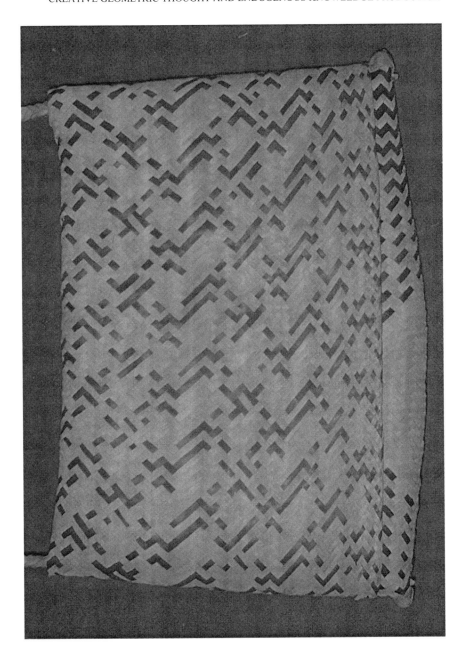

Figure 13. First face of the third purse

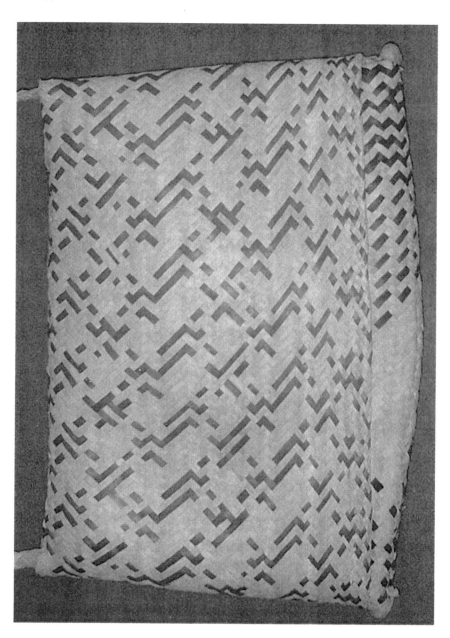

Figure 14. Second face of the third purse

Figures 13 and 14 present both faces of the third *gipatsi* purse. This time the basket weaver has produced a more complex design than in the previous two handbags.

T

X

M

Y

B

Figure 15. The different layers of the third purse (first face)

Repetition of design elements at regular distances characterizes the top (T), middle (M), and bottom (B) layers of the purse (see Figure 15). For instance, the middle layer M is the same as the bottom layer presented in Figure 11. In fact, the basket weaver has used the same period (8) and the same code 10100000, as Figures 16c and d illustrate for the top layer T, where she has interwoven the strands successively 'over three, under two, over three, under three, over two, under two' (see Figure 16a).

The X and Y layers appear chaotic: successive design elements appear completely different. The symmetry of the repetitive pattern of period 8 appears broken. How is this possible?

How could the basket weaver achieve this while using the same 10100000 code of period 8 for the whole purse?

(a) Weaving structure

10100000

(b) Introducing colored strands in one weaving direction

10100000

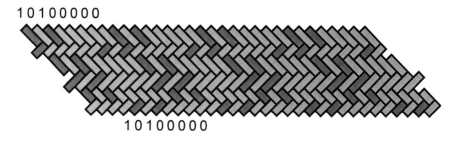

10100000

(c) Introducing colored strands in both weaving directions

10100000

10100000

(d) Visual image

Figure 16. Analysis of the top layer (T) of the third purse

Let us observe the weaving structure that characterizes the layers X and Y. In both instances it is the same. It is the weaving pattern of a strip pattern of period 10.

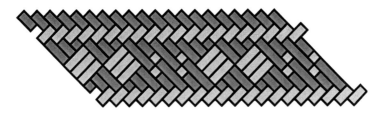

Figure 17. The weaving structure of layers X and Y: period = 3 + 3 + 2 + 2 = 10

As the basket weaver has introduced dyed strands (1) and naturally colored strands (0) using the code 10100000 of period 8, the weaving patterns of layers X and Y appear different (see Figures 18 and 19).

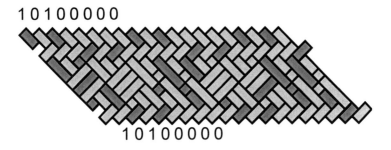

Figure 18. Coloring of the weaving structure in the case of layer X

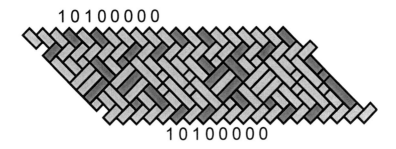

Figure 19. Coloring of the weaving structure in the case of layer Y

As the underlying strip pattern has period 10 and the coloring has period 8, the new strip pattern has the lowest common multiple of 10 and 8 that is 40 as its period. The apparent chaos of the layers X and Y dissolves in order and symmetry:

both layers are strip patterns of period 40. Figure 20 presents the visual image of the decorative elements of period 40 of both layers (compare this with Figure 15).

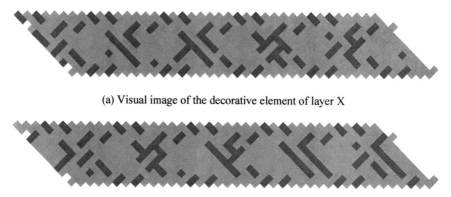

(a) Visual image of the decorative element of layer X

(b) Visual image of the decorative element of layer Y

Figure 20. Observe the visual image of the decorative elements
of period 40 of both layers

As the reader can observe in Figures 13 and 14, the basket weaver has repeated her decorative motifs of period 40 exactly three times around the initial woven cylinder, using 40x3 = 120 strands in each weaving direction. In other words, she started the weaving with 60 knots, 30 for each face of the purse cover, as from each knot there go two strands in each weaving direction.

When we examine the interior of the purse cover (Figure 21), we can see that the double knots are organized in groups of four: each time two successive 'mixed' knots followed by two 'white' knots (Figure 22). The 'mixed' double knots are made of two dyed strands (1) and two naturally colored strands (0): one dyed and one naturally colored strand going in one weaving direction and the other dyed and other naturally colored strand going in the other direction. In other words, the two 'mixed' double knots contribute the first half of the code in both weaving directions: 1010. The 'white' double knots are made of four naturally colored strands: two of them going in each weaving direction. The two 'white' double knots contribute the other half of the code in both weaving directions: 0000. As a consequence, the group of two 'mixed' knots and two 'white' knots has produced the coloring code 1010 0000 of period 8 in both weaving directions. When the basket weaver selected her code, she did not do it arbitrarily. On the contrary, she alternated pairs of 'mixed' knots with pairs of 'white' knots, generating 'automatically' the weaving code 1010 0000 of period 8. Because she wanted to use a strip pattern of period 10 simultaneously, she had to select a number of knots equal to a multiple of 10.

Figure 21. Interior of the purse cover with one and two-color start knots

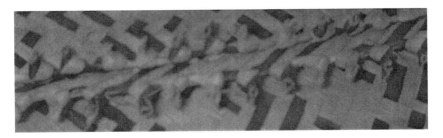

Figure 22. Alternating pairs of 'mixed' double knots with pairs of 'white' double knots

Behind the apparent chaos of layers X and Y on the twill-plaited purse lies perfect order and symmetry! Both layers with period 40 are the result of creative reflection and careful calculation. Even the coloring code 1010 0000 was generated at the start when the basket weaver opted for alternating pairs of 'mixed' and 'white' double knots.

The most recent example of experimentation and invention by *sipatsi* weavers, analyzed in the present chapter, reveals, once more, how lively and dynamic the *sipatsi* 'tradition' is. The creative idea of selecting alternating pairs of 'mixed' and 'white' double knots to start the weaving has led to the invention of a new coloring code applied in the three purse covers. The combination of this innovative idea with the use of a well-known strip pattern has resulted in a weaving process which is more complicated, and produces apparently irregular strips on the third purse cover – 'appearances of chaos.' The basket weaver, however, has consciously achieved a higher order of regularity, symmetry and beauty. She has demonstrated her capacity to produce strip patterns of a much higher period (40) than is usually the case, and to interweave them with bands of lower period (8). The basket weaver has created a new coloring code, opening up a new horizon, leading to new perspectives.

Example of Educational Exploration in Mathematics (Teacher) Education

The ideas involved in the making of the three purses we analyzed can be explored in many ways in the mathematics classroom. Here I present a few problems and questions for reflection, and some answers.

Problems and Questions for Reflection

1. Find all possible coloring codes of period 8 that may be generated by starting with 'mixed' and 'white' double knots. Let us suppose that the strands leave the 'mixed' double knots in the order [10] (as in the case of the third purse cover), and not in the other possible order [01].
2. Find all possible coloring codes of period 8 that may be generated by starting with 'mixed' and 'white' double knots. Let us suppose this time that the strands leave the 'mixed' double knots either in the order [10] or in the order [01].
3. Find all possible coloring codes of period 8 that may be generated by starting with 'white' and 'black' double knots. 'Black' double knots are made of four artificially dyed strands, two of them going in each weaving direction.
4. Find all possible coloring codes of period 8 that may be generated by starting with 'white,' 'mixed' and 'black' double knots.

Some answers

1. Besides the 10 10 00 00 coloring code of the third purse cover, there are two other really different codes: 10 00 00 00 and 10 10 10 00. In principle, there are $2^4 = 16$ possibilities, but some lead to codes of a period inferior to 8, and others lead to codes that are equivalent to others. For instance, the code 10 00 10 00 has period 4 and not 8. The codes 10 00 00 10, 00 10 10 00, and 00 00 10 10 are equivalent to the basket weaver's code 10 10 00 00.
2. In principle, there are $3^4 = 81$ possibilities, but some lead to codes of a period inferior to 8, and others lead to equivalent codes. For instance, the codes 00 10 00 00, 00 00 10 00, 00 00 00 10, 01 00 00 00, 00 01 00 00, 00 00 01 00, and 00 00 00 01 are all equivalent to code 10 00 00 00: only one dyed strand in eight successive strands. There are thirteen distinct codes:

$$10\ 00\ 00\ 00,$$
$$10\ 10\ 00\ 00,\ 10\ 01\ 00\ 00,\ 10\ 00\ 00\ 01,$$
$$10\ 10\ 10\ 00,\ 10\ 10\ 01\ 00,\ 10\ 10\ 00\ 01,\ 10\ 01\ 10\ 00,$$
$$10\ 01\ 00\ 01,\ 10\ 00\ 01\ 01,$$
$$10\ 10\ 10\ 01,\ 10\ 10\ 01\ 01,$$
$$10\ 01\ 01\ 01.$$

3. In principle, there are $2^4 = 16$ possibilities. Three of them lead to really different colouring codes:

$$11\ 00\ 00,\ 11\ 11\ 00\ 00,\ 11\ 11\ 11\ 00.$$

4. In principle, there are $4^4 = 256$ possibilities. Many are equivalent and some lead to codes with period 2 or 4. Find the codes that are really distinctive.

CONCLUSION

The example analysed above shows the experimentation and invention by *sipatsi* weavers, and reveals how lively and dynamic the *sipatsi* tradition is. The creative idea of selecting alternating pairs of mixed and white double knots to start the weaving has led to the invention of a new color code applied in the three purse covers. The combination of this innovative idea with the use of a well-known strip pattern has resulted in a weaving process, which is more complex, producing what appear to be irregular strips on the third purse cover. In so doing, however, the basket weaver has consciously achieved an even higher order of regularity, symmetry and beauty. In this apparently chaotic design, she has demonstrated her capacity to produce strip patterns of a much higher period than is usually the case, and to interweave them with bands of a lower period. In sum, the basket weaver has created a new color code, and opened up new horizons, leading to new perspectives. Behind the apparent chaos on the twill-plaited purse lies perfect order and symmetry! This decoration is the result of extensive creative reflection, careful calculation and highly developed awareness of order and logic.

The science and creativity of the Tonga basket weavers knows no limits.

REFERENCES

Eglash, R. (1998). *African fractals: modern computing and indigenous design.* Piscataway: Rutgers University Press.

Gerdes, P. (1994). *Sona geometry: Reflections on the sand drawing tradition of peoples of Africa south of the Equator.* Trans. Arthur B. Powell. Maputo: Universidade Pedagógica.

Gerdes, P. (1995). *Women and geometry in Southern Africa.* Maputo: Universidade Pedagógica.

Gerdes, P. (1998). *Women, art and geometry in Southern Africa.* Lawrenceville, NJ: Africa World Press.

Gerdes, P. (1999). *Geometry from Africa: Mathematical and educational explorations.* Washington DC: Mathematical Association of America.

Gerdes, P. (2003). *Sipatsi: Cestaria e geometria na cultura Tonga de Inhambane.* Maputo: Moçambique Editora & Lisbon: Texto Editora.

Gerdes, P. (2006). *Sona geometry from Angola: Mathematics of an African tradition.* Trans. Arthur B. Powell. Monza: Polimetrica International Science Publishers.

Gerdes, P. (2007). *African basketry: A gallery of twill-plaited designs and patterns.* Maputo: Centre for Mozambican Studies and Ethnoscience & Morrisville NC: Lulu.

Gerdes, P. (2009a). *Sipatsi: Basketry and geometry in the Tonga culture of Inhambane (Mozambique, Africa).* Morrisville NC: Lulu.

Gerdes, P. (2009b). *Sipatsi images in colour: A supplement.* Morrisville NC: Lulu.

Gerdes, P. (2010a). *Otthava: Making baskets and doing geometry in the Makhuwa culture in the northeast of Mozambique.* Nampula. Universidade Lúrio & Morrisville NC: Lulu (color edition, 2012).

Gerdes, P. (2010b). *Tinhlèlò, interweaving art and mathematics: Colourful circular basket trays from the south of Mozambique.* Maputo: Mozambican Ethnomathematics Research Centre & Morrisville NC: Lulu.

Gerdes, P., & Djebbar, A. (2007). *Mathematics in African history and cultures: An annotated bibliography.* Cape Town: African Mathematical Union & Morrisville NC: Lulu.

Gerdes, P., & Djebbar, A. (2011). *Mathematics in the history of Africa: AMUCHMA 25 years* (2 volumes). Maputo: African Mathematical Union & Morrisville NC: Lulu.

Gerdes, P., & Bulafo, G. (1994). *Sipatsi: Technology, art and geometry in Inhambane.* Trans. Arthur B. Powell. Universidade Pedagógica: Maputo.

Zaslavsky, C. (1973). *Africa counts: Number and pattern in African culture.* Brooklyn NY: Lawrence Hill.

SARFO K. NIMOH

8. INDIGENOUS TRADITIONAL MEDICINE IN GHANA

Tapping into an Under-Explored Resource

INTRODUCTION

This chapter is about the role of indigenous traditional medicine (hereafter referred to as ITM, traditional medicine) in Ghana. It is based on the premise that ITM has great potential of improving the health status of Ghanaians if it becomes more systematized, and if its worthiness is explored to a greater extent than it is now. Much needed resources, funds included, are being pumped into orthodox medicine when our main focus should be on less costly and easily available traditional medicine. The current medical system of Ghana mimics that of the developed nations, which are rich and can afford the use of more costly and sophisticated interventions in the treatment of diseases. It is true that the developed countries have had a more significant improvement in their life expectancy rates compared to developing countries in Africa, but does it merit an adoption of full-scale orthodox medicine? For instance, in a statistical release by WHO (2010), it was indicated that, life expectancy has increased among many nations around the world. People are living longer today than say a century ago. Life expectancy in the majority of nations in the developed world, especially that of women, has improved considerably (CDC, 2012).

Perhaps the reason African countries have low life expectancy rates is partly because African nations are not exploring their natural resources to their fullest potential, but are rather trying to duplicate the system in most developed countries. These systems, modeled after the orthodox system, have their own disadvantages that African countries such as Ghana need to be prudent not to replicate. There is the need to proceed with caution while exploring the full potential of ITM. Countries like China, Hong Kong, Japan, and Singapore have successfully depended on ITM alongside orthodox medicine with encouraging life expectancies comparable to countries with western-based medicine, such as the United States. This chapter provides an overview and examples of ITM as a knowledge system, a comparative analysis of ITM and orthodox western medicine, and highlights ways in which they converge and diverge. It highlights what Ghana is currently doing to systematize ITM, and then concludes with a discussion of implications and recommendations on how the ITM knowledge can be taught in schools and what can be done to maximize the role of ITM in Africa, with specific reference to Ghana.

G. Emeagwali & G. J. S. Dei (eds.), African Indigenous Knowledge and the Disciplines, 83–93.

OVERVIEW AND EXAMPLES OF INDIGENOUS/ TRADITIONAL
MEDICINE (ITM) AS A KNOWLEDGE SYSTEM

Indigenous or traditional medicine as a knowledgebase has been passed on from one generation to the other for thousands of years. For as long as humans have lived, indigenous traditional medicine (ITM) has been used in the treatment and prevention of common ailments and diseases. Traditional healers, medicinal herbs, and medicinal plants, collectively have all played important roles in serving our health care needs long before the emergence of mainstream medicine (Rios & Recio, 2005). The use of ITM is still fairly prevalent in the village where I grew up, where it was depended on for most of my medical needs. However, it is not accorded the same status as western orthodox medicine, and its knowledge base is not being preserved because most traditional healers have no western education; these healers are among some of the older generation who are slowly going to their graves with this valuable knowledge that should be more extensively cherished and preserved. Newly introduced orthodox/scientific alternatives to traditional medicines have diluted concentrations and thus are less potent with inferior efficacy, despite the use of the same plant extracts as ITM healers. It is therefore not farfetched to assert that western orthodox medicine has its roots in ITM because the latter was long in existence prior to the birth of the former. The reason one model of health care is seemingly more popular and universal than the other will be explored in later parts of this chapter. But for now, let us take a look at a classic example of ITM.

The use of "Bentoa" (a bulb syringe) as it is called locally, is very much prevalent among Akan and other African nationalities in Ghana. It provides the rudimentary methodology for treating common ailments and diseases such as constipation, nausea, indigestion, headaches, dizziness, that arise from a blocked colon due to constipation. Bentoa is used to introduce herbal medicinal potions into the lower part gastrointestinal (GI) tract via the rectum. Depending on the herbal medicinal content and how distant the accumulation occurs, relative to the stomach, different actions could occur. In the colon, the potion induces fluid accumulation either through concentration gradient or intestinal secretion, which in turn effects a cleansing action. The cleansing of the colon allows the bile to flow freely, thereby detoxifying the liver from harmful toxins, and of course allows regular intestinal movement to take place. These normal GI regulations cure many of the illnesses mentioned above such as constipation, nausea, indigestion, headaches, dizziness, that arise from a blocked colon. These remedies are among the herbal medicinal practices passed on to us from our ancestors. Today, there are all forms of copycats of this traditional knowledge in all parts of the globe known as *Enemas*, in a more refined prototype (Hamouy, 2006). In fact, the western approach of introducing medicine to the GI tract uses the same knowledge base as ITM, at least in the Bentoa model. It is true that, "significant contributions to global knowledge have originated from indigenous people ..." (The World Bank – KLG, 2004). Yet the Ghanaian government, leaders, and others continue to trust and follow the status quo, western medicine, pumping millions of dollars into it.

As developing countries such as Ghana continue to focus more on western medicine, much of the knowledge base in our traditional medicine will slowly become extinct because it is neither practiced as commonly as before, explored, nor are citizens encouraged to use ITM. The agony of all this is that the ill-effects of neglecting or suppressing ITM are, in many cases, not felt by lawmakers, but rather by those at the bottom who cannot afford western medicine. This group of people includes the beneficiaries, the practitioners of ITM, and all those whose survival in one way or the other depends on indigenous or traditional medicine.

Ghana, as a proud nation with strong roots to its traditional medicine, is vulnerable of losing most of its indigenous knowledge base because of its obsession with orthodox medical systems. There is no doubt that traditional medicine forms a major component of the health care system in Ghana. The local practictioners in various regions have built into their respective traditional medicine a sense of cultural heritage; ultimately, it has a great meaning to the people who use it. Surprisingly, curriculua in medical schools in Ghana have long been designed to cater to western medicine with relatively little attempt to incorporate one into the other. Efforts made to revive and improve ITM have been mediocre. This is counter to the warning of the World Bank and other global economic watchdogs, that the overzealous pursuance of western medicine can be detrimental to the developing countries' economic growth and development. "The tragedy of the impending disappearance of indigenous knowledge is most obvious to those who have developed it and make a living through it. But the implication for others can be detrimental as well, when skills, technologies, artifacts, problem-solving strategies and expertise are lost" (World Bank-Sub Saharan Africa, n.d.).

The over acceptance of orthodox systems could be seen as a declaration of war on indigenous knowledge. Specifically, there has not been a major and systematic analysis of the technical knowhow behind most indigenous practices, and the herbs involved. Current attempts to tap into, analyse, and systematize ITM have not included adequate input from traditional healers. Some researchers have complained about the reluctance of healers to release the knowledge base and other pertinent information about their practices. But this should come as no surprise because, as indicated by Milijoana et al. (2003), with no incentives and recognition, some of them [healers] have turned to the exploitation of 'underground' practices while hiding treatment information and knowledge from others. Clearly, with the disproportionate attention focused on western medicine, nothing significant, if anything, can come out of Ghana's inadequate investment in indigenous traditional medicine. This is rather unfortunate because ITM is a rich knowledge base that is being undermined. How, then, can ITM and western orthodox medicine be incorporated into each other to maximize their efficacies and promote more affordable health care for all Ghanaians? One step forward will be to analyze their similarities and dissimilarities. The next section of this chapter is a discussion of the way ITM and orthodox western medicine converge and diverge, in order to set the stage for suggestions on how ITM knowledge base can be taught in schools.

THE DIVERGENCE AND CONVERGENCE BETWEEN ITM AND ORTHODOX WESTERN MEDICINE: A COMPARATIVE

The most distinctive difference between indigenous traditional medicine and western medicine is the openness and the continual improvement of the latter. Western orthodox medicine is open to all and its transparency transcends beyond international and cultural boundaries. Countries around the world have taken advantage of this opportunity to use and to advance the cause of western medicine. As a result, western medicine has achieved huge success by becoming the most favorite brand in the field of medicine. If countries like Ghana, with such a rich indigenous culture, can boast of prestigious medical schools designed to yield a supply of doctors, nurses, and pharmacists modeled after western practitioners, it is quite a testament to the extent of adoption and contribution orthodox medicine has received.

Obviously, this is a sharp contrast to indigenous traditional medicine, which for decades has faced threats of extinction and degradation (World Bank-Sub Saharan Africa, n.d.). For many Ghanaians and younger generations, the provisions and exploration of indigenous medicine have virtually been lost and, at best, discouraged. Although it continues to flourish under the shadows of western medicine, many of the pioneers and subsequent generations that contribute heavily to ITM, have passed away or failed to make it open and transparent. I remember how my grandmother would collect local herbs, with palm fruits, and made soup for breast-feeding mothers to increase their breast milk supply for their babies. Following consumption of these soups, a gentle squeeze of the breast could spurt milk everywhere. To say the least, both my grandmother and an elderly man (a herbalist) in my village have both passed away, their knowledge in herbal medicine gone with them. My grandmother and the said herbalist kept no record of their knowledge. This has been a common occurrence as far as indigenous medicine and their practitioners are concerned. In Ghana and other countries around the world that are involved in traditional medicine, there is not much impetus or incitement for traditional healers to pass on their knowledge to others.

On the other hand, unlike ITM, the advancement of western medicine has depended on collective contributions from the world community. Contributions have come from schools of medicine, nursing, pharmacology and other health-related programs all around the world that are affiliated with western medicine. The sciences, mathematics, physics, biology, chemistry have all provided a solid foundation of research and improvement upon which orthodox medicine rests. Schools of medicine, nursing, pharmacology and other health-related institutions have all rooted their curricula in the sciences, in their efforts to prepare learners for research and scientific exploration. This form of education provides opportunity for knowledge transfer and improvement of western medicine. Besides, western medicine is well-regulated, well-documented, well-funded, and follows systematic research requirements. In many countries such as Ghana, China, and India, medicinal plants are cultivated and harvested locally, providing employment opportunities and also contributing to the local economy (Ghana – Ministry of

Health (GNDP), 2004). In the case of orthodox medicine, especially in Ghana, it is imported into the country from various countries around the world. It is estimated that Ghana spends approximately 60-80% of its total cost of health care on importation of drugs, production materials, and supplies (Ghana – Ministry of Health (GNDP), 2004). Unlike orthodox medicine, indigenous traditional medicine continues to be more available, with relatively fewer side effects, and much cheaper than orthodox medicine. Although it is in existence and somehow well-understood and widely accepted, there is little or no scientific basis for its use or effectiveness (Gov.CN, 2006).

Another major distinction that throws them further apart is cost. Western medicine is far more expensive than the traditional medicine, making the former less accessible and affordable for those living in Africa (Bodeker et al., 2005). Even in the United States, which is considered one of the richest countries and a mastermind of western orthodox medicine, approximately 49 million (or 16% of the population) were without health insurance in 2011 because of the exorbitant costs of health care in that country (US Census Bureau, 2011). In 2012, the average cost of health insurance cost per family in the United States rose to approximately $16,745, a 4% increase over the previous year, 2011. The 4% actually represent a decrease from the 9% trend as reported in the previous year (Kaiser Family Foundation, 2012). Similar complaints associated with higher cost of premiums regarding western medicine have been reported in places like Canada, Japan, China, and the United Kingdom. In a related research study conducted by Burke, Wong, and Clayson and reported in their work entitled "Traditional Medicine in China Today," it is stated that a significant number of Chinese citizens are unable to purchase health insurance due to higher cost of the premiums (Burke, Wong, & Clayson, 2003). Their findings blamed the emerging presence and an overly increased trend of acceptance of western medicine in China as the causal factor. The team claimed that western orthodox medicine has seriously impacted the growth of an already established traditional medicine in the country.

This is the case in Ghana too. Western orthodox medicine is beginning to exert similar economic pressure on Ghanaians. Unlike many of these countries, orthodox medicine in Ghana is significantly subsidized by the government. However, the out-of-pocket payments has become a burden for some and has disccouraged or prevented such people from seeking health care from the orthodox medical system. Many seek health care elsewhere. It has also been reported that in some African countries, including Ghana, families have resorted to borrowing and selling household properties in order to make out-of-pocket health payments for health care, and those without it are routinely turned away (Leive & Xu, 2008).

Another major difference or divergence between ITM and orthodox medicine can be found in their treatment approaches. Treatment approaches in ITM and western medicine are based on two different fundamental philosophies. Western medicine is vested in reactive care and treats mainly body parts, while traditional medicine treats the entire body. Traditional healers trust in nature and believe that the body can heal itself, and that homeostasis can be maintained through body, mind, spirit and the soul (Lewis et al., 2007).

For many traditional healers, treatment involves holistic treatment approaches based on their clients' cultural heritage. ITM healers may call on the local gods and spiritual entities and use counseling in a more personal fashion. Chanting and the use of spiritual charisma, prayers, touching and massaging, in addition, to the herbal therapy are not uncommon (Lewis et al., 2007). In contrast to these approaches used in ITM, orthodox medicine focuses mainly on physical variables – the body. Traditional medicine, on the other hand, blends several approaches into treatment therapy as described above, which make it more appealing to people who seek holistic treatment. The uniqueness of this approach can be found in its focus on the whole person, which Neuman and Fawcett described as consisting of five variables or systems, i.e., physiological, socio-cultural, developmental, psychological, and spiritual (Neuman & Fawcett, 2002).

Western or orthodox, conventional medicine, on the other hand, focuses on the various parts of the body using functioning as the basis of treatment. The three functioning conditions are: functioning, not functioning, or impaired functioning. Thus, parts that are not functioning or impaired are targeted with treatment options – such as medication or surgical procedures to remove or fix them. For example, in cases of cancerous tumor – the tumor is either treated with chemotherapy, removed, or devascularized. There is more to this than this brief explanation; however, it is beyond the scope of this chapter.

Convergence and divergence between ITM and western medicine in the area of diagnosis, is perhaps the least addressed area in the literature and in discussions of the differences between the two. It is however noteworthy that ITM and western medicines do diverge and converge at the same time in their approaches to diagnosis.

The commonalities include their mission to find the causes of the illness. What is going on wrongly and what led to or caused the illness? This question can be answered through the use of manual mechanisms for simple diagnostic procedures. For example, the traditional healer will perform body examination for skin color changes, joint movements, abnormal shapes, vomitus, stature and posture. The traditional healer also listens to unfamiliar body sounds. They also use touching to check for circulation, smoothness and at the same time palpate for evidence of incongruences or structural abnormalities such as in a broken bone or joint dislocation. These are common, simple, and non-invasive procedures that are common to both systems. They diverge significantly in areas where the natural body senses are limited in pointing out the cause of the illness. For example, in the case of blunt traumatic injuries, the ability of the natural senses to detect, identify, and envision the extent of bodily damage is very restricted. Without sophisticated and costly medical equipment or machinery, the natural senses cannot detect or identify the scope of tissue injury. This area, commonly referred to as acute care, is where western medicine excels and outperforms indigenous traditional medicine. Ultrasound or Magnetic Resonance Imaging captures cross-sectional images of organs and tissues of the body (FDA, 2012), These are examples of techniques that are usually used exclusively by western medicine.

This significant difference between ITM and western medicine does not discount the commonalities that exist in their approaches to diagnosis of illnesses. Besides their convergence in terms of simple manual procedures in diagnosis (mentioned earlier), there are other critical areas where the two share common features. For example, they are both rooted in the knowledge base of the field of medical practice. Practitioners in both medical systems possess expert knowledge that helps them make diagnosis. The traditional healers are able to measure, calculate what to give, how much to give, and keep record of available practices and technical know-how. This expert knowledge provides them the ability to apply their skills and knowledge in the diagnosis and treatment of diseases just like western medicine practitioners.

The traditional healers are able to employ their skills in the treatment of disease and illness without the benefits of computers, medical equipment, and sometimes without the financial incentives (salaries, bonuses, offers) that are available to western medicine practitioners. Whether ITM is an art or science, the recognition of its contribution to medicine can clearly be defined as significant. For thousands of years, its knowledge base has served as a medicinal database or resource from which western medicine was born. Borrowed ideas have been refined, polished, and disseminated for use. Therefore, although western medicine enjoys a reputable knowledge base equipped with all the available tools for perfection, it still shares commonalties with ITM from which it was derived in some cases. Some drug formularies mimic that of herbal extract formularies, because many drugs are manufactured from herbal or plant extracts.

Furthermore, there is a common concern by both ITM and orthodox medicine in their search for treatment whenever there is a dangerous disease outbreak such as HIV/ AIDS. This is of special concern for practitioners in both medical systems, especially in Africa. There have been various contributions towards the HIV/AIDS epidemic by both orthodox and traditional medicine. In South Africa, several medicine plants including Hypoxis, Sutherlandia frutescens, and Hypoxis hemerocallidea (known as African potato) have been used to help fight HIV, the virus that causes AIDS. These herbs have been officially recommended for HIV/ AIDS treatment in South Africa and 14 other African countries (Mills et al., 2005).

It is clear from the above that ITM and western medicine do have their similarities and dissimilarities and that they coexist in many countries. The former, however, is not accorded the attention it deserves as a comparable more affordable medical system. The next section discusses how and why the national health care system of Ghana can be improved by tapping into the underexplored resource of ITM.

THE RATIONALE FOR AND THE 'HOW TO' OF TAPPING
INTO THE UNDER-EXPLORED RESOURCE OF ITM

Developing nations around the world are more than ever adopting a western-style of health care, and using it alongside their indigenous traditional medicine (World Bank-Sub Saharan Africa, n.d.). It is a trend that is on the rise. This attraction to western medicine is based on the premise that its benefits outweigh the disadvantages. Little attention is being paid to the direction that this trend will lead to in terms of the financial and capital implications. One only needs to take a look at the case of the United States to learn that western medicine is not all that glorious. The United States is one of the major architects of western medicine and has a complete health care system that is a prototype of western medicine. Visits to alternative or complementary practitioners are not reimbursed or paid for by health insurance companies in many cases. However, the life expectancy of people in the United States is not any higher than that of Japan, Hong Kong, Singapore, or China. The United States spends a higher percentage of its GDP, approximately 19%, on health care but yet the life expectancy rate of Americans ranks 27th in the world. Countries like China, Hong Kong, Japan, and Singapore have successfully depended on ITM alongside orthodox medicine and have encouraging life expectancies comparable to countries with exclusive western-based medicine such as the United States. Hong Kong and Japan actually have outperformed the US.

This is one of the reasons there is a need to standardize and explore ITM to the fullest extent possible. There are various indications that point to change and restructuring of Ghana's indigenous traditional medicine. Standardization, expansion, and drug pharmacopoeia of medicinal plants have already taken place in several countries, including pioneering nations like China, Japan, India, Hong Kong, and others like Ghana (Sofowora, 1982; Yazdanpanah, 2004). Moderate developments have been seen in these areas in several African countries such as South Africa, Nigeria, and Ghana.

In Ghana, current and previous administrations have employed several initiatives to modernize and to improve the traditional medical industry. Some of the restructuring initiatives include the formation of the Ghana Psychic and Traditional Healers Association in 1961. The Ghana Psychic and Traditional Medicine Practitioners' Association was entrusted by the Traditional Medicine Practice Act 595 to license and register traditional healers. This is intended to make it possible to regulate the preparation and sale of medicinal herbs and plants. And, later in 1975, the Centre for Scientific Research into Plant Medicine (CSRPM) was formed by the government to oversee the usefulness of traditional medicine. Some of its success stories include the "Mist Tonica," one of the several herbal medicines made by CSRPM for the treatment of Anemia (CSRPM, 2008). The Ghana Federation of Traditional Medicine Practitioners' Associations was subsequently born in 1999 to oversee the traditional medicine industry. Today, apprenticeship and training are basic requirements for traditional healers before they can practice. The aim is to include traditional medicine in the medical school.

Furthermore, several legislations, proposals, and associations have been made to improve traditional medicine in Ghana: The Ghana Psychic and Traditional Healers Association in 1961, Centre for Scientific Research into Plant Medicine in 1975, and the Food and Drugs Board in 1992. In licensing and enforcing the law, the Food and Drugs Board certifies the sale of Traditional Medicine products to the public under the TMPC Act-575. This act ensured the establishment of Traditional Medicine Council, which is tasked with the responsibility of overseeing the registration of all Traditional Medical Practitioners in the country. Another noteworthy attempt to systematize and standardize ITM in Ghana, includes the contributions of the research institutes at Noguchi Memorial institute for Medical Research, University of Ghana and the University of Science and Technology, and Centre for Scientific Research into Plant Medicine. This has been a major milestone for the indigenous traditional medicine industry; however there is more work to be done. The question now is what role can schools play and how can schools contribute to the new trend of attempts to explore ITM? Subsequent paragraphs focus on introducing and incorporating traditional medicine in Ghanaian schools of higher learning.

With about 70% of the population in Ghana depending on traditional medicine (WHO, 2012), the need to move faster with efforts to advance ITM is all the more pressing. People are beginning to avoid health care due to out-of-pocket payments. For this group of people who cannot afford western medicine, traditional medicine is a viable option for them. There is an increasing trend of people turning away from orthodox medicine due to increasing cost of health care and the ratio of physician to patient are at its all-time high (1:12000 people). In fact, concrete steps need to be taken to address the situation, by way of advancing ITM and promoting its use. Restructuring the curricula in schools and introducing ITM in elementary, junior and senior high schools as well as degree-granting institutions is a step in the right direction.

A model that can serve, as inspiration, is the one found in China. In China, pioneers in the research and practice of traditional medicine have maintained and transformed it to tap its potential to the highest level possible. Today, China's export and import in Traditional Chinese Medicine have reached over $855 million (Gov. CN, n.d.). Countries across the world, including Ghana, patronize the ITM export system set up by China. Major importers of China's traditional medicine include Germany, Hong Kong, Japan, and South Korea. China exports ITM to about 135 countries worldwide. This comes as no surprise: China can boast of five large institutions of medicine dedicated to the advancement of traditional Chinese medicine. For example, the Guangzhou University of Chinese Medicine (GZUCM), founded in as early as 1956, has several degree programs and attracts student from about 103 countries. Today, GZUCM has 19 doctoral degree programs in Chinese Medicine and Chinese Herbal Medicine. There is the integration of Chinese medicine and Western medicine with 24 master degree programs in Chinese Medicine, a clear indication of how extensively traditional medicine is explored in China (GZUCM, 2006).

For Ghana to make any meaningful changes and advancements, structural changes should begin at the lower level of the economy. When degree programs are offered in indigenous traditional medicine, many more will begin to consider consuming products of ITM. There is no reason students at all levels of their education should not be introduced to the indigenous knowledge base embedded in ITM. Schools in Ghana should not only encourage students to develop an interest and curiosity in ITM, they should also employ people like my grandmother and the herbalist (as experts on ITM).

CONCLUSION

This chapter has discussed the role of indigenous traditional medicine (ITM) in Ghana. The assumption made throughout the chapter is that ITM has great potential of improving the health status of Ghanaians if it becomes more systematized and its worthiness explored to a greater extent than it is now. It is asserted in the chapter that much needed resources are being pumped into orthodox medicine when our main focus should be on less costly and easily available traditional medicine. The current medical system in Ghana is modeled after that of foreign countries. The author suggests otherwise: ITM is more affordable and, therefore, supplementing the current health-care system with a more systematized and standardized ITM can lead to a more efficient use of this underexplored resource. It is not a given that western medicine is capable of reaching the needs of all Ghanaians. In this chapter, therefore, it is recommended that ITM be modernized, systematized and standardized by essentially incorporating it into the education system.

It is argued that the reason African countries have low life expectancy rates is partly because African nations are not exploring their natural resources to their fullest potential, but are rather trying to duplicate the system in most developed countries. These systems, modeled after the orthodox system, have their own disadvantages that African countries such as Ghana need to be prudent not to replicate. It is noted that countries like China, Hong Kong, Japan, and Singapore, which have successfully depended on ITM alongside orthodox medicine, have encouraging life expectancies comparable to countries with western-based medicine – such as the United States; they should therefore serve as inspiration and models. The chapter provided an overview and examples of ITM as a knowledge system, included a comparative analysis of ITM and orthodox western medicine, highlighted ways in which they converge and diverge, and noted what Ghana is currently doing to systematize ITM. The author also discussed implications and provided recommendations on how the ITM knowledge can be taught in schools, and what can be done to maximize the role of ITM in Africa, with specific reference to Ghana.

REFERENCES

Adeline, G., & Khalsa, P. (2009). *NCCAM Complementary and Integrative Medicine Consult Service.* http://nccam.nih.gov/health/whatiscam/chinesemed.htm (accessed 2012).

Administration, US Social Security. (2009). *Ghana. Social security programs throughout the World: Africa.* http://www.ssa.gov/policy/docs/progdesc/ssptw/2008-2009/africa/ghana.html (accessed 2013).

Balch, P. A. (2002). *Prescription for herbal healing: An easy-to-use A-Z reference to hundreds of common disorders and their herbal remedies.* New York: Penguin.

Balch, P. A. (2006). Prescription for nutritional healing: A practical A-to-Z reference to drug-free remedies using vitamins, minerals, herbs & food supplements, Vol. 4 (4th ed.). New York: Penguin.

CDC. (2012). *Inventions improving women's lives.* http://www.cdc.gov/women/inventions/index.htm.

CSRPM. (2008). *Herbal products.* http://www.csrpm.org/ (accessed 2013).

Gov.CN. (2006). *Traditional Chinese medicine export reaches record high.* Chinese Government Official Web Portal. Edited by Lin Li. Xinhua. http://english.gov.cn/2006-05/06/content_274294.htm (accessed 2013).

le Grand, A., & Wibdergem, P. (1990). *Herbal medicine and health promotion.* Amsterdam: Royal Tropical Institute.

Martin, D. H. (2009). *Traditional medicine and restoration of wellness strategies* (pp. 26-42). National Aboriginal Health Organization (NAHO).

Naur, M. (2001). *Indigenous knowledge and HIV/AIDS: Ghana and Zambia* (pp 1-5). IK Notes Indigenous Knowledge (IK) Initiatives (Africa Region's Knowledge and Learning Center).

Neuman, B., & Fawcett, J. (2002) *The Neuman systems model. 4.* Upper Saddle River, NJ: Prentice Hall.

Rios, J. L., & Recio, M. (2005) Medicinal plants and antimicrobial activity. *Journal of Ethnopharmacology, 100,* 80-84.

Smith, J. B., Coleman, N. A., Fortney, J. A., Johnson, D. A., Blumhagen, D. W., & Grey, T. W. (2000). The impact of traditional birth attendant training on delivery complications in Ghana. *Health Policy and Planning, 15*(3), 326-331.

Sofowora, A. (1982). Medicinal plants and traditional medicine in Africa. In A. Sofowora (Ed.), *Medicinal plants and traditional medicine in Africa* (pp. 28-256). New York: Wiley & Sons Ltd.

Tabi, M., Powell, M., & Hodnicki, D. (2006). Use of traditional healers and modern medicine in Ghana. *International Nursing Review, 53,* 52-58.

Togola, A., Diallo, D., Dembele, S., & Paulsen, B. (2005). Ethnopharmacological survey of different uses of seven medicinal plants from Mali (West Africa) in the regions Doila, Kolokani and Siby. *Journal of Ethnobiology and Ethnomedicine, 7*(1).

UNAIDS. (2010). *Global report: UNAIDS report on the global AIDS epidemic, 2010.* Global AIDS Report: United Nations, Joint United Nations Programme on HIV/AIDS (UNAIDS).

UNICEF. (2012). *Ghana Health Service and UNICEF encourage mothers to deliver with help from skilled birth attendants.* http://www.unicef.org/infobycountry/ghana_62444.html (accessed 2013).

WHO, World Health Organization. (1946). Preamble to the constitution of the World Health Organization. http://apps.who.int/gb/bd/PDF/bd47/EN/constitution-en.pdf (accessed 2013).

Yazdanpanah, Y. (2004). Costs associated with combination antiretroviral therapy in HIV-infected patients. *Oxford Journal of Medicine, 53*(4), 558-568.

93

R. O. OLAOYE

9. AFRICAN TRADITIONAL MEDICINE (TM) AND SOCIAL MOVEMENTS IN NIGERIA

INTRODUCTION

The focus of the chapter is on how the knowledge of Traditional Medicine (TM) is acquired. Next is the mode of practice characteristic of aspects of TM. In the two regards, the chapter emphasizes as well how social movements are stimulated. The study then proceeds to underpin areas of human interaction between both the herbal practitioners and their clients in the field of traditional medicine.

KNOWLEDGE ACQUISITION IN TM

Like in any other vocation, acquisition of knowledge in TM is a necessity for those who choose to pursue a career in it. Even for the people that take casual interest in it, either for personal purpose or otherwise, skill acquistion in TM cannot be compromised. Indeed, the long history of TM implies that this aspect of knowledge should be assigned a prominent place in the science education domain (SED). In this respect, the process of teaching and learning, as in other branches of study, involves education in TM.

Those who possess the knowledge of any branch of indigenous TM do teach others. The teaching puts premium on trust or at times on oath, or both. Normally, people go to the custodians of the knowledge for training. This may involve travel within a particular geographical zone or travel which cut across geographical, cultural and ethnic borders. That is why, for instance, someone from Ibadan in Oyo State would not mind traveling as far as Bida in Niger State, once it is confirmed that the indigenous knowledge which he or she so much desires is available in the Gwari community.

The teaching and learning processes involved are indeed great stimulants of social movements. It does happen at times that the required ingredients such as herbs, roots, leaves, barks, soil materials and other medicaments are generally not available in a community where the training center situates. In this case, both the trainers and the trainees do travel far and wide in search of such materials. In the course of this exercise, there could be a relocation from one place to another, leading at times to the founding of new settlements. That was the case with a village called Ikotun in the Oyun Local Government Area of Kwara State, which was noted to have been founded by an indigenous medical practitioner, generally called 'baba Ikotun.'

Splinter groups of the 'wise' men and experts usually emerge from time to time. In particular, at the end of training, the new graduates could decide to leave their

G. Emeagwali & G. J. S. Dei (eds.), African Indigenous Knowledge and the Disciplines, 95–98.

teachers or masters and establish their profession elsewhere. In their new places of settlement, they do not only practice their profession but also engage in training others. Apart from this, there are occasions when those who have finished training would have cause to go back to their erstwhile masters for guidance in one aspect or another of their vocation. It does happen that the 'master' would see the need to contact his former apprentice for one obligation or the other. The result of all of this is the occurrence of movements and interaction between one area and another.

THE MODE OF PRACTICE

Those endowed with the knowledge of TM make use of one type of medium of instruction or the other. Each indigenous practitioner of TM has his field of specialization. But in spite of what may be the nuances, all the instruments of instruction have a common goal of bringing to knowledge what is unknown, and into open what is hidden. It should be noted that the level of competence differs from one practitioner to another. This, therefore, provokes movements of the clients who travel far and wide in search of those they regard as the most capable of solving their problems.

Treatment modalities depend on the nature of the problem which in most cases involves payment in cash and in kind. The cost of treatment varies with individual practitioners and of course, the nature of the problem of the client. Thus a comparative advantage of the cost-benefit of treatment vis-a-vis the actual solution to the problem, is always a consideration for a client in his choice of a specialist. This itself stimulates movements of people from place to place.

The trend today is for those who are into Traditional Medicine to establish centers where they practice their craft. It is this trend that leads to the spread of what is called herbal homes, herbal centers or clinics. In local parlance, especially in the Yoruba community, the homes are differently called Ile babalawo; ile adaunse; ile onisegun; ile yemi wo, etc. The homes are run in the manner of modern clinics or hospitals whereby patients come in for consultation and treatment. In the homes, provision is made both for in-and out-patients. Thus, it is not unusual to record movements of men and women who have come from far and near in search of a solution to their problems.

Of recent, networking among the indigenous scientists in the mode of group activities has been carried to a new level. This is expressed in what is known among the Yorubas as ipate isegun. In English words, this means 'trade fair.' Trade fair in this case involves public display and marketing of the products of indigenous science. Initially, the method was for an individual to go from one place to another to display his products. Furthermore, he also goes ahead to explain what each of the products does, how it works, the dosage and its efficacy. Naturally, people come to see and buy the products on display. In the course of that, news usually goes around, which in most cases leads to arbitrary and in some cases, "stampeded" movements among the people.

Beyond the level of individuals and localized merchandising of products, there is now co-operation and collaboration among the stakeholders for wider markets, especially in the urban areas of the country. The modernized mode of market strategy is all-involving. For example, a team is built, with each team carrying a label different from one another. Some of the labels, for example, read: Agbomola World-Wide; Olorun ni ologun; Aditu Baba Ewe; Aiye ni iro mo; Laola Shalasi heritage herbal centre; Yemkem International, Iyalode Anigbajumo Ogun, Atewo laba ila, etc. As akin to a formal trade fair, each team takes a stand, usually built in the form of a makeshift shed. Here, the leader employs a few hands, some on temporary and others on permanent basis. These constitute members of staff who take charge of advertising and sales matters. In this context, due to the size and scope of the fair, many people are involved and movements enhanced, cutting across geographical and ethnic boundaries.

PATRONAGE

Patronage for the products of TM is often informed by the needs of the people. Furthermore, in modern times, the advertisement of the products of indigenous science has expanded. For a long time, the practice was to hawk from place to place through trekking. With time, the use of bicycles in hawking the products came into vogue. This increased the volume of sales as well as areas of coverage. Gradually, a few rich ones among the practitioners/dealers in local herbs and related indigenous scientific products were able to purchase motorcycles to carry out the sales of their wares. From the use of motorcycles emerged the use of motor cars, which further increased mobility and the volume of sales. There was usually a sharp rise in the movements of those engaged in the selling and buying of indigenous herbal products, covering wide geographical areas.

Equally monumental is the increasingly popular trade fairs. This is now a new dimension to the market strategy adopted by the stakeholders in the products of indigenous science. Usually, the trade fairs are organized in collaboration with the relevant agencies of government, particularly the Ministry of Commerce and Trade. One important thing to note here is that apart from the movements that such fairs stimulate, there is also the aspect of recognition that the government has given to herbal products, and for that matter, traditional medicine in general.

The trade fairs often involve a lot of movements of the people across the States of Nigeria. The herbal practitioners usually see the occasion as an opportunity to showcase what they have, what they know, and the potentials they possess. Their respective clients also usually seize the opportunity of the fairs to come from different parts of the country for diagnosis and treatment of their ailments at prescribed fees. Because it is an occasional affair, ipate isegun is usually allocated a special space wherever it is staged. In Ilorin, the capital of Kwara State, the herbal trade fair has almost become an annual event. Two places have always been reserved for the event, namely the Kwara State Stadium complex and the Kwara State Trade Fair Center.

In 1988, when one was staged at the Kwara State Stadium complex, an estimated population of six hundred thousand (600,000) was noted to be involved. In 1999, the population was higher. And in 2000, when the Kwara State Trade Fair

Centre (a more expanded space) was used, the number of the participants soared and the whole state was teeming with activity. The subsequent ones in 2002, 2006, and 2008 had high attendance figures. Obviously, all these stimulated a great volume of socio-economic and cultural movements across borders.

CONCLUSION

The chapter reflected on the important role played by indigenous science in social movements in modern Nigeria. The point was raised that traditional practitioners usually showcased their products through several avenues, such as hawking and trade fairs that stimulated the movements of people. Finally, the work brought into a bold relief the fact that demand and supply involved in the products of TM naturally provided a leverage for the social movements that have occurred.

REFERENCES

Dei, G. J. S. (2000). *Indigenous knowledge in global contexts: Multiple readings of our world.* University of Toronto Press.

Dopamu, P. (2000). *Esu: The invisible foe of man, Ijebu – Ode.* Sebiotimo Publications.

Elebuibon, Y. (2008). *Invisible powers of the metaphysical world.* Ibadan: Creative Books.

Ezegbe, M. O. (1990). *The impact of modern science and technology on socio-cultural values in Nigeria, fourth dimension.* Owerri.

Interviews. (2010-2013). Interviews with traditional practitioners in Ilorin, Kwara State, Nigeria, 2010-2013.

Kalilu, R. O. (1993). *Medicine, divination and art: Osanyin among the Yoruba.* Lagos: CBAAC.

Lantum, D. N. (1996). *Searching for the African personality in the traditional medicine – Man of Africa...* CBAAC.

Olaoye, R. A. (Ed.). (2009). *History of indigenous science and technology in Nigeria.* Ibadan: Chresthill Publishers.

Tella, A. (1996). *African traditional medicine and modern health oractices...* Lagos: CBAAC.

Sofowora, A. (1984). *Medicine plants and traditional medicine in Africa.* New York: Wiley Publications.

PAUL OBIOKOR

10. ART EDUCATION

Curriculum, Traditional Knowledge and Practice in Nigeria

INTRODUCTION

Art education provides perspectives on the more challenging question of education in Nigeria. Nigeria's development, stability and prosperity are particularly relevant to problems related to Euro-centered educational practices. The colonial British education legacy of curricular and practice models in Nigeria is examined. Emphasis is put on the notion that learning resides in local culture. Lack of attention to local culture is an impediment to the transfer of knowledge to children, thereby eroding centuries of local traditions, knowledge and culture, the cornerstones of indigenous knowledge.

In Nigeria, educators favor the curricula and practice model of British colonial education. The mixture of, yet separate, local and colonial traditions of knowledge transfer complicate children's education. Economic disparity among local populations also causes timid commitments to western education. Different religious beliefs also distort the worth of and support for education. On the one hand, Christians welcome and support western education; on the other hand, Muslims are generally apathetic towards western education and perceive it with suspicion (Imam, 2012). Without a doubt, Christians and Muslims want the kind of modernization exemplified in western societies. Whereas, Muslims want modernization that is rooted in Islamic ideology. The result is intense disagreement on how to go about modernizing.

This chapter focuses on the relevance of the Nigerian education system to traditional knowledge. It outlines the legacy of British colonial education in Nigeria. Further, it illuminates the curricular and practice model of colonial British education and the effects on children's learning, and explores the importance of local context in children's learning. Furthermore, it uses art education as a window to discuss pertinent theoretical issues. Finally, the chapter offers some insights on developing art programs that better serve traditional value systems for children's learning in Nigeria.

THE NIGERIAN EDUCATION SYSTEM

The Nigerian education system is to a large extent oriented toward examinations because of the legacy of British colonial education. About three decades ago, Kurian (1987) described the Nigerian education system as restricted because "the requirements of examinations determine the curricular at every level rather than

G. Emeagwali & G. J. S. Dei (eds.), *African Indigenous Knowledge and the Disciplines*, 99–111.

vice versa" (p. 947). This has not changed fundamentally to date. The orientation of educational practice in Nigerian if compared to Britain is not a result of some peculiar mandate of British colonialism, but of the mindset of Nigerian educators who import educational models not in harmony with traditional values. The result has been a remarkable similarity, or maintenance of British colonial curricula and practice. Nduka (1980) and Tibenderana (2006) shed more light on the purpose of colonial education in Nigeria. To be sure, the British value education served as a process of transmitting culture, at least in part, from one generation to the next. However, colonial pioneers of education in Nigeria preserved and transmitted their culture rather than the indigenous one(s).

Not to overemphasize British self-interest, Nigerians had a system of education that some analysts defined as 'informal.' The British colonials replaced 'informal' education with 'formal' education, which, of course, did not come from a vacuum but from an existing discourse of European racial superiority. Although contemporary educational perspectives in Nigeria represent significant breaks from the myth and exigencies of colonial relationship, they still exemplify the pathetic and often ludicrous attempts to copy from Europe, uncritically. As Majasan argued: [Although] no nation can today reach the lofty heights of modern civilization without borrowing from the common pool of world culture, no nation can reach those heights of modern civilization without putting itself by its own very solid and meaningful cultural foundation (p. 139). Majasan understood that habitual borrowing from Europe means educating Nigeria's youth for Europe. The result is the contemporary flight of the educated class of Nigerians to Europe and North America in search of "the good life," rather than seek solutions to ailments of the local worlds of Nigeria.

Education is central to the quest for national development in Nigeria (Imam, 2012). Since 1983, however, education has been insignificant to Nigeria's development because of incessant military administrations and increase in corruption. Serious political factors mitigate education in Nigeria in the 21st century, but a key aspect of it is being ignored. What is being ignored is why western education is not yielding the same results in Nigeria as in Britain; that is, why is western education in Nigeria not translating into desired development? There are many reasons for the failure, but this chapter will focus only on one: the legacy of the colonial British

Rather than depend on wholesale foreign models, Nigerian educators should "sift the good and useful from the imports and align it with the valuable in the local culture to form a new and worthwhile one" (Adeyinka, 1981, p. 7). As yet, Nigerian education affirms the legacy of colonial British education that mostly emphasizes the "child's movement through invariant stages that are strongly supported by standardized examinations" (Walsh, 1992; Pressley & McCormick, 2007; Little, 2012). In that curricular and practice, the child is not seen as the biological being proposed by Piaget (Woolfolk, 2004), or as a sociocultural being proposed by Vygotsky (Hall, 2007), actively involved in his or her own development. Rather, the child is seen as waiting passively for nature and an "examination laden educational system" (Paton, 2009; Awiti, 2012) to run its course.

One result of the colonial British education system is that it reduces education to endless hurdles of standardized examinations. The theories of child development and current research findings in child development, if considered at all, are insignificant to whether or not developmental levels and/or the socio-historical environment mitigate a child's capability to learn and perform tasks. The emphasis of the Euro-centered model of education in Nigeria has been on preparing children to pass examinations. That emphasis has unfortunate consequences for students and teachers alike. Whereas students are victims of deep philosophical or conceptual disjuncture, teachers are "reduced to technicians who simply prepare students to take [examinations]" (Gilman & McDermott, 1994, p. 73). In preparing students for examinations, teachers tend to teach children content that is not necessarily relevant to daily life. As a result, teachers complicate instruction to the point of stripping it from the reality of what is being taught. Worse, if a child fails an examination, that child's future is jeopardized.

COLONIAL CURRICULA AND PRACTICE IN NIGERIA

Majasan was critical of the failure of making crucial distinctions in Nigerian education. He argued: "whether one is being educated in the most advanced society in the world or in the most primitive, the educational objective of passing on to the next generation the existing knowledge of the physical environment remains constant" (p. 5). The Euro-centered model has been under scrutiny for many years because students have learnt to overcome the system by stealing actual examination questions long before the examinations are written. Why? Because the examination content is far removed from what makes sense to the students. The system is disposed to using examinations as the sole indicator of knowledge, and the inattention to the social and cultural environment in knowledge taught at school, contributes to students' cheating. The Nigerian education enterprise remained seriously criticized in the late 1980s for not delivering on modernization and some of these criticisms remain valid. To better understand the failures of the Nigerian education enterprise, let's examine the emphasis on examinations.

STANDARDIZED EXAMINATIONS IN THE NIGERIAN EDUCATIONAL SYSTEM

The conception of examinations in Nigerian education is a powerful one. The practice became popular following the first Nigerian Education Ordinance of 1887 and has thrived until now. The following is a short description of how standardized examination became the cornerstone of Nigeria's education:

> The ordinance enforced teaching in every [aid-assisted] school [focus on] reading and writing of the English language, and arithmetic and in the case of girls, plain needlework. English grammar, English history and geography could [also] be taught as class subjects. This was a projection of the needs of

the Government (British) and mercantile houses for clerks and literate assistants. Government acknowledged also the importance of teachers in an educational system. [Thus,] teachers were to be trained, examined and awarded certificates and received stipulated salaries. (Taiwo, 1980, p. 18)

The emphasis on examinations has a history that favor credentials over actual knowledge. The problem is, this practice of placing high value on examinations has not stood up well under the test of modernization. Without doubt, the British legacy of education has not produced the kinds of citizen necessary for development, stability, and prosperity in Nigeria. Instead of using examinations as a sole indicator of knowledge, Nigeria's educators should strive with conceptions that speak to traditional values and indigenous knowledge. In practical terms, that means better incorporation of the best practices of British education with indigenous, traditional ones. Also, the use of examinations as the sole indicator of knowledge should be de-emphasized. The saying goes that one coat does not fit all; meaning if standardized examination model works for the British, the United States of America, Japan, China and Indonesia to catapult development, it doesn't mean the same can work in Nigeria for Nigerians. As a result, the informal traditional education model should be allowed to complement the western model in education in Nigeria. Local traditions should be revisited to encourage the study and furtherance of oral traditions with regard to history, folklore, agriculture, trade and commerce, and creative art, etc. The mentor-apprentice relationship in education that pervaded ethnic nationalities of Nigeria before the arrival of Europeans should again be allowed and encouraged.

WESTERN CONTENT IN NIGERIA EDUCATION

One of the broad objectives of education is inculcation of cultural values. Nigeria's educational model, by design, loathes indigenous values, including instilling locally desirable habits in the child. The Nigerian educational system cultivates in children "seeds of future alienation from the language and immediate environment" (Onwuchekwa, 1981, p. 17). Books written for pupils in Britain used by Nigerian pupils put children in a predicament of comprehension. Although Taiwo (1980) is less judgmental, he gives credence to the argument that until recent times many of the textbooks used in Nigerian schools at various levels were written outside of Nigeria for pupils in the environments where the books were written. Clearly, Nigerian children confronted the problem of comprehension by resorting to translating text from English to their first language. There have been efforts to rectify these concerns since independence in 1960, but much remains to be done. One area that has not been thoroughly explored in the efforts to reduce illiteracy is "writing." Writing should be encouraged to supplement oral culture.

At this time, the legacy of colonial British education in Nigeria remains stable. To be sure, English language remains the official language of instruction in Nigeria. Instructional materials are in English and make unclear the purpose of education for children. The result is a shaky foundation. No wonder that the investments in education in Nigeria are not translating to desired development. To reform education, visionary scholars have suggested that teachers employed in schools come from local communities so that they may better translate English textbooks into local languages. These teachers who, obviously, also have a better understanding of the language and local culture thereby make more meaningful connections between British instructional materials and local community life and experiences. The real goal is to replace educational materials that draw heavily upon European culture, with materials produced in Nigeria that embrace local traditions and global understanding. I will continue by emphasizing the social and cultural worlds, and show how critical they are to the education of children.

THE SOCIAL AND CULTURAL WORLDS IN EDUCATION

The social and cultural worlds are critical to children's education, but the legacy of British colonial education makes those worlds irrelevant to education. Because learning is an active process, however, context also has an important role in the process (Hall, 2007). For the learning of the Nigerian child to be authentic in the 21st century, the Euro-centered educational model in Nigeria should yield to the social and cultural worlds of Nigeria. Meaning, the Euro-centered educational model should be responsive to the traditional educational system that when children are born, culture is handed down to them in local communities. As children grow up, they inevitably learn about the local culture through negotiations with adults. Until a child learns the culture and proves him/herself by conduct and application, s/he is not seen as knowledgeable and a contributing members of community. In that sense, education is not a natural result of individual maturation but an invention of culture (Feldman, 1980; Rogoff, 1990; Scott & Palincsar, 2011; Phillipson, Ku, & Phillipson, 2013).

Rogoff (1990) discloses in her cross-cultural research that children's skill and knowledge of their world are achieved by cultural activities that socialize them in skilled roles. Lave and Wenger (1991) further explains that over time, children take on increasing responsibility for their own learning and participation in joint activity. Rogoff characterized this process as guided participation. Adeyinka (1980) offers a perspective on children discovering their own identity. He notes:

> The learner in [indigenous] education is a human being who undergoes training to fit into society and live a full life in which s/he participates from the beginning. [From the onset,] the child does not know what to develop into until he understands the system into which s/he must be [part]. (p. 11)

What I am suggesting is that growth in the child's knowledge occurs in the context of functional activities in local environment. Nigerian education policymakers often condemn such a view as being inconsistent with the Euro-centered education model. But without intervention, the Euro-centered education model in use in Nigeria will continue to undermine the education of children. No question that the transfer of local knowledge to children would remain obscure and thereby erode centuries of local culture and tradition.

A few years ago, I met a Nigerian graduate student in a "get-together" held in honor of new African students at the University of Illinois, Urbana-Champaign. This meeting was unusual because it altered my perspective on how big and small our world, at the same time, can be. To be sure, I hardly meet people in the United States of America who understand and speak my language. On this occasion, however, I met someone like that. When I told my new friend that I was studying toward a doctorate in art education, his interest peaked and wanted to know more about the kind of art I create and the medium(s) I work in. I told him, "I draw and paint representational and non-representational objects." What was of most interest to me is his remark as he reminisced his past in art classes in high school in Nigeria. He expressed an unfulfilled desire and condemned the experience, describing it as disconnected. He said, "I was taught about Michelangelo and others who I do not know, and how they did this and that. I wonder how many children in Italy, France or Spain, for that matter knew about Erabo Emokpae or Yusuf Grillo, accomplished Nigerian artists?"

The above anecdote illustrates some of the problems in curricula and practices' affecting education in Nigeria, and art education in particular. Children in Nigeria are not directly encountering colonial influence. But they encounter colonial influences through the adults around them who mediate, uncritically, Euro-centered models of education for use.

SOME THEORETICAL ISSUES OF CONTEMPORARY ART EDUCATION

Most subjects of learning and academic disciplines in Nigerian institutions of learning are rooted in western thought, and the art subject is no different. Art education in Britain as in North America draws upon various disciplines including the social sciences and humanities. Feldman (1996) makes the point that by habit and sentiment, traditional art education practices also rely on psychological theories. Western curricular and practices in art education are framed on "creative self-expression" (Efland, 1987, p. 10) with therapeutic benefit and personal growth. They are also mixed with the influence of John Dewey who triggered revisions in art teaching practices from kindergarten through the university. Additionally, Gestalt psychology in the 1950s added further weight to the arts in education. Furthermore, the writings of Rudolf Arnheim on art therapy were also particularly influential. Art therapy drew on many of the lessons of art psychology towards ego repair. However, the idea of "creative self expression" by Lowenfeld in the late 1980s gained immense popularity. In his book, *Creative and Mental Growth* (1987), Lowenfeld emphasized sequential stages in artistic development beginning with the toddler's early scribbles and climaxing in preadolescent's preoccupation with realism (Villeneuve, 1992). Lowenfeld also accentuated self-identification through creativity encouraged by spontaneous self-expressionist practice setting apart non-interference in children's artistic activity. What is troubling in Lowenfeld's description is the notion of "stages" and the "solitary artist." Lowenfeld's devised his scheme from Piagetian cognitive theory that is

104

markedly "romantic and maturationist," which are powerful notions. I will continue by attacking the notions of "stages" and the "solitary artist."

STAGES

Jean Piaget (1962) describes stages as all-encompassing, invariant, and universal. Gelman and Baillargeon (1983, p. 214) argue that "[there] is little evidence to support the idea of major stages in cognitive development of the type described by Piaget" as maturation of the child predisposes the child to learn (Mayer, 2009).

Walsh (1992) is more direct in his criticism: "The problem with stages as described by Piaget is that they have not stood up well under empirical test" (p. 3). To recognize that problem-solving and knowledge acquisition is not determined by stages as theorized by Piaget, Kayoko Inagaki (1992) argues:

In Piaget's theory, one's competence in problem-solving and knowledge acquisition is determined by one's structures of thinking, which are applicable across domains. Thus, preschool children whose structures are not so advanced are considered inevitably incompetent, whereas adolescents who have acquired formal operations can logically and systematically deal with problems in any domain. However, competence may vary from domain to domain. For example, even young children do show advanced modes of reasoning in a domain they know well; in other words, acquired domain-specific knowledge serves as a restraint in solving problems there. (p. 120)

What can be deduced from the above is the capability of children to learn. Clearly, when children are left long enough in a learning situation, they soon begin to perform tasks pertaining to the learning intended, and they sometimes perform better than most adults in similar situation. It is not too big a step to take, therefore, to conclude that children with all their incompetence according to Piaget are still capable of initiating the art-making process evidenced in professional artists.

SOLITARY ARTIST (INDIVIDUALISM)

The notion of the solitary artist lacks certainty, for it assumes that encounters are exclusive to the artist alone in the social world. To expose the falseness of this view, Walsh (1992) again argues that educational practice is dominated by emphasis on teaching children only what they are ready to learn, what they already know. To this extent, the child is seen as a solitary learner to the exclusion of the contexts in which he or she learns. Bruner (1987) critiqued the focus on the individual calling it "unmediated conceptualism," and describes it as:

[An assumption] that the child's growing knowledge of the world is achieved principally by direct encounters with the world rather than mediated through vicarious encounters with it in interacting and negotiating with others. [So this] doctrine of the child going it alone in mastering his knowledge of the world is vacuous [and cannot be taken with a grain of salt]. (p. 85)

To be specific about the development of cognition, Bruner argues:

> In the main, children do not construct a reality solely on the basis of private encounters with exemplars of natural states. Most beginning learner approaches to the world are mediated through negotiations with others. (1987, p. 93)

What follow is Vigotsky's cognitive theory as alternative theory that stresses the importance of the social and cultural world.

VYGOTSKY'S COGNITIVE THEORY

Vygotskian ideas of art education provide an alternative to the dominant stages and solitary adventurer described by Lowenfeld and derived from Piaget. Although Vygotsky did not create a full-fledged theory of art education, his work provides an original metatheoretical perspective on how children perceive and produce drawings (Stetsenko, 1995). For Vygotsky, the social is prior to the individual. Subsequently, development moves from the outside to within the child (Gauvin and Cole, 1997). Vygotsky proffers that:

> Every function in the child's cultural development appears twice; first, on the social level, and later, on the individual level; first, between people (interpsychological), and then inside the child (intrapsychological). This applies equally to voluntary attention, to logical memory, and to the formation of concepts. All the higher functions originate in actual relations between human individuals. (Vygotsky, 1978, p. 57)

Vygotsky promoted the cultural-historical bases of cognitive development. Haste (1987) wrote in support of the Vygotskian perspective that development "must ultimately be seen within the wider context of a cultural-historical framework which defines what is possible, what is legitimate, and what is, also, functional to the social system" (p. 173). This focus, then, brings cognitive development into existence as a social process that occurs through social interactions and "through mediation via semiotic systems, notably language, that are themselves products of socio-historical processes" (Cazden, 1989; Fávero, 2007; Bonicoli, 2011).

THE FUNDAMENTAL PRINCIPLE OF INDIGENOUS EDUCATION

The basic belief about traditional education is knowledge and skills are transferred from the older to younger generation to ensure the survival of the culture. Ultimately, the goal is to educate children through companionship and the support of adults who help to stretch children's imagination to understand the skills of using the tools of culture; that is, adults guide the participation of "children in activities that socialize them" (Rogoff, 1990).

INEXTRICABLE LINK IN VYGOTSKIAN THEORY TO TRADITIONAL EDUCATION

Vygotskian theory has an inextricable link to traditional education in that it clarifies that growth in knowledge and skills are rooted in the socio-cultural world. The customs and traditions of Nigeria are explicit about how the socio-cultural world is ordered – men, women and children – playing distinctive roles in the survival of all members of one big family who share a common life experience. So culture is handed down to children after they are born. That explains children don't have a priori knowledge of the culture they are born. Children don't know what to develop into until they understand the cultural system in which they must be a part. But for a child to understand the system, s/he must be inducted and guided as apprentice into the system. As a result, children gradually learn the necessary skills and knowledge of the culture through participation in cultural activities that socialize them (Rogoff, 1990; Kozulin, Gindis, Ageyev, & Miller, 2003; Hall, 2007). Although Vygotsky's theory is about child development and educational psychology, his supposition lends to the guiding beliefs of traditional education, at least in part, that development must be culturally relevant. I will continue with this line of thought and provide some insights on strategies to develop art education programs that affirm traditional values of Nigeria.

ART EDUCATION THAT AFFIRMS INDIGENOUS VALUES

Are the objects called *art* in the western world, *art* to the African? In many African languages, mine (Isoko) included, "there is no word that corresponds to 'art.' But many words define "the activities of art-making and expressions of qualitative judgment" (Geoffroy-Schneiter, 2000). Whatever it is about "art," we can agree that art generally mimics life and the values humans bring to it. In Nigeria, art is a system of values that are predominantly cultural. The manifestations of art are incredible, and are as many as the cultures that exist in the country. The Isokos, for example, are one of the many ethnic nationalities of Nigeria. Isoko art occasions the daily lives of the people. Isoko art manifests mostly in figurines, costumes, and handicrafts – animate and inanimate – with religious or clan importance. Yet, most of the artworks are indisputably decorative for purposes of honor and prestige. The wealth of Isoko aesthetics lies in decorations. With the legacy of colonial British education, the values of Isoko art are bound to lie dormant or sadly be lost to foreign domination.

Art in Nigerian schools is taught and expressed in a foreign context; that is, art education is totally disconnected from the local context. Art education should yield to the structures of local culture to enrich and foster the learning experiences of children. Because art is a hands-on subject that invigorates practice, the local context in Isoko, for example, should inform the teaching and learning of art. Children can and should learn to produce items such as drums, mortar and pestle, clay pots and dishes, handheld fans, hats, baskets, sleeping mats, doormats, ceiling or partitioning mats, and other locally valuable items. Handheld fans, for example, are made from sun-dried palm fronds and animal skin leather. Handheld fans may variously be decorated for different purposes. But in the school context, they could be limited to one or more combination of decorations. So also can the doormats, ceiling and partitioning mats, hats and baskets. Decorations alone are forms of art expression. They may be expressed variously with sun-dried color-dyed raffia to show clan identities, family occupation and careers, or religious belief and folklore. The decorations may focus on local permissions, or symbolic patterns. Dancing is another form of art expression of the Isoko people. Different dances are learnt and performed by different groups: boys, girls, men, and women, in revolving seasons. Dance groups are usually formed into "clubs." These clubs perform their dances, especially during festivals. The dances could be replicated in the schools to the extent that a member of a dance group could be invited to teach the children different dance steps and moves.

To bring local context into schools, art education programs should reform and be child-centered, rather than Euro-centered. The curricula should be planned with serious consideration of philosophical and psychological perspectives through the lenses of local custom and traditions. Teachers should spend less time on the blackboard and desk, and shift their focus to a more pragmatic role of a doyen; that is, be more involved in proximal guidance of the learner, rather than be a "talking head" at the learner. Children should occasionally be allowed to inform the planning of the curricular. It is important to note, however, that many children will grow up, live, and die in their original localities, but some will move on to study in worlds beyond. So teachers should as much as possible embrace in- and out-of-classroom learning experiences for the children.

ART RESOURCES IN THE LOCAL WORLDS OF NIGERIA

Art resources abound in all communities in Nigeria. "African art," as we know it, is produced mostly from local materials: wood, leather, cane, raffia, palm fronds, coconut shell and fiber, bamboo, palm fronds, broom sticks, melon gourds and other more durable materials such as terra-cotta, tusks, animal horn, etc. Material choices are numerous, interesting, and meaningful to occasions. Art techniques, forms and styles that have been perfected over time because of available materials, are readily available for use. Local artists such as potters, carvers, weavers, musicians, and dancers are among the human resources that can be tapped and brought into the classroom to augment the education of children.

CONCLUSION

I will conclude by reiterating that the most resounding problem of the legacy of western education in Nigeria is the disconnection between knowledge taught in schools and the values of the local culture. Rogoff (1990), Kozulin, Gindis, Ageyev and Miller (2003), and Hall (2007) emphasize that the construction of meaning is culturally situated. Santrock (2008) reiterates that Vygotsky perceived learning from a collective and social perspective; and thus, learning was only as prevalent and powerful as the community surrounding the child. Yet, curricula and practice in art education in Nigeria is pitiful and painfully slow to consider the context of the local culture in children's learning. When the Nigerian child's thinking about art moves beyond a locally supportive context, it becomes far-fetched, abstracted, and dislodged. For the Nigerian child, this can be a devastating problem because it leads to easy errors that are a result of departure from what makes sense to the child. The human mind dies without culture. As Bruner (1996) points out, "Mind could not exist save for culture, [and] education is a major embodiment of a culture's way of life, not just a preparation for it" (p. 13). The art education of children in Nigeria must be developed with a view of indigenous peoples' humanness – the indigenous humanness of Nigerians – to produce the kind of results that better serve Nigerian value systems. The Nigerian education system should reflect indigenous cultures as a top priority. Finally, the Nigerian education system should firmly ground the learning experiences of Nigerian children in a local context.

REFERENCES

Adelusi, I. O. (1981). General problems of educational development in Nigeria: Economic, manpower needs, responsibility control, diversification of the system, and curriculum. In P. A. I. Obanya (Ed.), *Education and the Nigerian society* (pp. 19-34). Ibadan, Nigeria: Ibadan University Press.

Adeyinka, A. A. (1981). The educational ideas of Professor James Majasan. In P. A. I. Obanya (Ed.), *Education and the Nigerian society* (pp. 1-8). Ibadan, Nigeria: Ibadan University Press.

Awiti, A. (2012). *High stakes tests killing education.* www.the-star.co.ke/news/article-9444616/

Bronicoli, M. P. (2011). *Cultural-historical theory: A theoretical framework for changing the way we think about learning and education technology.* http://library/view/BONICOLI2011CUL

Bruner, J. S. (1996). *The culture of education.* Cambridge, MA: Harvard University Press.

Bruner, J. S. (1987). The transactional self. In J. S. Bruner & H. Haste (Eds.), *Making sense: The child's construction of the world* (pp. 81-96). London: Methuen.

Cazden, C. B. (1989, March). *Vygotsky and Bakhtin: From word to utterance and voice.* Paper presented at the annual meeting of the American Educational Research Association, San Francisco. Conference of African states on the development of education in Africa (Addis Ababa, Ethiopia, 1961). UNESCO.

Donaldson, M. (1978). *Children's minds.* New York: W. W. Norton & Company.

Efland, A. D. (1989). Curriculum antecedents of discipline-based art education. In R. A. Smith (Ed.), *Discipline-based art education* (pp. 57-94). Urbana: University of Illinois Press.

Feldman, E. B. (1996). *Philosophy of art education.* Upper Saddle River, New Jersey: Prentice-Hall, Inc.

Gauvain, M., & Cole, M. (1997). Reading on the development of children. www.psy.cmu.edu/~siegler/vygotsky78.pdf

Gelman, R., & Baillargeon, R. (1983). A review of some Piagetian concepts. In P. H. Mussen (Ed.), *Handbook of child psychology, Volume III, Cognitive development* (J. Flavell & E. M. Markham, volume editors) (pp. 167-230). New York: Wiley.

Geoffroy-Schneiter, B. (2000). *Tribal arts.* New York, NY: The Vendome Press.

Gilman, D. A., & McDermott, M. (1994). Portfolio collection: An alternative to testing. *Contemporary Education, 65*(2), 73-76.

Hall, A. (2000). Vigotsky goes online: Learning design from a socio-cultural perspective, learning and socio-cultural theory. *Exploring Modern Vygotskian Perspectives International Workshop 2007, 1*(1).

Haste, H. (1987). Growing into rules. In J. S. Bruner & H. Haste (Eds.), *Making sense: The child's construction of the world* (pp. 163-195). London: Methuen.

Imam, H. (2012). Educational policy in Nigeria from the colonial era to the post-independence period. *Italian Journal of sociology of Education, 1*, 2012.

Inagaki, K. (1992). Piagetian and post-Piagetian conceptions of development and their implications for science education in early childhood. *Early Childhood Research Quarterly, 7*, 115-133.

Kurian, G. T. (1988). Nigeria. In G. T. Kurian (Ed.), *World education encyclopedia* (pp. 945-952) New York: Facts on File Publication.

Lave, J., & Wenger, E. (1991). *Situated learning: Legitimate peripheral participation*. New York: Cambridge University Press.

Little, J. (October, 2012). *Importance of cognitive development. Parents teach kids blog: Hopes and wishes become real for everyone*. http://blog.parentsteachkids.com/importance-of-cognitive-development/

Lowenfeld, V., & Brittain, W. L. (1987). *Creative and mental growth* (8th ed.). USA: Macmillan Publishing Company.

Mayer, S. J. (2009). Dewey's dynamic integration of Vygotsky and Piaget. *Education and Culture, 24*(2), 6-24.

Majasan, J. A. (1975a). *The indigenous for national development*. Ibadan, Nigeria: Onabanjo Press.

Majasan, J. A. (1975b). *Indigenous education and progress in developing countries*. Ibadan, Nigeria: Ibadan University Press.

Nduka, O. (1964). *Western education and the Nigerian cultural background*. London: Oxford University Press.

Obameata, J. O. (1981). Social class, language and the intelligence of Nigerian children. In P. A. I. Nya (Ed.), *Education and the Nigerian society* (pp. 35-54). Ibadan, Nigeria: Ibadan University Press.

Onwuchekwa, J. N. (1981). Traditional education as an asset to formal education. In P. A. I. Obanya (Ed.), *Education and the Nigerian society* (pp. 9-18). Ibadan, Nigeria: Ibadan University Press.

Paton, G. (May, 2009). Half of adults 'would fail exams second time around.' *The Telegraph*. http://www.telegraph.co.uk/education/educationnews/5351635/

Phillipson, S., Ku, K., & Phillipson, S. (2013). *Constructing educational achievement: A sociocultural perspective*. New York: Routledge.

Pressley, M., & McCormick, C. B. (2012). *Reflection M4: Piaget and information processing theory. Child and adolescent development for educators*. New York: The Guilford Press.

Rogoff, B. (1990). *Apprenticeship in thinking: Cognitive development in social context*. New York: Oxford University Press.

Santrock, J. W. (2008). *A topical approach to life-span development* (3rd ed.). New York, NY: McGraw-Hill.

Scott, S., & Palincsar, A. (2012). *Sociocultural theory*. www.education.com/reference/article/sociocultural-theory/

Sheninger, E. (2012). *Standardization will destroy our educational system, if it hasn't already*. www.huffingtonpost.com/eric-sheninger/standardization-will-dest_b_1703357

Stetsenko, A. (1995). The psychological function of children's drawing: A Vygotskian perspective. In C. Lange-Kuttner & G. V. Thomas (Eds.), *Drawing and looking* (pp. 147-158). New York: Harvester Wheatsheaf.

Taiwo, C. O. (1980). *The Nigerian education system: Past present & future*. Ikeja, Nigeria: Thomas Nelson (Nigeria) Limited.

Tibenderana, P. (2006). *Education and cultural change in Northern Nigeria, 1906-1966: A study in the creation of a dependent culture*. Fountain Publishers.

Villeneuve, P. (1992). *Contending art education paradigms and professionalization*. Doctoral Dissertation, University of Arizona.

Vygotsky, J. V. (1978). *Mind in society: The development of higher psychological processes*. Cambridge, MA: Harvard University Press.

Walsh, D. J. (1989). Changes in kindergarten: Why here? Why now? *Early Childhood Research Quarterly, 4*, 377-391.

Walsh, D. J. (1992). *Some implications of post-Piagetian perspectives for early childhood education: Helping children make sense.* Paper presented at the seminar on Early Childhood Education, Taipei Municipal Teachers College.

Woolfolk, A. (2004). *Educational psychology* (9th ed.). Boston, MA: Allyn and Bacon.

EDWARD SHIZHA

11. INDIGENOUS KNOWLEDGE SYSTEMS
AND THE CURRICULUM

INTRODUCTION

The school system in many regions of Africa does little to cater for the unique challenges to psychosocial adjustment and cultural identity development that students experience when they enter the school gate. Schools and the education system in general promote poor academic performance, low self-esteem, and high dropout rates for students who do not identify with the schools' cultural capital. The school systems ignore cultural capital that learners bring to school and thus fail to provide a supportive home-school learning environment. In the end, teachers and education policymakers, and those who conduct evaluation end up inappropriately "blaming the victim" for their failure. African education has been colonized for over a century. The education system that was introduced by colonial regimes and still continues to be provided in African schools is largely dependent on imported systems, which are Eurocentric in nature. However, reforming African education curriculum in the light of the concept of indigenization or Africanization appears to be at the core of current educational reform debates across Africa. Okeke (2010) argues that although much has been said about indigenization, transformation and renaissance in African education, education policy-makers have yet to forge a new identity to cope with the pressures of frustration amongst Africans. Most policy statements on indigenizing education have been at most rhetorical and political. They have not been acted on or legislated. Any attempt toward the rethinking of the African curriculum must take into account the role and value of indigenous knowledges, which has been a much neglected aspect of Africa's educational reform. An indigenized school curriculum will enhance success, cognitive development and academic achievements for students. The purpose of this chapter is to discuss the benefits of indigenizing the school curriculum in Africa, and the role of indigenous knowledge or traditional ecological knowledge in the indigenization process. The chapter uses a postcolonial or anticolonial discourse to analyze school curriculum in African schools.

WHAT IS CURRICULUM?

There are various ways in which curriculum issues can be approached. Ornstein and Hunkins (2009, p. 15) contend that curriculum development encompasses how a "curriculum is planned, implemented and evaluated, as well as what people, processes and procedures are involved ...." Lopes and Macedo (2011) argue that investigations into curriculum practices have always had great prominence in the

G. Emeagwali & G. J. S. Dei (eds.), African Indigenous Knowledge and the Disciplines. 113–129.

curriculum field, to the point where the notion of curriculum in action has become one of the most powerful concepts in curriculum theory. Curriculum in action is a model that focuses on school daily life and teaching knowledge that is based on the experiences of students and on questioning the prescriptive approaches to curriculum. Although there are different models that are used in designing curriculum, Ornstein and Hunkins (2009) submit that although curriculum development models are technically useful, they often overlook the human aspect such as the personal attitudes, feelings, values involved in curriculum making. The questions that need to be noted when designing the curriculum are: What is valid knowledge? Whose knowledge? What is the purpose of that knowledge? Who decides on curriculum knowledge? The decision on the knowledge that is to be taught in schools and how it is taught is based on politics. Education is a key 'regime of power' through which a culture's conception of truth is maintained, and as such can play a critical role in the marginalisation of epistemological diversity (McCarter & Gavin, 2011). The politics of knowledge determines how knowledge is created, used, and disseminated. The decisions on curriculum content are made by those who are in positions of power and control. It is also essential to ask how power affects knowledge. Michel Foucault observes that the criteria of what constitutes knowledge, what is to be excluded, and who is designated as qualified to know involves actions of power (Foucault, 1971). To the extent that knowledge and curriculum are a political text, Marxist theoretical approaches argue that curriculum is characterized by ideas of centralized power in the state apparatus (Pinar et al., 1995, cited in Lopes & Macedo, 2011). In African schools, power and decision on curriculum issues are mainly controlled by the elite who were schooled under colonial education systems.

Curriculum is the term that is frequently used to refer to the content of teaching and learning activities. Many conceptions of curriculum have been postulated in many textbooks on curriculum and educational theory which conceptualize curriculum that emphasizes content, learning experiences, and behavioural objectives. Other explanations advocate curriculum that has a nontechnical and more philosophical, social, and personal approach. According to one theorist, Basil Bernstein (1973), curriculum is "what counts as valid knowledge" (p. 85). When it comes to what is defined as valid knowledge Shizha (2005) argues that there are existing debates and contentions on "how to define and validate knowledge, particularly the official curriculum in the face of globalization, and the internationalization of knowledge" (p. 65). Knowledge is diverse, especially in Africa where there are thousands of ethnic groups and sub-cultural groups. Cultural pluralism in contemporary Africa leads to an elusive definition of valid knowledge that can be institutionalized for the official curriculum.

VALID KNOWLEDGE: THE DEBATE

There are two schools of thought that attempt to explain what knowledge is valid for curriculum development. According to Shizha (2005), knowledge entails the total experiences that an individual has and the ways that individuals look at and give meaning to experiences in their natural, cultural, and social worldviews. From a traditional view, knowledge constitutes facts, concepts, and skills that must be mastered through memorization and drill. In this case knowledge that is regarded as valid is pre-planned, programmed, and prescribed. It is then the role of the schools and teachers to disseminate the knowledge to willing learners, who should then be assessed to determine how much knowledge they have acquired. The traditional perspective deems it necessary for schools to return to the essentials or to basic education and high standards (Tanner & Tanner, 2007). Accordingly, schools must systematically teach basic knowledge and not be afraid to stress hard work and discipline. What is questionable in this perspective is: what is factual knowledge and who determines standards and how are they defined? The perspective ignores the existence of multiple cultural knowledges, the importance of personal experience, and the effect of social and cultural capital on learning. Knowledge is generally regarded and interpreted as an objective, impersonal, value-free commodity, of which it is not. Curriculum is based on the values of the powerful and reproduces the values of the powerful. However, what schools should do is be inclusive and offer opportunity for other ways of knowing to be included in the curriculum and teaching programs. Sadly, knowledge that is validated in African schools and presented as curriculum is a colonial and Eurocentric cultural reproduction that is structured in ways that alienate African students.

To the extent that the knowledge is predetermined and structures, it does not value independent thinking that could be promoted by indigenizing the curriculum. Indigenous knowledges that reflect the experiences of students and their communities encourage students to think reflectively and to be proactive learners. The knowledge instills in students a sense of ownership, control, and social responsibility. According to Eggleston (1977), "differences in thought processes and differences in perceptions of events and worldviews lead to differences in the store of knowledge possessed by each society and each group" (p. 1). These stores of knowledge are spatial and temporal as experience and history affects them. Therefore what counts as valid knowledge for curriculum development in African schools should take into consideration the cultural identities and experiences of the African society (Shizha, 2005). The continued use of knowledge and curricular that were adapted before decolonization is a disservice to our own African identities. The significance of knowledge for African school curriculum should be of great concern to African sociologists, educationists, academics, researchers, and curriculum developers.

The validation of knowledge for curriculum development can also be approached from a progressive (Tanner & Tanner, 2007) or critical anticolonial perspective. Critical anticolonial paradigm favours curriculum knowledge that is inclusive. It is a decolonizing perspective that views schooling, knowledge, and learning as an interactive and meaningful experience. From a progressive anticolonial approach, curriculum comprises common beliefs and values, and a progressive orientation with emphasis on making meaning. It fosters critical thinking linked to life situations, and yields a more thoughtful approach to learning. Kohn (2008) describes this approach as atraditional. It is an approach that involves students in experiencing schooling as a community of learners who have shared experiences. This perspective is shared by Tanner and Tanner (2007, p. 121) who offer an explanation that was derived from Dewey's definition of education that posits, "That reconstruction of knowledge and experience that enables the learner to grow in exercising intelligent control of subsequent knowledge and experience." The approach provides avenues through which the learners extend and deepen their learning capabilities. Therefore, a critical anticolonial approach is student-centred and takes into account the different social and cultural backgrounds of the learners. In addition, the curriculum conceptualizes a multidirectional approach to knowledge and learning. In the African context, an indigenized curriculum provides an educational system that respects all sources of experience and offers a true learning situation that is historical, social, and dynamic. Such a curriculum has the effect of promoting principles of continuity and interaction in experiences that students and teachers bring to their classrooms.

INDIGENIZATION: THE CONCEPT

Indigenization is an important concept to discuss in order to understand what entails an indigenized African school curriculum. Many formerly colonized nations have in one way or another attempted to indigenize their educational programs, although not much has been achieved in this direction. Countries differ not only in their socio-economic and political structures, but also in their definitions of indigenization and authentication of knowledge (Ferguson, 2005). Nonetheless, the presence of curriculum models that are not culturally appropriate in many African countries has precipitated the call for indigenization of the western models that were inherited after attaining independence. Indigenization has its conceptual roots in academia in Latin America derived from scholars who were disillusioned by the use of western theories and practices in the region (Ferguson, 2005). In countries where indigenization has been adopted, it is perceived as a revolutionary policy. However, we should note that developing a curriculum that works is an evolutionary process.

Proponents of the indigenization policy claim that many of the ideas, values, and methods used in developing countries require modification if they are to be an appropriate response to the social problems and needs of people. The concept of indigenization, which Okeke (2010) describes as *Africanization*, implies that things are not the way they should be within the African educational, economic, political, and social lives. Indigenization demands a re-narration of the African existence and it is meant to bring about equal opportunities to the previously marginalized, and promotes indigenous knowledges and resources. For example, in Nigeria, the indigenization decree was to give Nigerians the opportunity to demonstrate the ability to assume ownership, control, and management of a greater part of the nation's economy (Udoh & Udeaja, 2011). In Zimbabwe, the rationale for the indigenization policy is to empower indigenous populations who were disadvantaged in the colonial era; to give them a chance to take part in the national economy through ownership of corporate businesses (Zhou & Zvoushe, 2012).

Conceptually, indigenization connotes a process through which a country experiences discontent with the imported western models of development in the context of the local political, economic, social, and cultural structures. Such models are viewed as inappropriate to the aspirations of local people and are targeted for change or transformation to fit the local contexts. Weightman (2008) points out that contextualization is a key ingredient in the indigenization process; without contextualization, indigenization of any type will suffer.

INDIGENIZATION OF THE AFRICAN SCHOOL CURRICULUM

One of the most insightful definitions of indigenization of education comes from Magagula and Mazibuko (2004), who state:

> By indigenization of formal education from a cultural perspective is meant the inclusion of African indigenous cultural values, beliefs, practices, norms, and the indigenous social institutions, or the indigenous cultural ways of life of African societies, into the content of the formal educational systems at all the levels of education in Africa. (p. 89)

There is very little empirical research on African education that is inspired by indigenous conceptions and methodologies in curriculum development and implementation. Even though there emerged a flurry of studies examining indigenizing or Africanizing curriculum in several countries from the early 1970s to mid-1980s. Few such efforts survived the initial euphoria. Shizha (2011) argues that while curriculum changes were deemed necessary to refocus knowledge and pedagogy on African perspectives, research indicates that most curriculum changes were promoted by outsiders, mainly Western governments and donors. For example, in Francophone Africa, curriculum changes were borrowed from France and implemented with little or no local input (Holsinger & Cowell, 2000 in Shizha, 2011). Even in Tanzania, which is usually credited with implementing an indigenized curriculum dubbed Education for Self-reliance, the content of the science curriculum for primary schools was borrowed from the USA and Britain (Osaki, 2007 in Shizha, 2011). Education planners and curriculum developers are to blame for the failure to indigenize African curriculum. The content of education in Africa, especially in Sub-Saharan Africa, continues to imitate former colonial values, beliefs, practices, norms, and socio-political structures and institutions. The content continues to neglect and demean indigenous knowledge in favour of Western knowledge that denies students the cultural values needed to develop and advance their socio-economic and political worlds (Semali & Stambach, 1997).

Curriculum frameworks should engage productive inquiry and produce useful knowledge that provides a sufficient epistemology or methodology for using indigenous knowledge. It is important at this juncture to point out that indigenizing the curriculum refers to the reintroduction of indigenous practices into the school system and a de-emphasis or decolonization of Western education. However, it does not mean doing away with the current system, but making sure that indigenous knowledge systems are highlighted and given more prominence than

117

before. Education systems that do not reflect indigenization in their formal curriculum reconstruction in post-colonial Africa, mainly in their textbooks, syllabi, policy documents, and teachers' resource materials, are not performing their intended task for sustainable social and economic development.

INDIGENIZING CURRICULUM CONTENT

Positive relations have been noted between cultural knowledge, school curriculum, and the academic achievement of students (Deasy, 2002). In a review of research on the influence of arts education on academic outcomes, Morin (2004) reported that such programs enhance spatial-temporal reasoning skills, understanding of structures and structural relations, object relations, and planning activities. Morin (2004) also reported positive relations between participation in music classes and spatial-temporal reasoning skills, the introduction of drama and improvement in language arts, including oral understanding of stories, reading readiness, reading achievement, and writing. These reports point to the desirable adoption of indigenous arts into African schools. A program of artistic teaching presentations in the curriculum provides scheduled series of learning experiences that should lead to lasting systemic improvements in cognitive and psychosocial development and self-esteem. Knowledge that is derived from the communities' arts should be made the foundation of arts education. In addition, knowledge that should be found in the humanities and social sciences should be drawn from the cultural history of indigenous African societies or communities.

According to Shizha (2005), the community provides alternative ways of explaining social phenomenon, which is critical in fostering cognitive development among students. Cognitive development is enhanced by the emphasizing of indigenous knowledges or indigenous historical commemorations in curriculum development. Curriculum that contains indigenous histories and indigenous sciences helps to democratize African knowledges in education. Democratization involves a redefinition of knowledge such that the local and diverse are both valued as legitimate forms. Local and diverse knowledge are viewed as indispensable because they are rooted in the community from which they arise. Being contextualized, local knowledge is concrete and part of what is real to those who live in the local communities (Semali & Stambach, 1997, p. 20).

When school curriculum is designed from indigenous knowledges, it transforms itself into a living entity. The concretization of curriculum through the use of local knowledges helps African students to identify with its content and pedagogical implications. It deconstructs the misconception that valid and authentic knowledge exists outside African society.

TRADITIONAL ECOLOGICAL KNOWLEDGE (TEK) AND THE CURRICULUM

For centuries, African people have depended heavily on traditional ecological knowledge, and botanically based traditional medicine, to cure and treat a variety of diseases. Traditional ecological knowledge refers to the knowledge, practice, and belief concerning the relationship of living beings to one another and to the physical environment, which is held by peoples in relatively 'non-technological' societies with a direct dependence upon local resources (Berkes, 1999). Indigenous worldviews emerged as a result of the people's close relationship with their natural environment and their lived experiences. According to Asabere-Ameyaw, Dei, and Raheem (2012), Studies of African Indigenous Knowledge Systems attest to how the physical environment has been an important source of knowledge about herbal pharmacology and herbatology, indigenous farming technologies, traditional arts and crafts, including folkloric productions, knowledge of climatic changes and patterns, as well as local soil and vegetation classification systems (p. 5).

From an indigenous African perspective, the natural environment is significant in understanding indigenous science/ecological knowledge. The physical environment is the source of scientific knowledge and it contributes to health promotion for both humans and animals. TEK is rational and reliable knowledge that has been developed through generations of contact by indigenous peoples with their lands. Today, TEK is being recognized as having equal status with scientific knowledge and has been termed the "intellectual twin to science" (DeLoria, 1995 in Kimmerer, 2002, p. 433). However, some western scientists continue to resist the formalization of indigenous knowledges in school curriculum (Berkes, 1999). Knowing about indigenous forms of knowledge is a crucial basis for survival, especially where Western medicine is unavailable or expensive to access. Currently, more than "80% of the world's population depends on indigenous healthcare based on medicinal plants" (Eyong, 2007, p. 125), while indigenous people use at least 20,000 plant species for medicines and related purposes (Melchias, 2001, cited in Eyong, 2007). Studies on rural South African and Botswana communities revealed that about 80% of these communities rely on indigenous herbal plant medicines to sustain their health needs (Ntsoane, 2000). The preservation of the African physical environment as an important source of local cultural knowledge is critical to the lives of people in Africa. Consequently, it is important and imperative for curriculum and policymakers as well as educators to revise science education content and upgrade how science is taught in African schools. These stakeholders and other groups interested in indigenizing school curriculum should collectively discuss and build on ideas for introducing and emphasizing traditional ecological knowledge (TEK) in science education. The stakeholders should facilitate the collection of ideas from a diverse group of people on the broad topic of TEK to be used in science education. The use of TEK in mainstream education will make it more widely recognized and respected for its usefulness (Armstrong, Kimmerer, & Vergun, 2007) in science education, research, and sustainable ecological management.

Education in Africa should emphasize the interdependence of society, culture, and TEK, and the necessity for communities to be in harmony with their physical environments for collective survival. The current curriculum programs are based on western models that are typically linear, even though most of the systems that are examined in learning are complex cycles of relationships (Andrews, 2012). The incongruence in indigenous and western pedagogies has been seen as an impediment to deeper understanding of science and traditional knowledge systems in Africa. In countries like Canada, TEK is increasingly being sought by academics, scientists, and policymakers as "a potential source of ideas for emerging models of ecosystem management, conservation biology, and ecological restoration" (Kimmerer, 2002, p. 432). It has been recognized as not only complementary, but also equivalent to scientific knowledge. TEK has been recognized and acknowledged for its contribution to our understanding of ecological systems (Folke, 2004). It has also been acclaimed as a source of new biological insights and models, in both conservation biology and ecosystem management (Armstrong et al., 2007). The acknowledgement of TEK in the school curriculum relies on the formation of equitable partnerships with indigenous communities, but many school curricula, particularly in science education, portray knowledge that is unfamiliar and incongruent with the cross-cultural realities and perspectives necessary for social development required in Africa.

Although TEK is increasingly valued for its potential contribution to education, it is not currently included in mainstream school courses. Armstrong et al. (2007) conclude that there is a strong need for educational efforts to build bridges between school knowledge and TEK knowledge systems, so that the strengths of both approaches are brought to bear on socio-economic development and ecological problem-solving. Therefore, there should be clarity in the purposes, content, and organisation of the curriculum in order for schooling to provide students with holistic learning experiences. The content of an indigenized curriculum should promote a common vision to extend educational experiences and inspire learners. In that context, a curriculum that emphasizes indigenous knowledges offers students an educational experience that takes account of learners' views, feelings, and socio-cultural characteristics. Such a curriculum would be presented in ways that are meaningful to learners and would excite their imagination.

Curriculum content that is derived from TEK can help preserve the knowledge of communities when it is used and valued for intellectual purposes (Shizha, 2010). A community knowledge transfer is possible when learning content or knowledge for formal learning is established from TEK resources for public education. However, indigenization or curriculum renewal has many challenges, especially if the changes are to include recognition of indigenous knowledge as foundational to an educational program. The challenge for curriculum indigenization is the dominance of western science in the African school curriculum, and how it influences assumptions, motivations, and values that become part of what and how teachers teach. Curriculum reform initiatives attempting to offer alternative perspectives to the dominant Western Eurocentricism, require an understanding that the curriculum is a cultural practice where beliefs, values, and meaning are drawn upon to make sense of the world (Kanu, 2009 cited in Andrews, 2012). Western models have failed to guarantee students' academic success. Teachers have to motivate their learners through indigenized curricula that guarantee success. Hussey and Smith (2003) maintain:

... accepting that student motivation is an essential element in learning, we propose that those who teach should begin to reclaim learning outcomes and begin to frame them more broadly and flexibly, to allow for demonstrations and expressions of appreciation, enjoyment and even pleasure. (p. 367)

Enjoyment and pleasure in learning for African students can be achieved if they are able to make sense of their learning and their world. Indigenous knowledge in the curriculum provides possibilities for successful learning outcomes.

INDIGENOUS PEDAGOGICAL PRACTICES IN SCHOOLS

Pedagogy is a vital process that promotes success or failure in African schools. Pedagogy is "the practice of teaching framed and informed by a shared and structured body of knowledge" (Pollard, 2010, p. 5). It can be described as art to impart collectively created knowledge. Evidence is accumulating from around the world that the single most significant means of improving the performance of national educational systems is through excellent teaching (e.g., Barber & Mourshed, 2007). The quality of pedagogy, of what teachers actually do, and the methods that teachers utilise and the way they communicate knowledge to students are of critical value for indigenizing curriculum. Researchers and curriculum developers should stimulate a debate with teachers and other partners on developing a shared pedagogical language for indigenizing teaching (Shizha, 2008). This calls for a critical pedagogical approach. Critical pedagogies are needed to challenge the assumptions, practices, and outcomes taken for granted in dominant culture and in conventional education (Gruenewald, 2003). Chief among these are the assumptions that education should mainly support individualistic and nationalistic competition in the global economy and that an educational competition of winners and losers is in the best interest of public life in a diverse society (Apple, 2001).

Indeed, teachers are the main mediators of formal school knowledge and should employ critical pedagogy. Critical pedagogy encourages teachers and students to reinhabit their places, that is, to pursue the kind of social action that improves the social and educational aspirations of students. For Freire (1972), critical pedagogy begins with recognizing that human beings exist in a cultural context. The ways knowledge, concepts, skills, values, and attitudes are learned in formal education depend very much on cultural context and the pedagogical creativity of the teachers. It is important that teacher-learners build on existing knowledge to strengthen dispositions to learn (Pollard, 2010).

Students learn best when curriculum or knowledge is mediated in a manner that is consistent with methodologies that students are used to or familiar with. Teachers should be knowledgeable about indigenous knowledge in the curriculum and assessment principles as a part of their pedagogical expertise. These principles should reflect an understanding of the cultural backgrounds of students. In African schools, the main perception is that teachers are there to impart knowledge and maintain discipline. The transmission model of knowledge places the teacher and

121

the content at the centre of teaching and learning. In most cases, learners are regarded as empty vessels or *tabula rasa* waiting for the teacher to spoon feed them with knowledge. This banking concept (Freire, 1972) is against the principles of indigenized teaching and learning. Indigenization of teaching and learning means that teachers have to implement methods of learning that take into account the previous knowledge students bring to school. Although other methods can be incorporated into the teaching and learning process, the methods that students are used to should take precedence. In Zimbabwe, for instance, Shizha (2009) found that when teachers focused on the transmission model of teaching, students were turned into passive learners and they did not show excitement in learning. On the other hand, in cases where teachers led students into using storytelling as a way of sharing knowledge, learners became involved and enthusiastic about their learning.

Storytelling is critical narratology (Haymes in Gruenewald, 2003), a very important methodology that is used by indigenous communities to share knowledge, values, and skills. Stories are intriguing, engaging, and easily recalled, and are therefore highly effective in transferring knowledge (Armstrong et al., 2007). Traditional stories told by indigenous peoples often incorporate ecological lessons; they contain information about ecosystem structure and function at specific locations. Narratives simplify knowledge and enhance understanding of abstract concepts. Kimmerer (2002) argues that the oral tradition of TEK offers a detailed prescription for "living in place," and includes both empirical and metaphorical elements; many indigenous stories arose as vehicles for teaching and have great value in the classroom. Teachers should recognize the value of cultural stories, learn how to communicate them in culturally appropriate ways, and then share them in lessons. Narratives encompass the intellectual achievement of indigenous peoples accumulated over generations, knowledge that has survived extinction through oral discourses. Teachers have to be culturally sensitive and commit to culturally appropriate skills, knowledge, and judgement for the public good. However, the question quickly arises about how such commitment and expertise is to be developed, maintained, and renewed. Pollard (2010) argues that this is where reflective practice comes in. Reflective practice is used when a teacher feels that students appear unsettled, or they find the curriculum uninteresting. A reflective teacher would, in this case, invariably apply narratives or storytelling to excite students' interests. The value of reflective activity is that it can improve the quality of teaching and learning.

Indigenous communities are practical in their approach to transmitting knowledge. As a result, indigenous African students learn best when they participate in hands-on and fun activities while engaging in investigative problem-solving. Investigative learning involving observation and manipulation of learning material promotes hands-on experience to generate and communicate knowledge. Students could be asked to keep an observation notebook in which to write information that interests them. Students can also show their mastery of learning by carrying out community projects that show the relevance of school knowledge to their community life and realities. Dweck (2006) contrasted pupils with a mastery orientation from those who develop learned helplessness in school. Those who identify school knowledge with their home experiences are likely to master concepts and knowledge, while those whose community knowledge is neglected by the school are likely to be helpless in their learning (cf. Shizha, 2011). The conditions and experiences of classroom life contribute to such self-beliefs. By creating opportunities for learners to take independent action and experience success, teachers support the development of self-confidence and positive learning dispositions. In Africa, indigenous knowledges contribute to independent action in learning which is facilitated by teachers in terms of what Freire premises as liberating education that is "co-intentional" (Freire, 1972, p. 56). This means that students and teachers should collaborate and engage in dialogue, investigating knowledge as equals and creating new understandings of the world together.

Indigenous learners prefer working in groups, unlike the western models of learning that emphasize individual effort. Participation in communal activities is the cornerstone of indigenous communities. Again, as Dei (2004) argues, the pedagogic, instructional, and communicative approach to synthesizing different knowledges in the classroom must first allow indigenous learners to produce and control knowledges about themselves, their communities, and their societies. Collaborative learning between and among students empower them with control over knowledge creation. This collaboration is relevant in centring local knowledges, cultures, values, languages, and worldviews in the school curriculum (Adjei & Dei, 2008). The collaboration between learners and the knowledge they create and share brings society and the school in a close relationship. At the end of the day, teachers need to consider whether or not they have been able to enrich the lives of learners and increased their life chances (Pollard, 2010). Indigenized teaching practices should develop students with self-confidence and a stronger sense of personal and cultural identity, and students who will be functional in their communities. It is certainly important to affirm the role of teachers to apply indigenous African philosophy in facilitating indigenization in education and in producing confident individuals and future citizens who are proud of their culture and identity.

INDIGENOUS LANGUAGES AND THE CURRICULUM

One of the major constituents in indigenizing school curriculum in Africa is the language used in school instruction. Language plays a critical role in school instruction and in comprehending the teaching and learning that is planned in the curriculum. In Africa, the colonization process introduced a foreign language that excluded the majority of learners from effectively participating in formal learning. In the continent, the enthusiasm for the use of indigenous languages and scholarship has remained relatively moderate as scholars are conflicted in their loyalty to imperial languages (Moshi & Ojo, 2009). According to Ngugi wa Thiong'o (1986) in *Decolonizing the Mind*, language is central to the way we define ourselves in relation to the ecological and social environment. During colonization, foreign languages such as English, French, Portuguese, Italian, and Afrikaans (Dutch derived), had disastrous effect on African students' personal and cultural identity. As Wa Thiongo noted, "But obviously it was worse when the colonial child was exposed to images of the world as mirrored in the written languages of his impressionable mind with low status, humiliation … non-intelligibility and barbarism" (1986, p. 18). Even in this age when Africa has been decolonized and emancipated, foreign languages continue to be used in African schools. These foreign languages operate to silence, deny and marginalize the voices of indigenous African students (Shizha, 2012). Language is the medium through which we read our world and if language is the medium through which we articulate our world, and make sense of our cultural reality, it is high time that African indigenous languages are used in schools. It is educationally wrong for African education, knowledge production and reproduction to continue exclusively in English, French, or Portuguese. Prah (2006) contends that in Africa, knowledge, its production and reproduction, is negotiated in the languages of a European minority that silences indigenous languages in favour of a dominant minority Eurocentric culture. The attitude towards the use of African languages by African leaders has also hampered scholars' efforts to create and sustain the needed visibility for African languages around the world (Moshi & Ojo, 2009).

Arguments against the use of indigenous languages as languages of instruction in Africa justify the hegemony of foreign languages. For example, Shizha (2012) points out that the usual excuse is that English, for example, is an international language and a language for technological advancement. Others argue that African languages have limited vocabularies, hence there are no sufficient academic textbooks written in African languages (Shizha, 2010). More significantly, at the social level in many parts of the continent, African languages are now perceived as inadequate means of communication (Moshi & Ojo, 2009). However, Asian countries like Malaysia, China, Japan, Korea, and even Russia use their languages for communication and as languages of instruction and are all living examples of excellence through mother-tongue teaching. These countries have made tremendous socio-economic progress while using their own languages in education. Prah argues:

Thus while an Africa-centred approach would be misplaced if it was suggested as a developmental paradigm for contemporary Britain, Ireland, Germany, France, or Sweden, where Africans are minorities, in Africa it is only natural that the African cultural and historical belongings of the people should be provided relevant space. When this is resisted, the development of South Africa is restricted and the cultural rights of the majorities dismissed. (2006, p. 24)

It is mainly in Africa that indigenous languages are marginalized in education and the main reason given is that foreign languages, especially English, must receive priority and that African languages are restricted to Africa where there are no opportunities arising from mother-tongue proficiency. Noting the marginalization of indigenous languages in Africa, Anchimbe (2006) laments,

The dilemma of African languages in the wake of globalisation and the continuous empowerment of other languages qua languages of industrialisation, technology, and international currency, is one that has occupied one of the most obscure positions in the national agenda of many African states. With less and even lesser attention paid to the functional empowerment of these indigenous languages, since a greater attention is paid to developing and promoting bilingualism, or an imposed second official language or a national cross-cultural language, the fear of their extinction is becoming higher. (p. 94)

Africa should not be an exception to implementing indigenous languages in its schools. For most African children, school knowledge and the language of instruction are disconnected from the children's home experiences and from interactions with teachers. Research has revealed benefits that are derived from using the mother-tongue as the language of instruction in schools. Classroom observation studies in several countries in Africa (Botswana, Burkina Faso, Ethiopia, Ghana, Mali, Niger, South Africa, Tanzania, and Togo), reveal that the use of unfamiliar languages forces teachers to use traditional and teacher-centered teaching methods that undermine teachers' effort to teach, and students' effort to learn (Alidou & Brock-Utne, 2006). Closing the communication gap between the teacher and students is a crucial and rewarding undertaking for both teachers and students, if they can use the collective language to share learning experiences that employ forms of communication that create situations whereby meaning can be derived and learning becomes a lived-experience (Shizha, 2012). Like other critical pedagogues, an indigenous language is a "language of possibility" (Giroux, 1988) through which relations of domination and colonization are transformed.

Indigenous languages have been found to be critical in enhancing students' academic performance and achievement. Heugh (1999), who studies language education models in Africa, concluded that indigenous languages contribute positively towards improved provision of education for children. A longitudinal study conducted by Bamgbose (2005), which compared the use of the home language, Yoruba, and English as languages of instruction in Nigeria, concluded that children who were taught in Yoruba performed significantly better than those who had been taught in English, although those who were taught in English had a specialist teacher of English. In Ghana, Wilmot (2003) studied classes in which the medium of instruction was changed from English to the children's mother tongue, and found that children knew much more and learned much better when taught in a language familiar to them than in a foreign language. Chekaraou (2004) conducted a comprehensive study of the use of Hausa in primary schools in Niger, and observed that teaching in these schools through a home language fostered active teacher-student interactions that enabled students to develop their critical thinking skills. This was transferable to all learning experiences, even when the first language ceased to be the language of instruction in upper grades. As a start, we need to promote the teaching of African languages while simultaneously developing academic books in African languages. Researchers and academics should vigorously campaign for language policy reforms and advocate for the promotion of indigenous languages as languages of instruction in schools.

CONCLUSION

The importance of indigenizing the school curriculum in Africa cannot be overemphasized or ignored. The role of active advocacy work and campaigns cannot be overstated. This should involve both academic and professional organizations, the state, and civil society organizations. The point that must be forcefully made is that indigenous African knowledges, not Eurocentric or former colonial knowledge, are fundamental for socio-cultural and socio-economic development in Africa. Curriculum planning and development need to be considered in terms of whom the curriculum is being designed for, the purpose to be served by validated knowledge in the curriculum, and the effect it will have on learners and society. It is a human right for African students to learn curricula that are designed from their indigenous knowledges. Beyond the issue of rights, it is important to note that indigenized school knowledge and the use of indigenous languages enhance literacy and are very crucial for societal development. A society develops when its citizens are literate in their languages, the languages of the majority. It is not possible to reach 'modernity,' as defined by the people, if the curriculum for formal education is only within the intellectual domain of a small minority. A people's culture is at the heart of their identity, social cohesion, and the development of a knowledge-based economy. Emphasizing traditional ecological knowledge in the curriculum can increase the participation of Africans in the scientific community of their countries. The understanding of traditional knowledge, and its introduction into the school curriculum, can foster creative collaborations between learners, local peoples, policymakers, and nongovernment organizations to the benefit of communities. Traditional knowledge recognizes the different strengths of multiple understandings and explicitly includes the culture of learners into their learning experiences.

REFERENCES

Adjei, P., & Dei, G. (2008). Decolonizing schooling and education in Ghana. In A. A. Abdi & S. Guo (Eds.), *Education and social development: Global issues and analyses* (pp. 139-153). Rotterdam: Sense Publishers.

Alidou, H., & Brock-Utne, B. (2006). Experience 1 – Teaching practices – Teaching in a familiar language. In H. Alidou, A. Boly, B. Brock-Utne, Y. S. Diallo, K. Heugh, & H. E. Wolff (Eds.), *Optimizing learning and education in Africa – The language factor: A stock-taking research on mother tongue and bilingual education in Sub-Saharan Africa*. Paris: Association for the Development of Education in Africa (ADEA).

Anchimbe, E. A. (2006). Functional seclusion and the future of indigenous languages in Africa: The case of Cameroon. In J. Mugane, J. P. Hutchison, & D. A. Worman (Eds.), *Selected proceedings of the 35th annual conference on African linguistics*. Somerville, MA: Cascadilla Proceedings Project.

Andrews, C. A. G. (2012). *Integrating traditional ecological knowledge into western science based environmental technology curriculum – An examination*. Unpublished Master of Arts Integrated Studies Project, Athabasca, Alberta.

Apple, M. (2001). Markets, standards, teaching, and teacher education. *Journal of Teacher Education*, *52*, 182-196.

Armstrong, M., Kimmerer, R. W., & Vergun, J. (2007). Education and research opportunities for traditional ecological knowledge. *Front. Ecol. Environ.*, *5*(4), W12-W14.

Asabere-Ameyaw, A., Dei, G. J. S., & Raheem, K. (2012). The question of indigenous science and science education: A look at the current literature. In A. Asabere-Ameyaw, G. J. S. Dei, & K. Raheem (Eds.), *Contemporary issues in African sciences and science education* (pp. 1-28). Rotterdam: Sense Publication.

Bamgbose, A. (2005). Mother-tongue education. Lessons from the Yoruba experience. In B. Brock-Utne & R. K. Hopson (Eds.), *Languages of instruction for African emancipation: Focus on postcolonial contexts and considerations.* Cape Town: CASAS.

Barber, M., & Mourshed, M. (2007). *How the world's best performing school systems come out on top.* London: McKinsey & Company.

Bernstein, B. (Ed.). (1973). *Class, codes and control, Vol. 2: Theoretical studies towards a sociology of language.* London: Routledge & Kegan Paul.

Berkes, F. (1999). *Sacred ecology: Traditional ecological knowledge and resource management.* Philadelphia, PA: Taylor and Francis.

Chekaraou, I. (2004). *Teachers' appropriation of bilingual educational reform policy in Sub-Saharan Africa: A socio-cultural study of two Hausa-French schools in Niger.* Ph.D. Thesis, Indiana University, Bloomington.

Deasy, R. J. (Ed.). (2002). *Critical links: Learning in the arts and student and academic and social development.* Washington, DC: Council of Chief State School Officers. Retrieved October 16, 2012, from http://www.aep-arts.org

Dei, G. J. S. (2004). *Schooling and education in Africa: The case of Ghana.* Trenton, NJ: Africa World.

Dweck, C. S. (2006). *Mindset: The new psychology of success.* New York: Random House.

Eggleston, J. (1977). *The sociology of the school curriculum.* London: Routledge & Kegan Paul.

Eyong, C. T. (2007). Indigenous knowledge and sustainable development in Africa: Case study on Central Africa. In E. K. Boon & L. Hens (Eds.), *Indigenous knowledge systems and sustainable development: Relevance for Africa, tribes and tribals special* (pp. 121-139). Delhi: Kamla-Raj Enterprises.

Ferguson, K. M. (2005). Beyond indigenization and reconceptualization: Towards a global, multidirectional model of technology transfer. *International Social Work, 48*(5), 519-535.

Folke, C. (2004). Traditional knowledge in social-ecological systems. *Ecol. Soc., 9*, 7.

Foucault, M. (1971). The order of discourse. In R. Young (ed.), Untying the text: A poststructuralist reader. London: Routledge and Kegan Paul.

Freire, P. (1972). Pedagogy of the oppressed. New York: Herder and Herder.

Giroux, H. (1988). *Teachers as intellectuals: Toward a critical pedagogy of learning.* South Hadley, MA: Bergin Garvey.

Gruenewald, D. (2003). The best of both worlds: A critical pedagogy of place. *Educational Researcher, 32*(4), 3-12.

Heugh, K. (1999). Languages, development and education in South Africa. *International Journal of Educational Development, 19*, 301-313.

Hussey, T., & Smith, P. (2003). The uses of learning outcomes. *Teaching in Higher Education, 8*(3), 357-368.

Kimmerer, R. W. (2002). Weaving traditional ecological knowledge into biological education: A call to action. *BioScience, 52*(5), 432-438. Retrieved October 29, 2012 from http://www.esf.edu/nativepeoples/weaving.pdf

Kohn, A. (2008) Progressive education: Why it's hard to beat, but also hard to find. *Independent School.* Retrieved October 13, 2012. http://www.alfiekohn.org/teaching/progressive.htm

Lopes, A., & Macedo, E. (2011). Curriculum, policy, practice. *Transnational Curriculum Inquiry, 8*(2), 1-3. Retrieved October 30, 2012 from http://nitinat.library.ubc.ca/ojs/index.php/tci

127

Magagula, C. M., & Mazibuko, E. Z. (2004). Indigenization of African formal education systems. *The African Symposium*, 4(2), 89-99. Retrieved November 1, 2012 from http://www.ncsu.edu/aern/TAS4.2/TAS4.2.pdf

McCarter, J., & Gavin, M. C. (2011). Perceptions of the value of traditional ecological knowledge to formal school curricula: Opportunities and challenges from Malekula Island, Vanuatu. *Journal of Ethnobiology and Ethnomedicine*, 7(38). Retrieved October 24, 2012 from http://www.ethnobiomed.com/content/7/1/38

Morin, F. (2004). The arts and academic achievement: A review of research. *Educators' Notebook*, 15(4), 1-4.

Moshi, L., & Ojo, A. (Eds.). (2009). *Language pedagogy and language use in Africa*. London: Adonis & Abbey Publishers Ltd.

Ntsoane, O. (2000). *Implications of intellectual property rights on indigenous knowledge systems Southern Africa: A comparative study of selected rural communities in Botswana and South Africa*. Unpublished Master's Thesis, North-West University, South Africa.

Okeke, C. I. O. (2010). A neglected impediment to true Africanisation of African higher education curricula: Same agenda, differential fee regimes. *JHEA/RESA*, 8(2), 39-52.

Ornstein, A. C., & Hunkins, F. P. (2009). *Curriculum foundations, principles and issues* (5th ed.). Boston: Allyn and Bacon.

Pollard, A. (Ed.). (2010). *Professionalism and pedagogy: A contemporary opportunity. A commentary by TLRP and GTCE*. London: TLRP.

Prah, K. K. (2006). *Challenges to the promotion of indigenous languages in South Africa*. Cape Town: Center for Advanced Studies of African Society.

Semali, L. & Stambach, A. (1997). Cultural identity in an African context: Indigenous education and curriculum in East Africa. *Folklore Forum*, 28(1), 1-27.

Shizha, E. (2005). Reclaiming our memories: The education dilemma in postcolonial African school curricula, In A. A. Abdi & A. Cleghorn (Eds.), *Issues in African education: Sociological perspectives* (pp. 65-83). New York: Palgrave Macmillan.

Shizha, E. (2008). Globalization and indigenous knowledge: An African postcolonial theoretical analysis. In S. Guo & A. A. Abdi (Eds.), *Education and social development: Global issues and analysis* (pp. 37-56). Rotterdam: Sense Publishers.

Shizha, E. (2009). Chara chimwe hachitswanyi inda: Indigenizing science education in Zimbabwe. In D. Kapoor & S. Jordan (Eds.), *Education, participatory action research, and social change: International perspectives* (pp. 139-154). New York: Palgrave Macmillan.

Shizha, E. (2010). Rethinking and reconstituting indigenous knowledge and voices in the academy in Zimbabwe: A decolonization process. In D. Kapoor & E. Shizha (Eds.), *Indigenous knowledge and learning in Asia/Pacific and Africa: Perspectives on development, education and culture* (pp. 115-129). New York: Palgrave Macmillan.

Shizha, E. (2011). Neoliberal globalization, science education and indigenous African knowledges. In D. Kapoor (Ed.), *Critical perspectives on neoliberal globalization, development and education in Africa and Asia* (pp. 15-31). Rotterdam: Sense Publishers.

Shizha E. (2012). Linguistic independence and African education and development. In H. K. Wright & A. A. Abdi (Eds.), *The dialectics of African education and Western discourses: Counter-hegemonic perspectives* (pp. 148-162). Peter Lang Publishers, New York.

Tanner, D., & Tanner, L. N. (2007). *Curriculum development: Theory into practice*. New York: Macmillan.

Udoh, E., & Udeaja, E. A. (2011). Ten years of industrial policies under democratic governance in Nigeria: "New wine in old bottle." *European Journal of Social Sciences*, 20(2), 248-258.

wa Thiong'o, N. (1986). *Decolonising the mind: The politics of language in African literature*. London: James Currey.

Weightman, D. A. (2008). *Defining the essential components of indigenization: A roadmap for parachurch mission agencies serving in the Bahamas*. Unpublished Master of Arts in Religion Integrative Thesis, Faculty of Reformed Theological Seminary.

Wilmot, E. M. (2003). *Stepping outside the ordinary expectations of schooling: Effect of school language on the assessment of educational achievement in Ghana.* Paper presented at the 47th Annual Meeting of CIES March 12-16, New Orleans.

Zhou, G., & Zvoushe, H. (2012). Public policy making in Zimbabwe: A three decade perspective. *International Journal of Humanities and Social Science* [Special Issue], *2*(8), 212-222.

E. FREDUA-KWARTENG AND F. AHIA

12. LEARNING MATHEMATICS IN ENGLISH AT BASIC SCHOOLS

A Benefit or Hindrance?

INTRODUCTION

In this chapter, we draw mainly from our experiences as mathematics educators and from the research literature, with the primary intent to answer this question: How does the learning of mathematics in a colonial language[1] (English, French, Portuguese, Afrikaans, etc.) at the basic school level help or hamper students' development of mathematical proficiency? To answer this question, we used basic school students' learning of mathematics through English in Ghana as our case study. A case study is an intensive scholarly inquiry that deals with a unit of a phenomenon, and it allows us to understand the phenomenon much better than studying all students on the African continent learning mathematics through the different colonial languages (Merriam, 2001; Dooley, 2002; Yin, 2003). With this unit of the phenomenon thoroughly analyzed, it is then possible to make generalizations to the entire phenomenon to which the unit is a member (Cohen & Manion, 1994).

In Ghana, English is the language of government and administration, the learned professions and much of the media.[2] English is also the Language of Learning and Teaching[3] (LOLT) in Ghanaian schools from primary 4 (Ampiah, 2010), though earlier policy had sanctioned English only as the LOLT throughout the school system (Owu-Ewie, 2006). Like many other policies in African countries, the use of Ghanaian languages as LOLT from pre-school to class three is hardly monitored in Ghana, leaving teachers to use their own discretion to adopt any LOLT they find appropriate. According to Ampiah (2008), observational studies indicated that in rural, urban, and private elementary schools (k-6) in Ghana, English language alone is used as the LOLT for mathematics due to the limited mathematics register in Ghanaian languages. A similar observation was made in junior high schools (1-3), though the use of Ghanaian language was dominant in teacher-student classroom interactions in rural schools (68%), 37% in urban schools, and almost 100% in private schools. The same author reported that in private elementary schools, teachers and students use only English for classroom interactions, compared to 6-13% for rural schools and 11-60% for urban public schools. We recognize that the English-only policy is vigorously enforced in private schools,[4] where the development and attainment of English language oral fluency is a cardinal focus of schooling.

G. Emeagwali & G. J. S. Dei (eds.), African Indigenous Knowledge and the Disciplines, 131–164.

Many reports and scholarly articles have been written about poor mathematics performance of Ghanaian basic school students. The common proxies used to determine student mathematics achievement are the results of public examination such as Basic Examination Certificate Examination (BECE) and international assessments like Trends in International Mathematics and Science (TIMSS) (Adetunde, 2007; Adetunde et al., 2010; Anamuah-Mensah & Mereku, 2005; Ministry of Education, Youth & Sports, 2004; Mullis et al., 2008; Ottevanger et al., 2007; West African Examination Council, 2006). For example, Anamuah-Mensah and Mereku (2005) attributed the poor performance of Ghanaian junior high school students (JHS 2) in the TIMSS 2003 to the inability of teachers to fully cover the mathematics curriculum content domains of number concepts, algebra, measurement, geometry, and data management. They also stated that the national mathematics curriculum puts an undue emphasis on number concepts or computational skills, knowledge of facts and procedures rather than problem-solving. Lastly, they argued that the Ghanaian national mathematics curriculum (or syllabi), textbooks, and teacher handbooks for JHS are out-of-date and do not meet international standards. Adetunde et al. (2010) advocated better remuneration for mathematics teachers in public-funded schools and government or society incentives for students, especially girls, to cultivate a positive attitude toward mathematics learning.

None of these researchers and scholars has included English as language of learning and teaching mathematics in the catalogue of probable causes for dismal mathematics achievement. We wonder why, knowing very well that almost all the teachers and students in basic schools are incompetent users of the English language.

The absence of English language proficiency from the core analysis of poor mathematics performance of Ghanaian students in those examinations motivated us to write this chapter. As a matter of fact, the act of speaking, listening, and writing through English is something that is not constantly thought of among Ghanaian scholars, researchers, and policymakers. They may trivialize or ignore the fact that in the mathematics classroom, language is the basic means students use to express the knowledge they have acquired as well as their understanding of mathematical ideas and formulae (Yushau, 2004). This is why, we believe, less attention has been given to the language factor in analyzing poor mathematics achievement.

This chapter is organized as follows. The first part discusses the research method and conceptual framework for the chapter. In the second portion of the chapter, we have analyzed the effects of mathematics learning and teaching through English language for basic school students[5] whose mother tongue is a Ghanaian language rather than English. In the conclusion, the final part, we argued that learning mathematics through English hinders student development of mathematical proficiency. We also discussed other factors that might contribute to the dismal mathematics learning outcomes in African schools, besides the use of colonial languages. However, for the English-learning African students the use of a colonial language itself for learning mathematics could be a considerable source of anxiety, which we defined as the state of emotional discomfort, uncertainty, and despair of doing mathematics. We also touch on the issue of developing a mathematical register in Ghanaian languages.

RESEARCH APPROACH

We have been mathematics educators for a long time now, with a mix of Ghanaian and Canadian professional experience. The second author has more than two decades of professional experience as a mathematics and science educator, having taught in secondary schools and a university in Ghana before coming to the University of Toronto, Canada, to pursue a doctorate degree in mathematics and physics. After completion of his doctoral studies, he taught mathematics at the community-college level and then later on moved to the University of Toronto. At these levels, he taught mathematics to heterogeneous students from Africa, Asia, North America, and South America, a vast majority for whom English is a second or perhaps a third language.

The first author started teaching mathematics and science in Toronto inner-city elementary and middle schools for four years after obtaining his undergraduate degrees in mathematics and education from York University, Toronto. He also obtained a master's degree in mathematics education from the same university. Later on, he taught mathematics and science for six and half years in a secondary school in Nunavut, Canada's newest territory, where the students were Inuit Aboriginal people. In all, he has more than 15 years of experience teaching elementary, middle, and high school mathematics and science. Above all, both of us were mathematics and science students in Ghana and Canada before we became educators. The first author completed secondary school calculus and other mathematics courses in Ontario before enrolling in a university undergraduate mathematics program. The second author studied advanced mathematics courses at the secondary school, undergraduate, and master's program in mathematics at the Kwame Nkrumah University of Science and Technology, Kumasi, Ghana. Our previous status as students of mathematics has enriched our professional experience and understanding as mathematics educators, in terms of teaching and learning mathematics through English as a second language.

Consequently, as mathematics educators we have valuable, insightful experiences to share about mathematics teaching and learning of students whose indigenous language or mother tongue is a non-European language. Qualitative researchers may regard our professional experiences as stories or narratives. They may also say that we lead storied lives (Connelly & Clandinin, 1990; Creswell, 2008). These authors may characterize our professional narratives or stories as similar in character to interviews, letter writing, journal records, field-notes, autobiography, and biography that constitute the major approach to data collection in qualitative research methodology. Using professional education narratives as data is increasingly acceptable in the field of qualitative research (Gardner, 2001; Stoddart, 2001) and nursing (Eubanks, 1991; Scherting, 1988). It is also an accepted part of qualitative research that requires examination of one's personal practice or experience, like action research (Dick, 1992; Greenwood, 1994;

Greenwood & Levin, 1998), and of other research traditions, such as ethnography, where the personal experience of the researcher is considered inseparably bound up with the data collection and interpretation activities (Ellis, 1995; Hannabuss, 2000). On our part, we opted to use our professional experiences because they helped us to supplement the paucity of literature we found on teaching and learning mathematics in colonial languages by continental Africans.[6] In addition, the use of our professional experiences, we hope, would allow the reader to understand where we are coming from in terms of our mathematics teaching and learning experiences and how practical this chapter is for improving mathematics education in Africa. As our research approach is qualitative or interpretative (Denzin & Lincoln, 1994), it allowed us to critique or corroborate with the literature in the field using our combined practical teaching experiences. Teachers' practical knowledge has epistemic merit as Fenstermacher (1994) asserted:

> The concept of practical knowledge is a legitimate epistemological category so long as we attach to it demands for justification or warrant in the same way that demands are attached to formal knowledge. (p. 47)

In this quote, Fenstermacher (1994) is suggesting that knowledge gained from experience is of value, relevance, and meaning in qualitative research provided we are able to demonstrate that such claims are practical and fairly logical within the context of such experience. We have provided evidence for our assertions rather than relying merely on our accumulated experiences as mathematics educators.

Those narratives (or professional experiences) have shaped and continue to shape our professional lives as we interact with students, prepare lesson plans, design mathematics activities, assess student mathematics performance, or engage in any professional development activities. It is therefore irresistible for us to write about teaching and learning mathematics without drawing on those stories. However, those narratives are not merely incidents, events, or observations of what happened in our professional lives. We produced our narratives through critical reflection on our accumulated professional experiences over the years in teaching students whose primary language is non-English. As we reflected on our experiences we met face-to-face in our offices or engaged in phone discussion once a week from October 10, 2012 to January 25, 2013 to discuss those reflections. Our research question, conceptual framework, and the following questions guided our individual as well as our collective reflections: (a) How is it like teaching or learning mathematics in English? (b) What problems do English-learners encounter in the mathematics classroom and how do teachers respond to those learning problems? (c) Do teachers actually know that English-learners have linguistic problems learning mathematics in English? (d) How do you assess English-learners' knowledge of mathematics? (e) What are the learning effects of using both the indigenous language of the student and English to teach mathematics? (f) What are the practical benefits of using students' indigenous language to teach them mathematics?

A face-to-face meeting for the research could last between 1.5 hours, but each of our phone conservations exceeded 2 hours most of the time. During the meetings we shared our reflections and provided opportunities for each to ask questions of the other's reflections. Sometimes our reflections led us to more questions than answers as we focused on the question we were trying to answer in this chapter. In all, we had a total of five meetings, seven sessions of phone conversation and 10 electronic correspondences (emails). We took notes of all those final reflections, used themes to summarize and analyze those assertions we found relevant to help us to answer the major research question. In the analysis we moved between the final reflections and the field literature repeatedly to compare them. Some of the results of the comparison were expected, but others were unexpected. Our definitions of *expected* and *unexpected* conform to those of Cole (1994). The author used *expected* to refer to data that support ideas of authors in the literature, and *unexpected* for those that do not confirm ideas of the authors of the literature in the field. The email communication exchanges between us focused on clarifying meanings, reinterpretation of reflections, justification of reflections, additional reflections, questions for further reflection, and possible answers to precious questions or new questions for reflection.

Reflection is an indispensable characteristic of effective mathematics teachers. The research literature suggests that teachers learn effectively through their reflections (Berliner, 1994; Dewey, 1933; Jaworski, 1998; Mason, 2002). Jaworski (1998) and Mason (2002) distinguished between reflection-on-action as thinking back after the fact and reflection-in-action as being aware of inner thoughts and feelings while engaging in an act of teaching. Mason (2002) added a third category of reflection: Reflection-through action. It is about teachers' awareness of patterns of their own professional practices. According to Dewey (1933), reflection is different from other forms of thinking in that it involves: (i) "A state of doubt, hesitation, perplexity, mental difficulty in which thinking originates and (ii) an act of searching, hunting, and inquiring to find material that will resolve the doubt, to settle and dispose of the complexity" (p. 538). Dewey (1933) went on to suggest that critical reflection has three main attributes: Openness, responsibility, and wholeheartedness. Yost et al. (2000) explained that openness relates to having the desire to listen to alternative views and having the courage to question one's own teaching beliefs and practices. They defined responsibility as the desire to search actively for truth and apply the findings obtained to resolve problems. Finally, they stated that wholeheartedness has to do with an attitude for making changes and critical evaluation of ourselves as mathematics educators, our organization, and our society. Our reflections produced and utilized in this chapter bear those characteristics of reflection-on-action and reflection-through action.

Besides our professional narratives or experiences, we also made an increasing use of the international research literature. We used the University of Toronto electronic databases and the internet search engines like Ultra Vista, Google, and Yahoo to search for literature in the field of interest. Using descriptors "learning mathematics through second language," "learning mathematics using mother-tongue," "and mathematics education in Ghana/Africa," and "teaching and learning mathematics in English" interchangeably, we searched in the following database: ERIC, EBSCO, JSTOR, PROQUEST, Education Full-Text, and Wilson Education

Abstract. These databases displayed more than 200 articles, research reports, monographs, and conference papers. However, we confined our search to peer-reviewed sources because they were easier to locate and are more authentic relative to others.

We also used the same descriptors or phrases in the databases to search the world web via Ultra Vista, Google, and Yahoo. The search netted more than 320 documents, including conference proceedings, academic articles, and research and project reports. Using our major research question and guided reflection questions, we determined which of the documents were relevant to assist us to answer the questions. Much of the literature was generally about teaching or learning in second languages or L2, rather than mathematics specifically. A majority of the mathematics-related literature in the field come from the United States of America. Nevertheless, we were interested in the literature related to English-learners learning mathematics through English language. In the United States many of such learners speak Spanish as their primary language of communication (Khisty, 2006; Khisty & Chval, 2002; Moschkovich, 1999, 2002, 2007). South Africa, with its multilingual classrooms and one of the best research traditions on the African continent, has produced numerous papers in the field of mathematics teaching and learning through English, a second or third language[7] to the majority of South Africans. Unfortunately, only a few of the literature is useful in helping us to answer our research question.

CONCEPTUAL FRAMEWORK

The conceptual framework of research consists of concepts, assumptions, beliefs, and theories that support and contribute to shaping the research (Miles & Huberman, 1994). According to these authors, a conceptual framework "explains either graphically or in narrative form the main things to be studied – the key factors, concepts, or variables – and relationship among them (Miles & Huberman, 1994, p. 18). A conceptual framework is thus a set of concepts that assists researchers to address either the research question(s) or purpose (s). In the case of this chapter, our conceptual framework is made up of dimensions of mathematics proficiency: teacher knowledge for teaching mathematics effectively, and language and thinking. Each of these will be discussed briefly in the following subsections.

TEACHER KNOWLEDGE FOR TEACHING MATHEMATICS

We agree with researchers that effective mathematics teachers must possess subject-matter knowledge, pedagogical knowledge, curricular knowledge, and knowledge of students (An et al., 2004; Fennema & Franke, 1992; Shulman, 1986). These authors agree that subject matter knowledge includes understanding of the nature of mathematics, mathematical concepts, and their interrelationships, rationale underlying mathematical procedures, rules, formulas, algorithms, and how the field is organized. They also defined knowledge of pedagogy as the ability to prepare lesson plans, using appropriate teaching strategies and assessment

136

practices that provide authentic information about each learner. Knowledge of the curriculum relates to knowing the official goals for different grade levels, how to use different teaching resources such as textbooks, technology, and concrete materials to teach mathematics.

Knowledge of students, which is our primary concern here, focuses on the characteristics of students: their interests, aspirations, difficulties learning mathematics, and attitude toward mathematics. While those researchers agree on the interrelated nature of the four strands of teacher knowledge, we noted that in practice, mathematics teachers tend to pay much attention to the first three to the exclusion of the last strand. As a matter of fact, knowledge of students includes their indigenous or home languages and "informal" mathematical procedures and concepts that they bring to the mathematics classrooms from their culture. As Bishop (2004) has indicated, all cultures and societies have developed six categories of mathematical activities: counting, locating, measuring, designing, playing, and explaining. Counting answers the question how many, while measuring deals with how much. Locating involves navigating or finding one's way around in the spatial features of one's environment. Designing focuses on making shapes and structures to serve different social, esthetic, and economic purposes, whereas playing has to do with games that involve puzzles, logical paradoxes, and decision-making. Explaining relates to mental abilities: logical and verbal reasoning about why and how things happen the way they do. Particularly, "in mathematics we are interested in, for example, why number calculations work, and in which situations, why certain geometric shapes do or do not fit together, why one algebraic result leads to another, and with different ways of symbolizing these relationships" (Bishop, 2004, p. 7).

MATHEMATICAL PROFICIENCY

Basic school mathematics curriculum in African countries, as in different parts of the world, includes number concepts, operations with numbers, measurement, geometric shapes, fractions, and percentages. However, attaining mathematics proficiency goes beyond knowledge of these concepts. Mathematics proficiency involves knowledge, skills, and attitude in five strands (Kilpatrick et al., 2001). The five interrelated strands are conceptual understanding, procedural fluency, strategic competence, adaptive reasoning, and productive disposition. Conceptual understanding is about comprehension of mathematics concepts, operations, and their relationships. Students who have conceptual understanding of mathematics know more than isolated number facts, and are able to explain similarities and differences between number concepts, operations, and relationships between them. Procedural fluency refers to the knowledge and skills to apply mathematical procedures flexibly and appropriately. Strategic competence is the ability to formulate, represent, and solve mathematical problems. That is, it is about using mathematics to solve problems as well as pose problems. Adaptive reasoning relates to the capacity to explain things using logic, thought reflection, and justification. Productive disposition is "the habitual inclination to see mathematics as sensible, useful, and worthwhile, coupled with a belief in diligence and one's own efficacy" (Kilpatrick et al., 2001, p. 5). In other words, productive disposition involves the development of positive attitude toward mathematics.

From this discussion, it is clear that these five strands also define teachers' subject matter knowledge. To illustrate, it may not work very well for teachers to help students to develop mathematics proficiency if the teachers have a negative attitude toward mathematics, or refuse to provide justification for using specific procedures or algorithms to solve mathematical problems.

LANGUAGE AND THINKING

The last part of the conceptual framework is language and thinking. Both psycholinguists and sociolinguists agree that language performs three major functions: (1) Providing new ideas; (2) changing or maintaining beliefs, values; and (3) assisting memory (Shakur, 2009; Steinberg, 1982). Language is needed for rational thought in that it assists our memory and helps us to label abstract ideas with words, numbers, and sounds for ease of identification and processing by our brains. In this case, language provides order for thought and thought also in turn provides organizational framework needed by language. Sometimes we use language for ordering as well as for organizing our thoughts. Without language we can only express our thoughts through gestures, facial expression, and other artistic forms. However, linguists share the common view that language does not entirely influence the nature, context, and direction of human thought and that there are other factors as well (Bloom & Keil, 2001; Boroditsky, 2001; Shakur, 2009; Steinberg, 1982). Culture is another factor that influences human thinking processes (Allan, 2011). The fact is that language spoken, written, or gestured provides a medium to express, create, and interpret meanings and to establish and maintain social and interpersonal relationships, but it does not mean that language is the basis of thinking. While language is independent of thinking, language can exercise some influence on thinking (Boroditsky, 2001; Steinberg, 1982; Slezak, 2002).

To conclude this section, it should be noted that teacher's knowledge, mathematics proficiency, and language and thought are related. Teachers and students in mathematics classrooms need language to express themselves to each other and to engage in discourses. Similarly, it is impossible to attain mathematical proficiency without a language facility – a language to understand mathematical concepts, to problem-solve, pose problems, to communicate explanation, thought reflections, and justification for specific procedures. Mathematics teachers also need knowledge of students, particularly mathematics concepts, strategies and understandings that they bring from their homes into the classroom, and their linguistic backgrounds in order to assist them to develop mathematics proficiency.

DEVELOPING STUDENT MATHEMATICAL PROFICIENCY:
DOES LANGUAGE MATTER?

In the previous section, researchers, educators, and scholars were quoted asserting a positive correlation between education in a foreign language and African educational failures like school dropout rates, low graduation rates, and poor mathematical achievement. A group of researchers and scholars wants to improve education quality in Africa through the adoption of indigenous languages as LOLT (Alidou & Brock-Utne, 2011; Bamgbose, 2007; Owu-Ewie, 2006; Obanya, 1980). Generally, the literature suggests that the use of a colonial language as official language negatively affects attainment of development goals, achievement of mass literacy, participation in international discourses, and knowledge production (Bamgbose, 2007; Robinson, 1996; Wolf, 2011). So, what do these have to do with developing the mathematical proficiency of African children and adolescents? In this section we argue that the use of English as a LOLT in basic schools in Ghana hampers the students' development of mathematical proficiency. Using the student's home or familiar language as the LOLT has psychological, sociological, and educational benefits:

> Psychologically, it is a system of meaningful signs that his mind works automatically for expression and understanding. Sociologically, it is a means of identification among members of the community to which he/she belongs. Educationally, he learns more quickly through it than through unfamiliar linguistic medium. (Todd, 1988, p. 165)

In the past, researchers and policy-makers generally accepted that language influenced learning, but not so much on the acquisition of mathematics skills, concepts, and problem-solving (Cuevas, 1984; Flores, 1997; Gutierrez, 2002). That is, the prevalent notion was that a student's proficiency[8] of LOLT has a minimal effect on learning mathematics. This was because mathematics was conceptualized as having to do with numbers, calculation with numbers, shapes and manipulation of symbols (Hansen-Thomas, 2009; Janzen, 2008; Lager, 2006). Nonetheless, in the last two decades or so, researchers have observed that English language learners[9] (ELLs) who learn mathematics through English need proficiency in English in order to develop their mathematical proficiency (Abedi & Lord, 2001; Beal et al., 2010; Parker et al., 2009; Schleppegrell, 2007). English language proficiency will ensure that these students are able to comprehend and apply mathematics skills and concepts to solve problems (Garrison & Mora, 1999; Mestre, 1988; Moschkovich, 1999).

The influence of English language on mathematics learning can be viewed in two ways: natural language and technical language, both of which form the mathematical register. Certain phrases and words have been adopted from the English language and given special meanings. These include line, point, angle, sum, average, variable, mean, table, range, set, field, difference, degree, addition, set, and input, even and odd numbers. Apart from these terms, mathematics also uses the same English pronoun, connectors, punctuation, transitional words, and other syntax. Technical words or vocabulary in mathematics include parabola, x-axis, y-axis, hypotenuse, distribution, parallelogram, asymptotic, standard deviation, symmetry, compound interest, coefficient, term, sine, cosine, radian, equation, and rational numbers (Ernst-Slavit & Slavit, 2007a). Thus, ELLs who learn mathematics through English have to master the technical English language usage, along with ordinary English, to understand what their teachers teach in order to develop their mathematical proficiency (Nordin, 2005). They would rather learn mathematics more quickly and grab mathematical ideas comfortably if instructed in a familiar language.

EXPLAINING, COMMUNICATING, JUSTIFYING MATHEMATICALLY

In the case of Ghanaian basic school students, a vast majority of them are ELLs and have problems with ordinary English language, let alone the specialized words borrowed from English and the technical mathematics vocabulary. Accordingly, the second author provided the following reflection:

> The main problem with Ghanaian students (in Ghana) is not necessarily mastering the technical language of mathematics or the special mathematical meanings assigned to certain English words or phrases. It has more to do with expressing themselves in ordinary English sentences and making sense in those expressions. It is a problem most students at that level may deny because to admit it openly suggests one is stupid, knowing that in Ghana English language proficiency is equated with intelligence ... though there is no connection whatsoever between the two. Students have a strong preference for number skill questions or those requiring procedural or computational fluency rather than those that require analysis, reasoning, and communication. As a consequence most mathematics teachers avoid assigning to students activities that involve explaining mathematical concepts, supplying justification, or making arguments ... not that Ghanaian students are incapable of reasoning mathematically, but they can't do it with ease when using English.

The first author made a similar reflection on the same issue, emphasizing that the problem of explaining, communicating and justifying mathematically are prevalent among ELLs:

> I found the difficulties ELLs experience in explaining and justifying similar among that population of students .... Even where I gave written explanations or analyses of concepts they would try to memorize them and reproduce them, most of the time, inappropriately in other contexts. They usually show frustration on their faces when I pointed out to them the inappropriateness of their explanations or justifications. No wonder these students often chose questions that involved calculation rather than those that required them to explain by comparing one thing with another; choosing one procedure/formula over others; justifying a solution/answer/procedure;

demonstrating the effects of procedures on specific social variables; what some concepts mean .... But as mathematics educators we fail to consider or underestimate the implications and challenges of teaching and learning through a foreign language (English language). This failure or underestimation is more likely to have a negative impact on the quality of teaching and learning outcomes in mathematics .... ELLs at that basic level cannot engage in analyzing, communicating, and justifying mathematically until they have attained English proficiency. By that time they might have lost interest in mathematics!

To develop mathematical proficiency, Ghanaian basic school students need more than procedural skills or computational fluency. As we have noted about mathematical proficiency, students also need conceptual understanding too, which demands language proficiency for communicating or expressing their conceptions of mathematical ideas (Brodie, 1989). If mathematics learning were merely number crunching or manipulating there would be no problems for most ELLs. However, the learning of mathematics in the last few decades has taken the direction of analysis, communication, and exploration – all of which require language proficiency (Ernst-Slavit & Slavit, 2007b).

The National Council of Teachers of Mathematics (1991) stressed that students should spend more time on reasoning, problem-solving, communicating ideas, exploring the relationship between representations of mathematical forms and making connections between concepts. We found this suggestion crucial for developing mathematical proficiency. Unfortunately, the mother tongue of most basic school students in Ghana is non-English with the result that mathematics learning is a formidable challenge for them. How can the child learn mathematics effectively or successfully through English in which he/she is weaker? The situation is more dangerous when mathematics teachers are unaware of the language implications of teaching and learning mathematics through English and reason, erroneously, that since they were able to do it the ELLs should be equally able to do it. Indeed, at the commonsensical level, the mother tongue of the child is the language he/she is familiar with and can comfortably use for communication, analysis, and exploration of mathematical objects and concepts (Sua & Raman, 2007). As Obanya (1980) carefully observed 32 years ago:

It has always been felt by African educationalists that the African child's major problem is linguistic. Instruction is given in a language that is not normally used in his (or her) immediate environment, a language which neither the learner nor the teacher understands and uses well enough. (p. 88)

The myth that mathematics learning transcends English language proficiency is to deny basic school students in Ghana the opportunity to develop mathematics proficiency through their home languages – languages they are familiar and comfortable with. We have not even mentioned those basic school students who have learning difficulties with their own mother-tongue. How would such students fare in learning mathematics through the English language? In a research in South

Africa, students reported that the use of their home language helped them to develop conceptual understanding of mathematics they were learning. Others indicated that the use of their home language allowed them to develop a positive or productive disposition toward mathematics (Langa, 2006). It is for this reasons we are arguing that learning mathematics through the indigenous languages of basic students in Ghana would assist them to develop their mathematics proficiency. We know from our experiences that ELLs would have no difficulties to explain, justify, or communicate mathematical ideas if they were to use their indigenous languages.

MATHEMATICAL PROBLEM-SOLVING

Mathematical problem-solving is considered the heart of mathematics learning more than learning to compute with numbers and identifying geometric shapes (Eshun, 2000; Halmos, 1980). Problem-solving is a goal-oriented, cognitive activity entailing analysing and interpreting a situation mathematically (Lesh & Zawojewski, 2007). A definition we find more acceptable is the view that mathematical problem (often called word problem) is any problem amenable to representation, analysis, and possible solution using mathematics methods, principles, algorithms, operations, or theorems. It involves language, strategic thinking, and links to mathematics concepts. It also ranges from real-life problems to contrived puzzle-like problems. Mathematical problems may be solved by seeking patterns, trying out possibilities, drawing a picture or graph, working backward, listing or arranging elements, or using special cases as models. Problem-solving provides students opportunities to learn analysis, reasoning, and to assess their understanding of a combination of mathematical skills and concepts.

However, mathematical problem-solving is the Achilles' heel of ELLs who learn mathematics through English. They often make different types of errors that are purely linguistic in nature (Abedi & Lord, 2001; Feza-Piyose, 2012; Lager, 2006; Setati, 2005b; Zevenbergen, 2001). Zevernbergen (2001), for instance, gave an example of the use of the English prepositions to, by, and from, in relation to a temperature word problem for which ELLs may be vulnerable: The temperature fell to 10 degrees, the temperature fell by 10 degrees, and the temperature fell from 10 degrees. According to the author these prepositions signify either an increase or decrease in temperature, which require students to use addition or subtraction symbols to represent the temperature. Generally, most ELLs have difficulties in understanding subtle meanings embedded in words used in mathematical problems (Durkin & Shire, 1991). For example, most Australian Aboriginal students lack intuitive understanding and use of the English language. Therefore, it is not surprising that they have difficulties engaging in problem-solving activities (Christie, 1985). A long time ago, Mestre (1988) argued that the language proficiency of the student mediates cognitive functioning, and identified four forms of language proficiency influencing mathematical problem-solving: (a) language proficiency in general; (b) proficiency in the technical language of the domain, and (c) proficiency with the specific symbolic language of the domain. The last two on

Mestre's (1988) list constitutes the mathematical register that we have already talked about in the last subsection.

The Ghanaian basic school students also have difficulties with word problems. According to Awanta (2009), students showed confidence in solving mathematical problems, especially numerical and routine problems. However, their confidence level with word problems drops as they move up the grade ladder when mathematical problem-solving becomes more complicated as a result of the abstract nature of the English language. The author admitted that students' low competence in the English language is a possible cause of the difficulties they experience with mathematical word problems. Other researchers noted that mathematical problems are difficult for Ghanaian basic students to read, understand, and interpret (Mereku et al., 2005). In Ghana's basic schools, problem-solving is hardly emphasized or made the central goal of mathematics teaching and learning, though the national mathematics syllabus requires teachers to organize lessons around investigation and inquiry (Ministry of Education, Science and Sports, 2007a, 2007b). These problem-solving and problem-posing activities involve the English language, the LOLT, of which the majority of the students are not proficient. The second author provided the following critical reflection to explain why Ghanaian teachers minimize the teaching of word problems:

> The English language is again the main problem, though conceptual and situational knowledge are needed as well to solve word problems comfortably. For word problems, students have to read the information carefully, analyze the information; determine the procedure to apply; apply the determined procedure to solve the problem; and justify their solutions. The English language is heavily involved in these processes. It is very frustrating for teachers to teach problem-solving in the math classroom because both the teachers and students have a limited English proficiency. The teachers have difficulties explaining things clearly and students don't have the English comprehension skills to understand or make sense of the problems to be solved. When mathematical problems are assigned, students tend to spend excessive amounts of time cognitively processing the linguistic aspects of the problems. Some teachers try to help by separating the language in which the question is embedded from the mathematics, and this is often a frustrating exercise. The fact is the language and the mathematics is bonded up together such that one cannot explain the mathematics without explaining the language. The net result is that teachers give up on teaching problem-solving, or they teach the very basic ones that is minimally English-dependent, and whose solutions are simple at best.

Frequently, the English language and mathematics are so bounded up together in word problems that it is futile to separate the two – sorting out the linguistic and mathematical aspects of the problem. This is not the case with native speakers of the English language, who focus mainly on the cognitive or mathematical aspects of the problem-solving:

> In mainstream settings, native speakers, for whom English is nearly automatic, can focus primarily on the cognitive tasks of an assignment – uearning new information, procedures, etc. – however, the student with limited ability in English must focus on both cognitive and linguistic tasks-learning new vocabulary, structures and academic discourse. (Anstrom, 1997, p. 5)

Similarly, the first author observed that Ghanaian basic school students who transferred to Canadian schools encounter the same linguistic difficulties, along with the cognitive aspects, in mathematical problem-solving since most of them do not have adequate understanding of the English language. This contrasts sharply with Asian students of basic school, who had learned mathematics in their own languages and transferred to Canadian schools. For these students, the linguistic aspects of problem-solving are their major concern, not the mathematical part. Once they have mastered the linguistic component, they excel far better than their Ghanaian counterparts who were taught in and learned mathematics through English language in Ghana (Fredua-Kwarteng and Ahia, 2005).

We agree with Barwell (2010) that for ELLs, sometimes "Sorting out the language of the question also entails sorting out the mathematics. In this case, attention to language is relevant and contributes to mathematical thinking and understanding." So, teachers face a double challenge of teaching mathematics in English language while the students are still learning the language (Ferreira, 2011). This divided attention between language learning and mathematics learning is frustrating to both teachers and students. This may well explain why the Ghanaian basic school teachers give up on teaching word problems. The first author asked the following poignant question: "How do you teach word problems effectively to students in English, a majority or all of whom are deficient in that language?" A fitting answer to that question is that the mathematics teacher also has to assume the role of a teacher of English. He or she has to combine the teaching of mathematics with the teaching of English. This role, we have to admit, would be very difficult for most mathematics teachers to assume.

According to Schleppegrell (2007), language and learning school mathematics cannot be separated from each other, and that language proficiency is needed to learn and make sense of mathematics. Research has shown that poor language proficiency, especially reading, can impede ELLs mathematics learning; hence, their attainment of mathematical proficiency. For instance, Parker et al. (2009) maintained the position that English language proficiency in reading and writing scores are significant predicators of scores on mathematics assessment for 5th and 8th grade ELLs. This view is consistent with those researchers who posited that the mathematics performance of ELLs increases as their reading proficiency in English also increases (Abedi & Lord, 2001; Beal et al., 2010; Larwin, 2010). These researchers share the common view that reading proficiency of ELLs is a strong predictor of mathematical achievement, particularly problem-solving.

In spite of the overwhelming research evidence that English proficiency is needed to attain mathematical proficiency, Manu (2005) has challenged this empirical assertion. Researching in the context of mathematics teaching and learning through English in the nation-state of Tonga, Manu (2005) argued that there is a difference between inadequate mathematical understanding and inadequate language understanding. He went on to say that students' mathematical understanding and development of mathematical proficient depends significantly on the images students are able to associate in their first or indigenous language. He added that by switching languages in the process of doing mathematics Tongan students are able to perform as much as their monolingual English speakers.

We do not doubt the veracity of switching languages during mathematics in order to make sense of what an ELL is learning; for we have done it many times before during the learning of mathematics in our elementary and secondary school days. Nevertheless, is it an efficient way of learning mathematics? How long does it take for one to make the switch from English to Tonga or from English to Akan[10] in the process of making sense of a specific mathematics concept? Obviously, native English speakers who do not have to make any switches have a great cognitive advantage over Tongan students learning mathematics. In addition, Manu (2005) stated that the understanding of mathematics is conditioned on the images the students are able to link to their first language. Thus, for understanding of mathematics to occur, Tongan students or any ELLs have to first create images about the mathematics concept or problem and, second, link them to their first or home language. What about if the student is unable to create such images? What about if they create the wrong images? The consequences, we venture to say, would be terrible for the student. We believe that overburdening ELLs with switching between languages and creating images are unnecessary for them to learn mathematics proficiently. If the first or home language is good enough as a medium of sense-making, why is it that students are not taught mathematics in their own Tonga language? It is for this reason that we argue that the development of basic school students' mathematical proficiency would be hampered if they are taught mathematics continuously in English.

Moreover, it is tempting to confuse the Ghanaian basic students' low mathematical problem-solving ability with mathematics learning abilities as it has happened to immigrant children to the United States (Salend & Salinas, 2003). That to say, the linguistic factor in mathematics learning has made it almost impossible to assess the true mathematical learning abilities of basic school students in Ghana. That is one of the reasons we have argued that the mathematical proficiency of these students would be hampered if they are taught and learned mathematics through English language.

To help students to attain mathematical proficiency, some Ghanaian mathematics teachers switch code – they change from English to the indigenous languages of the students. The second author offered the following reflection:

> I have used code-switching to the home language of students countless times when I was teaching junior secondary school students in Ghana. And I have found it to be an effective tool to teach and to help students to learn mathematics much more effectively. I used code-switching in one-on-one

tutoring of students who were having difficulties in understanding or making sense of mathematics problems I taught in class. I also used it to teach mathematics concepts and associated problem-solving that I thought the students would find difficult to make sense of. In addition, I found code-switching extremely useful for linking mathematics to the students' life-world or cultural communities. I did this linking easily because I did not have to make any translations from the student home language to English ... communication flew naturally for me. For this reason, I must say that code-switching is not only for the benefit of the students; the teacher also benefits because it made teaching easier.

Research has consistently demonstrated that using African languages in the mathematics classroom enrich students' understanding of mathematical concepts and problem-solving (Adler, 1998; Ampah-Mensah, 2009; Nicol, 2005; Matang, 2006; Setati, 1998, 2002, 2005a; Setati & Adler, 2001; Setati & Barwell, 2006; Whale, 2012). In Malaysia, too, researchers have found that some teachers have been code-switching from English to Malay despite a government policy that made it mandatory to teach science, mathematics, and technology exclusively through English[11] (Lan & Tan, 2008). Thus, instead of Ghanaian indigenous languages being banned in the mathematics classroom, they should be used as the LOLT; indeed, it is a valuable cultural capital that allows students to learn and teachers to teach mathematics more efficiently and effectively. Students use their mother tongue for three fundamental functions: sense-making, understanding of new ideas, and participation in conceptual discourses in the classroom (Setati, 1998, 2005; Setati & Adler, 2001). As a matter of fact, the use of students' home language helps them significantly to integrate known to the unknown mathematically, possibly leading to internalization of mathematical concepts and procedures. It also allows students to internalize and personalize mathematical ideas and apply them in various cultural contexts (Feza-Piyose, 2012). We found during our reflections that students are able to connect mathematics to their cultural or indigenous communities when the LOLT is their home language.

MATHEMATICS CLASSROOM PARTICIPATION

In the mathematics classroom, teachers must create opportunities for students to participate in mathematical discourses (Boulet, 2007). Participation would allow students to seek clarification of mathematical concepts, learn from their peers, and for the teacher to assess student understanding. Simply put, students' participation in the mathematics classroom assists them immensely to develop their mathematical proficiency. Nevertheless, the use of English as LOLT has the potential to stifle student participation even where the teacher is English proficient. In fact, the situation is terrible where English is a foreign language to both the teacher and student as it is the case in Ghana. The teachers tend to adopt teacher-centred teaching strategies:

Classroom observation studies conducted in several countries in Africa (Benin Botswana, Burkina Faso, Ethiopia, Ghana, Guinea-Bissau, Mali, Mozambique, Niger, South Africa, Tanzania, and Togo) reveal that the use of unfamiliar languages forces teachers to use traditional and teacher-centred teaching methods. Teachers do most of the talking while children remain silent or passive participants during most of the classroom interactions. Because children do not speak the language of instruction, teachers are also forced to use traditional teaching techniques such as chorus teaching, repetition, memorization, recall, code-switching, and safe talk. (Alidou & Brock-Utne, 2011, p. 160)

While we agree to the import of the authors' narrative quoted above, we have to make little comment on memorization. Memorization in mathematics education has for the most part received negative connotations. Yet as Knight (1997) has stressed, "Memory does have a part to play in thinking, in reasoning, in explaining, and in justifying. In our anxiety to avoid the dangers of rote learning, we have, we believe, forgotten the essential role that memory plays in all cognitive activity "{including mathematics}" (p. 2). Indeed, memorization and recall sometimes play a significant role in mathematics learning by aiding imagination, which makes our sensory experience meaningful through interpretation and sense-making (Thomas, 2004). Memorization and recall allows some students to reflect over and over again on their mathematics learning and infuse it into their life experiences. Nonetheless, it is very worrying when mathematics learning becomes merely memorization activities or memorization is seen as an end in itself (Kennedy, 2002).

Similarly, repetition of practice in mathematics learning may also be necessary in some situations to enable students to gain competence in a procedure before the students could understand the mathematical concepts underlining the practice (Leung & Park, 2002). Cases in point are the multiplication and metric system tables. Moreover, a recent research report indicates that the speed at which mathematical facts are recalled, is a predictor of one's performance on standardized tests, mathematical problems, word problems, data interpretation, and mathematical reasoning activities, as well (Cholmsky, 2011). We want to emphasize that mathematics teaching does not necessarily follow a linear process or prescription; one approach does not always work effectively for all mathematics topics or concepts. It is a grave error if mathematics teaching or learning is entirely and consistently based on chorus repetition and memorization by a class of students.

It may be argued that Ghanaian mathematics teachers use teacher-centred teaching techniques because of their desire to maintain autocratic control over their classrooms, rather than to shield their English language limitations or those of their students. However the first author made the following observation:

It may be true that some teachers desire autocratic control of their classrooms. But why is it that all these autocratic teachers always ask their students the following question at the end of math lessons: Do you understand? Normally, when this question is asked, the students are silent and

147

look at the teacher or each other. The students may have questions, suggestions, or comments to make but they lack the English proficiency to do so. There are some teachers who will not ask such a broad question like, "Do you understand?" Instead, they will ask specific questions like these to encourage discussion or discourse: Explain how we got to this part of the procedure or how we obtained this answer? What is the difference between the previous mathematical question and this one (pointing to the chalkboard)? Yet students still sit down and say nothing! Why? I believe there would be lots of responses if the students were to ask those questions in their home language .... Some teachers used a more aggressive method by calling on individual students – they are put on the spot in a military fashion – to answer specific math questions as a means of encouraging participation. They sometimes yelled and insulted students as dumb, though these students have some ideas but lack general English proficiency to express themselves.

The above reflection is in line with Brock and Alidou's (2011) review of the literature on general student participation in classrooms across Africa. They noted that generally, students' lack of proficiency in the LOLT precludes them from effective participation in classroom discourses, which certainly includes the mathematics classrooms. According to these researchers, African teachers view this lack of proficiency as an indication of laziness, stupidity, and uncooperative attitude on the part of the students. They added that this teacher attitude stifles student motivation to participate in classroom discourses, especially among girl students, who are normally shy and easily hurt emotionally with words. The second author noted:

when students are put on the spot to answer mathematics questions in English and are derided as dumb or shouted at for not being able to do so, it psychologically discourages them from mathematics learning; they begin to have fears for mathematics learning; They begin to doubt their ability to do mathematics. The consequences are much worse when the teacher metes out corporal punishment to students who refuse to participate in classroom discourses or give wrong responses. Such draconian measures used to force students to participate in classroom discourses through English have bad consequences for mathematics education in Ghana. It has attracted only a few disciples for the discipline, so to speak .... These student-victims are invariably part of those who habitually skip math classes or fail mathematics courses .... The situation would be totally different if students were invited to participate in mathematics classroom discourses in their indigenous language.

We believe that students in those situations are less likely to develop any positive mathematical identities, which are shaped by factors such as culture, learning preferences, and experiences with mathematics learning (Berry, 2003). Martin (2007) referred to mathematical identity as one's belief about:
a) their ability to do mathematics;
b) the significance of mathematical knowledge;

c) the opportunities and barriers to enter mathematical field; and

d) the motivation and persistence needed to obtain mathematical knowledge (p. 19).

A majority of students in basic schools in Ghana do not develop a positive attitude toward mathematics, due in part to their negative experiences with mathematics learning in basic schools. As Awanta (2009) indicated, students in basic schools show remarkable interest in how mathematical formulas came about rather than how to use them to solve problems. However, who will help to illustrate or explain that to them? Awanta (2009) went on to say that students in basic schools, particularly junior high school (JHS), demonstrate interest in mathematics, but such interest drops substantially as they enter senior secondary school (SHS). In fact, the development of a positive mathematical identity, one of the strands of mathematical proficiency, is important for students to sustain their interest in mathematics education through the school grades to tertiary educational institutions.

It is possible that teacher conceptions of the nature of mathematics are a motivational force for maintaining or adopting teacher-centred pedagogy. A sterling example is a conception of mathematics as a fixed and sequential body of knowledge that is learnt by rote, algorithmic, and repetitive procedures (Wilcox et al., 1992). The other example is mathematics as a body of absolute truths which exist separate from the learner or as a toolkit of rules, formulas, and procedures that are used to attain specific purposes (Mayers, 1994). We wonder if these conceptions of mathematics will influence a teacher to ask students questions or prevent students to ask questions. It is probably true that if students are not getting what they perceived as satisfactory responses to their questions, they will not be encouraged to ask questions.

From our perspectives, most Ghanaian basic school teachers adopt the traditional, teacher-centred teaching methods as a cover-up for their own lack of proficiency in the English language rather than their subject-matter knowledge. Mereku's (2003) research demonstrated that 83% of Ghanaian primary school teachers surveyed admitted that they never gave meaningful answers to their students' questions in the mathematics classroom, and about 79% of them used teaching methods that do not promote discussion. More recently, a majority of students in basic schools (junior secondary) reported that their mathematics teachers used teacher-centred strategies that promoted passivity on the part of the students (Ampadu, 2012). Certainly, the teacher-centred pedagogy includes safe-talk as Alidou and Brock-Utne (2011) have identified – structuring mathematics teaching in such a way that it leaves no room for discussion, debate, or questions. It also includes dictating notes to the students to write and copying volumes of notes from the chalkboard, even where the students have access to approved textbooks. Why would teachers promote discussion in the mathematics classroom when they, like their students, struggle with the English language (Brock-Utne, 2005)? Naroth (2010) stated that teachers in South Africa revealed that they limit discussion in the mathematics classroom due to student English language limitations. Therefore, both teachers' and students' lack of English proficiency, negatively affects the development of the students' mathematics proficiency.

Nevertheless, based on Brock-Utne and Alidou's (2011) review of the literature, teachers allowed more discussion and are more confident in their teaching abilities when they use familiar or home language of the students as a LOLT. On the part of the students, when the LOLT is their home language they are more active, confident, and comfortable participating in classroom discourses and other learning activities as the second author stated in his reflection. Moschkovich (2002) made the same observations with Spanish speakers in the United States. That is why we are arguing that using English language as the LOLT in basic schools in Ghana would hamper the students' development of mathematical proficiency. Both teacher and student need to use a language they are comfortable with, so that they can express their thoughts, feelings, and cultural elements in the mathematics classroom without fear, shame, or humiliation.

STUDENT CULTURE AND MATHEMATICS LEARNING

In the previous subsections, we argued that the development of basic school students' mathematical proficiency requires that the LOLT should be their home language. The use of student s' home language has a higher probability of opening up opportunities for incorporating elements of their community mathematics culture[12] into school mathematics. Such incorporation is extremely important for developing basic school students' mathematical proficiency. The first author offered the following insight:

> Infusing the mathematics classroom with students' mathematics culture has the purpose of eliminating the gap between students' home mathematics practices and those of the school. Home mathematics practices use different procedures; they are unwritten; and do not use symbols. But incorporating them into the classroom practice could help students to make a smooth transition into school mathematics and develop positive attitude toward mathematics … students immediately realize that mathematics is part of their culture rather than being separate from it and that one does not need the brains of an elephant, so to say, to engage in it and enjoy it. In problem-solving, the first rule of thumb is that students must be interested in the problems they are asked to solve. So if problems are from students' culture, they would be motivated to commit more effort because problems would be those that are relevant to them emotionally, intellectually, and culturally.

This quote is consistent with that of Polya (1962), a passionate advocate of problem-solving pedagogy, who stated that students should cognitively and emotionally own the problems they are asked to solve before they would have the desire to solve them. As Wilson (1992) observed, a good deal of the education of African children and adolescents occurs "around the village, in the market, among peers, and while watching adults perform traditional tasks or hunt or make music or exercise skills in one of Africans' many crafts. Schools on much of the continent derived from the West, and came as a package complete with Western-styled curricula, books, examinations, and often Western language" (p. 126). Thus, mathematical concepts and problem-solving activities should be related to those sources where Ghanaian children and adolescents receive their prime socialization. But this is difficult to occur smoothly unless basic school's LOLT is a Ghanaian language.

Researchers agreed that the socio-cultural environment in which children and adolescents are parented and socialized into the world have influences on their development of pre-school number concepts and problem-solving strategies (Allardice & Ginsberg, 1982); Charbonneau & John-Steiner, 1988). Students bring these understandings and meanings of mathematical concepts, measurement, and procedures into the mathematics classroom and use them to conceptualize mathematics they are taught (Abreu et al., 2002; Fleer & Robins, 2005). These mathematical understandings and meanings should be utilized and made the starting point of mathematics education in basic schools (Wilson, 1992; Gerdes, 2008). Second, the incorporation of student mathematics culture into the school mathematics classroom would facilitate the transfer of knowledge acquired in the classroom to problem-solving in different situations in the student community (Carraher & Carraher, 1984). We view as a travesty of mathematics, education that begins at the door of the classroom and ends at the same door when the students leave for their homes. Is mathematics only practiced in and relevant to school? No, we do not think so!

Further, we believe that incorporating students' mathematics culture into mathematics education would help them to make sense of the mathematics they learn at basic school, especially in their early formation of mathematical concepts (Okpoti, 2001). Sense-making has to do with developing understanding of mathematical concepts, principles, or procedures by connecting them to existing knowledge or previous experiences. Students make sense of mathematical concepts and procedures by constructing their own meanings through a combination of personal experiences and cultural traditions (Pirie, 1998). Furthermore, children and adolescents are most likely to participate actively in mathematics activities familiar to them and the result is that they could easily acquire new mathematics skills and concepts (Okpoti, 2001). The author added that Ghanaian parents and the society as a whole, whose participation in their children's mathematics education has been marginalized and alienated as a result of the mystification of school mathematics, could have opportunities to contribute.

Invariably, when basic school students in Ghana learn and are taught mathematics through English, their mathematics culture is ignored and this severely affects their mathematical proficiency development. The students only learn the colonial language of English without learning the culture that goes with that language. The full participation in any culture includes its language and the culture the language represents (Gollnick & Chinn, 2006). It is almost impossible for students in Ghana to participate in an English culture in any form. This is why Ghanaian language should be used as the LOLT, so that students could relate what they learn to their past experiences, apply it to their lives, and make what they learn part of themselves (Chickering & Gramson, 1987). From our reflections, student mathematics culture in Ghana consists of how the larger society conceptualizes quantity, measurement, design, navigation, and rationalization in various activities (Bishop, 2004). They include the following:

1) sorting and grouping farm produce into subsets based on size, shape, and shades of colour;
2) counting and multiplying in sets of 2s, 3s, 4s, 10s, 20s, etc; doubling and halving for addition and multiplication;
3) subtracting without borrowing[13];
4) measurement based on volume[14] rather than mass; for example, using containers of different sizes to measure gari, beans, rice, cassava flour, corn flour, palm nuts, palm nut oil, palm kernel oil, peanut oil, etc;
5) traditional[15] games such as oware, ampeh and atotomma that are played in almost all regions in Ghana;
6) farm[16] and land navigation, including dividing up land or farms for sale or inheritance; travelling from one location to another;
7) traditional procedures for determining the mass of pieces of gold and diamond;
8) drawing of various geometric shapes embedded in rattles and shakers worn around hands, wrists, and legs of traditional dancers; baskets, wooden stools; houses of different shapes: cone, square, rectangle, etc; and
9) designing artifacts such as basket weaving, sewing, palanquins, boats, housing construction, wooden sculptures, etc.

These valuable areas and practices of student mathematics culture are significant for mathematical education research in Ghana. As Zevenbergen (2008) stated in reference to Australian Aboriginal peoples, "It would help to identify the mathematics in cultural activities in order to provide legitimation of those activities, so as to illustrate the indigenous people are capable of undertaking the mathematics of school activities" (p. 510). While we are not sure of the mathematical or quantitative methods used in all the activities in the student mathematical culture listed above, we are very sure that some of them, such as subtracting without regrouping, counting in blocks; adding and multiplying using doubling and halving; measuring quantities using metal, plastic, and gourd containers, could be used to develop many cognitively intriguing but mathematically challenging activities for basic school students.

A basket weaver, for example, starts with making a perfect circle as the bottom part of the basket. A perfect circle has equal radii from the centre to any point on the circumference. How do basket weavers get almost proportional circles? How do they determine the centre of the circle? Sometimes the bottom part of the basket is made up of concentric circles – series of circles with a common centre. While the radius is different for each circle forming the concentric circles, how does the weaver ensure that the distance between each circle is equal or almost equal? Concentric circles are a fascinating pattern in that they are found in many other Ghanaian artifacts such as textiles (patterns in kente and smock), footwear, and pottery products. They show the relationship between mathematics and art. Okpoti (2001) also observed that the "oware game" played in almost every region of

Ghana, involves domains of counting, ordinal, base four, probability, and grouping; ampeh game also entails counting, ordinal, base four, probability, and sequencing; while atotomma game is an excellent source of learning and teaching counting, ordinal numbers, area, and geometric shapes (examples are square, rectangle, rhombus, and circle). Certainly, this is a subject of another book chapter or journal article. It is a viable area of research for those who want to improve mathematics teaching and learning in Ghana and the rest of Africa

As well, we believe that embedding mathematics teaching and learning in the rich geometric cultural practices of student communities such as basket, mat, cloth, and hat-weaving, have been noted as a means of galvanizing student interest, enthusiasm, and self-confidence in mathematics learning (Gerdes, 2008). Ghanaian society, like their counterparts in other parts of Africa, has developed sophisticated geometric concepts that should be part of the mathematics curriculum and of teaching practices in basic schools (Gerdes, 2003). This is only possible if such geometric sources are made part of teacher knowledge of the subject matter of mathematics and of students.

We noted that student mathematics culture is termed ethnomathematics or mathematics of other cultural groups or non-western societies in the research literature (D'Ambrosio, 1985, 1999; Yusuf et al., 2010). The prefix "ethno" is referred to identifiable cultural groups such as national tribal societies, professional classes and labour groups; while "mathema" means explanation, understanding and management of realities by counting, measuring, classifying, ordering, and modeling patterns arising from one's cultural environment (Yusuf et al., 2010). While we share the majority of the ideas of ethnomathematics, we are apprehensive about the use of that label to describe student mathematics culture. First, it is acknowledged that mathematics is universal; that is, every society has a conception of quantity, and the understanding of the relationships between quantities and space (Burton, 1998; Hammond, 2000). However, Burton (1999) reminded us that approaches to thinking about quantity, relationships, and space vary between cultural groups.

According to Devlin (1994), mathematics is now widely accepted as the study of patterns: real or imagined, visual or mental, stemming from within the human mind or the natural environment. Visual and mental patterns are embedded in student mathematics culture. Why should their mathematical ideas and practices carry the label alternative mathematics or ethnomathematics? From our perspective, it should not be called alternative mathematics; it is just as mathematics as any other! Nevertheless, the mathematics methods and practices of non Euro-American societies have been criticized as nonmathematical. Rowlands and Carson (2000) in an end note to their article wrote: "Any practice may be described mathematically, but that does not mean to say that practice is mathematical. For example, laying the dinner table may be described as a mapping of 1 plate, 1 knife etc. with each tablemat, but laying the table is not a mathematical activity" (p. 90)! Does mathematical activity always involve calculation or handling of numbers or both? Does it involve logical decision-making or direction-making using numbers? We find the authors' statement a big leap because they did not describe what constitutes a mathematical activity. Accordingly, we found Hammond's (2000) critique instructive here and an indirect response to Rowlands and Carson's (2000) statement:

> Other cultures, although they do have the ideas or concepts that we deem as mathematical, do not distinguish them and classify them together as we do. The definitions of mathematics are based solely on the Western experience, even though they are often phrased universally. Even within the Western culture, the definition of mathematics can become confused and is generally defined to include whatever the Western professional class called mathematics or what their mathematicians do (p. 14).

Again, Rowlands and Carson (2000) in their comment on poverty and material deprivation in developing countries, stated: "Ethnomathematics runs the risk of maintaining the status-quo through the glorification of the knowledge that already exists rather than transforming knowledge to the level that has been utilized in that domination" (p. 89). We believe that when the student mathematics culture is made part of the national mathematics curriculum of basic school in Ghana, and when teacher knowledge of the subject matter and mathematics practices in the classroom is emphasized, the teaching of mathematics will be transformed. We recognize that mathematical ideas and practices evolve over time when humans make conscious efforts through research and other forms of intervention to develop them. For this reason, we reject the widespread belief that mathematical knowledge is neutral, value-free, objective, and completely detached from people who either created or use it (Bishop, 1990; Izmirli, 2011). Therefore, no matter how we view mathematical knowledge – theoretical, practical, logical, philosophical, or historical – the fact remains that it is created by humans in the context of culture, and it involves counting, locating, measuring, designing, playing, and explaining (Bishop, 2004; Izmirli, 2011).

CONCLUSION

In this chapter, our primary objective is to answer this question: How does the learning of mathematics in a colonial language[17] (English, French, Portuguese, etc.) at the basic school level help or hamper students' development of mathematical proficiency? Using Ghanaian basic school students as our case study, we found that learning mathematics through the English language hinders the development of mathematics proficiency of these students. These students encounter tremendous difficulties expressing their thoughts on mathematics concepts through English, engaging in mathematical problem-solving, participating in discourses in the mathematics classroom and, on top of that, they are unable to bring their home or community mathematics practices and ideas into the classroom. Unfortunately, researchers and scholars on the African continent have paid little to no attention to the language factors in all facets of mathematics teaching, learning, and assessment.

We acknowledge that learning and teaching mathematics in any language entails a range of difficulties even when both teacher and student are proficient in that language. The situation is more serious in basic schools in Ghana where both the teacher and student are not fluent in the English language used as LOLT. In this case, the teachers tend to use more teacher-centred teaching strategies while the students are passive receptacles of mathematical knowledge and skills transmitted to them. In fact, student mathematical proficiency is undeveloped when they merely parrot mathematical knowledge that they do not understand and found irrelevant to either their life world or that of their communities. Consequently, our conclusion is that it is a massive hindrance psychologically, sociologically, and educationally for basic school students in Ghana to learn mathematics through the English language. Our position differs from other researchers and scholars, who acknowledge the value of students' home language for enriching their mathematics learning, but do not advocate replacing the colonial language with an African language as LOLT. They want mathematics teachers to switch-code or use African language as supplemental LOLT where necessary. Most South African researchers and scholars of LOLT mathematics belong to this group.

Basic school students in Ghana need to develop their mathematical proficiency for personal, career, and humanistic purposes. Personally, mathematics education should help basic school students to develop mathematical concepts and skills for solving a variety of everyday problems in their own society and natural environment. In terms of career development, mathematics education should provide students a solid foundation on which to build a range of specialized skills and knowledge for their future career pathways. Humanistically, mathematics education should assist students to understand that mathematics is part of their cultural heritage, in so far as counting, measuring, designing, playing, and explaining are part of every culture. However, we found that in Ghana, basic school students are unable to develop mathematical proficiency when the LOLT is the English language. This finding is equally applicable to other African students on the continent who are forced to learn mathematics through other colonial languages rather than their own.

Nevertheless, some people may argue that lack of textbooks and teaching resources are to be blamed for the inability of basic school students to develop their mathematical proficiency, rather than language limitations. Of course, as a developing country Ghana has problems of inadequate funds and bureaucratic ineffectiveness to ensure that its basic schools are well-supplied with appropriate mathematics textbooks and teacher resources. But our position is that when the LOLT is a Ghanaian language or the home language of the students learning and teaching, resources should not be critical problems for mathematics education in Ghanaian basic schools. On the contrary, teacher knowledge, which as we have indicated should include student home language and student mathematics culture, is the critical factor for the development of student mathematical proficiency.

Admittedly, teacher mathematics subject knowledge depends significantly on the development of an appropriate mathematics register in Ghanaian languages. Though Ghanaian languages have been offered at the undergraduate and graduate levels in premier universities in Ghana, mathematics registers in Ghanaian languages are yet to be developed. For instance, the University of Ghana, Legon, and the University of Cape Coast, Cape Coast, offer graduate degree programs in Akan (Twi and Fante), Ga, and Ewe. In addition, the University of Education, Winneba, offers undergraduate programs in Akan (Twi and Fante), Ewe, Nzema, Ga, Ga-Adamgbe, Gonja, Dagaare, Dagbani, Kasem, and Gurune. As far back as the 1930s, Twi, Fante, Ga, and Ewe were General Certificate Ordinary Level (GCE 'O' Level) examination subjects and were counted towards exemption from the matriculation examination of the University of London (Owu-Ewie, 2006).

It may also be argued that mathematics anxiety, not the foreign LOLT, is what contributes to undeveloped mathematical proficiency of basic school students. Undeniably, mathematics anxiety or phobia as the state of emotional discomfort with mathematics learning contributes to the difficulties in developing mathematical proficiency. Mathematics anxiety could stifle the motivation or interest a student would otherwise have for learning mathematics. Such a student hates mathematics and anything associated with it. But once the language factor is unresolved, it is hard to say with any degree of certainty that it does not itself contribute to mathematics anxiety for many basic school students. That is, the language factor could constitute a great source of mathematics anxiety for basic school students in Ghana.

Finally, another group of Ghanaians or Africans may accuse us of impatience. For them, basic school students need sufficient time to acquire the elements of English proficiency necessary for them to learn mathematics effectively and efficiently. Their caution is based on the premise that when one uses a language over and over for a reasonable length of time, one eventually attains proficiency in that language. The problem we have with this theory is that mathematics education does not have the patience to wait for students with linguistic weaknesses. Sooner or later it squeezes these students out psychologically or physically. Psychologically, these students would stay in mathematics classes just to get a pass or the required grade to move onto the next rung of the education ladder, without developing any emotional or romantic attachment to mathematics, but harboring a simmering hatred for the subject. Physically, these students drop out of school completely harbouring a deep-seated revenge for mathematics and none for the English language. Eventually, these school drop-outs are seen engaged in farming, trading, sewing, carpentry, weaving, and masonry and begin to have an intimate relationship with mathematics. They are those most likely to warn their children or offspring to stay off the tracks of school mathematics, adding them on to the population of "math-phobians" in Ghana and other African countries.

NOTES

[1] We used colonial language, Euro-colonial language and foreign language to mean the same thing. That is, languages which are not the indigenous languages of the countries where they have been adopted as official/national language and LOLT.

156

[2] Recently, some FM radio stations have designed programming in Akan and other Ghanaian languages. Ghana Broadcasting Corporation (GBC), the state-owned news media, has also had news programming in Akan, Ewe, Ga, Hausa and Nzima for more than four decades.

[3] In accordance with Setati (2005), we preferred to use language of learning and teaching (LOLT) rather than medium of instruction or language of instruction. It reflects realistically what goes on in the schools. That is because students are required to use the language of teaching to learn; the textbooks and other classroom materials used in schools are written in the language of teaching as well as examination papers and answers that students are expected to provide. LOLT is a much clearer indication of what happens in Ghana's schools than of other terms or labels.

[4] Private elementary and junior high schools are owned and funded by private business people through tuition charges. Some of them, particularly those in the Ghanaian capital city, charge U.S dollars for tuition. Private schools are called different names such as international schools, experimental schools, and preparatory schools. Most of the students are from economically well-to-do parents/guardians.

[5] Basic school is used here to refer to students in the first 9 years of schooling (primary one to junior high school form three).

[6] We used continental Africans to denote Africans who were socialized in the indigenous language or culture (or both) of the continent. They are distinguished from Africans in the Diaspora in the United States, Europe, South America, and the Caribbean. We admit that the distinction between the two groups in some cases is not a clear-cut.

[7] We will use second language and additional language interchangeably.

[8] Language proficiency or linguistic proficiency is viewed in terms of four discrete macro skills: reading, writing, speaking and listening.

[9] We prefer the term English Language Learners (ELL) to English as a second language (ESL). The reason is that in the context of Ghana, English may be third or even fourth language to some students.

[10] Akan is one of the major linguistic groups in Ghana.

[11] The Malaysian government has reversed the policy that required teachers to teach science and technology exclusively through English.

[12] We used student mathematics culture synonymously with community mathematics culture.

[13] Subtracting by borrowing is a typical approach to numeracy in elementary schools in Ghana. But it is a stumbling block to numeracy development in lower elementary grades. People in the Ghanaian marketplace do subtraction calculations conveniently without borrowing.

[14] In school, mathematics volume is distinguished from mass, as it is in traditional activities. Mass is measured by weighing an object along with an object of known mass on a scale. Volume is a measurement of the space that an object occupies. The measurement is done by using containers of known or predictable volume. In the Ghanaian market place, volume is the dominant measurement of most farm produce and foodstuffs.

[15] We are using the word "traditional" to imply games or activities that are indigenous to Ghana or the African continent.

[16] Traditionally, how could a cocoa, coffee, or maize farmer know that his/her farm is bigger than that of another farmer? Is the total yield of the two farms a determining factor or how long it takes to harvest or cultivate each farm? In addition to measurement of volume using containers or jute bags, how is quantity determined for the purpose of comparison?

[17] We used colonial language, Euro-colonial language, and foreign language to mean the same thing. That is, languages which are not the indigenous languages of the countries where they have been adopted as official/national language and LOLT.

REFERENCES

Abedi, J., & Lord, C. (2001). The language factor in mathematics tests. *Applied Measurement in Education, 14*(3), 219-234.

Adetunde, I. A. (2007). Improving the teaching and learning of mathematics in second cycle institutions in Ghana. *Pakistan Journal of Social Sciences, 4*(31), 340-344.

Adetunde, I. A. (2009). Improving the teaching and learning of mathematics in second cycle institutions in Ghana (paper 2). *Report and Opinion, 1*(3), 33-35.

Adetunde, I. A., Oladejo, N. K., & Asare, B. (2010). Analysis of the performance of second-cycle students in core mathematics in Kassena-Nankana and Asuogyaman districts of Ghana. *European Journal of Social Science, 13*(1), 7-12.

Adler, J. (1998). A language of teaching dilemmas: Unlocking the complex multilingual secondary mathematics classroom. *For the Learning of Mathematics, 18*, 24-33.

Alidou, H., & Brock-Utne, B. (2011). Teaching practices – Teaching in a familiar language. In A. Ouane & C. Glanz (Eds.), *Optimizing learning: Education and publishing in Africa: The language factor* (pp. 159-184). Hamburg, Germany: UNESCO Institute of Lifelong Learning.

Allan, M. (2011). *Thought, word and deed: The roles of cognition, language and culture in teaching and learning in IB schools.* Genève, Switzerland: International Baccalaureate Organization.

Allardice, B., & Ginsberg, H. (1982). Children's psychological difficulties in mathematics. In H. Ginsberg (Ed.), *The development of mathematical thinking* (pp. 319-350). New York: Academic Press Inc.

Ampadu, E. (2012). Students' perceptions of their teachers' teaching of mathematics: The case of Ghana. *International Online Journal of Educational Sciences, 4*(2), 351-358.

Ampah-Mensah, A. (2009). Teachers' use of language in teaching mathematics in basic schools in Cape Coast, Ghana. In M. Joubert (Ed.), *Proceedings of British Society for Research into Learning Mathematics.* Bristol University, June 19-20th.

Ampiah, J. G. (2008). An investigation of provision of quality basic education in Ghana: A case study of selected schools in the Central Region. *CICE Hiroshima University. Journal of International Cooperation in Education, 11*(3), 19-37.

Ampiah, J. G. (2010). *Quality basic education in Ghana: Prescription, praxis and problems.* Paper presented at the Experience Sharing Seminar, Accra, Ghana, January 17-19.

An, S., Kulm, G., & Wu, Z. (2004). The pedagogical content knowledge of middle school, mathematics teachers in China and the U.S. *Journal of Mathematics Teacher Education, 7*, 145-172.

Anamuah-Mensah, J., & Mereku (2005). Ghanaian JSS2 students' abysmal mathematics achievement in TIMSS-2003: A consequence of the basic school mathematics curriculum. *Mathematics Connection, 5*, 1-13.

Anstrom, K. (1997). *Academic achievement for secondary language minority: Standards, measures and promising practice.* Accessed from http://www.ncela.gwu,edu/pubs/reports/acadach.htm

Awanta, E. K. (2009). Students' view of mathematics: A survey of junior and senior high schools in the Ashanti and Brong Ahafo regions. *Ghana Policy Journal, 3*, 90-109.

Bamgbose, A. (2007). Language and literacy issues in Africa. In N. Alexander & B. Busch (Eds.), *Literacy and linguistic diversity in a global perspective: Intercultural exchange with African countries* (pp. 23-30). Graz, Austria: European Centre for Modern Languages.

Barwell, R. (2010, May). Tension in teaching mathematics through a second language. *The American Council on Immersion Education (ACTE) Newsletter, 13*(3).

Beal, C. R., Adams, N. M., & Cohen, P. R. (2010). Reading proficiency and mathematics problem-solving by high school English language learners. *Urban Education, 45*(1), 58-74.

Berliner, D. C. (1994). Teacher expertise. In B. Moon & A. S. Mayes (Eds.), *Teaching and learning in the secondary school* (pp. 107-113). London: Rouledge.

Berry, R. Q. (2003). Mathematics standards, cultural styles and learning preferences: The plight and promise of African-American students. *Clearing House, 67*(5), 244-249.

Bishop, A. (1990). Western mathematics: The secret weapon of cultural imperialism. *Race & Class, 32*, 51-65.

Bishop, A. (2004). *The relationship between mathematics and culture.* Opening address delivered at the Iranian Mathematics Education Conference in Kermanshah, Iran.

Bloom, P., & Keil, F. C. (2001). Thinking through language. *Mind & Language, 16*(4), 351-367.

Boroditsky, L. (2001). Does language shape thought? Mandarin and English speakers' conceptions of time. *Cognitive Psychology, 43*(1), 1-22.

Boud, D., Keogh, R., & Walker, D. (1985). *Reflection: Turning experience into learning.* London: Kogan Page.

Boulet, G. (2007). How does language impact the learning of mathematics? Let me count the ways. *Journal of Teaching and Learning, 5*(1), 1-12.

Brock-Utne, B. (2005). *Education-job no 1: What education, for whom? Reactions to policy paper: Education job no. 1.* Washington, DC: International Monetary Fund.

Brock-Utne, B., & Alidou, H. (2011). Teaching practices – Teaching in a familiar language. In A. Ouane & C. Glanz (Eds.), *Optimizing learning: Education and publishing in Africa: The language factor* (pp. 187-215). Hamburg, Germany: UNESCO Institute of Lifelong Learning.

Brodie, K (1989). Learning mathematics in a second language. *Educational Review, 41*(1), 35-39.

Burton, B. (1998). *Ethnomathematics and philosophy.* Paper presented at the First International Conference on Ethnomathematics: International Study Group on Ethnomathematics. Granada, Spain September 2-5.

Burton, B. (1999). Ethnomathematics: A political playing. *For the Learning of Mathematics, 19*(1), 32-35.

Carraher, D. W., Carraher, T. N., & Schliemann, A. (1984). Having a fee for calculations. In P. Damerow, M. E. Dunkley, B. F. Nebres, & B. Werry (Eds.), *Mathematics for all* (pp. 87-89). Reports and papers presented in Theme Group 1, Mathematics for All at the 5th International Congress on Mathematics Education. Adelaide, Australia, August 24-29.

Charbonneau, M., & John-Steiner, V. (1988). Patterns of experience and the language of mathematics. In R. R. Cocking & J. P. Mestre (Eds.), *Linguistic and cultural influences on learning mathematics: The psychology of education and instruction* (pp. 91-100). Hillsdale, NJ: Lawrence and Erlbaum Associates Inc.

Chickering, A. W., & Gamson, Z. F. (1987). Seven good principles of good practice in undergraduate education. *American Association of Higher Education (AHE) Bulletin, 39*, 3-7.

Cholmsky, P. (2011, March). *From acquisition to automaticity: The reflex solution for math fact mastery.* Charlottesville, VA. Retrieved from http://www.reflexmath.com

Christie, M. J. (1985). *Aboriginal perspectives on experience and learning: The role of language in Aboriginal education.* Victoria, Australia: Deakin University Press.

Cohen, L., & Manion, L. (1994). *Research methods in education* (4th ed.). London: Routledge.

Cole, P. M. (1994, Spring). Finding a path through the research maze. *The Qualitative Report, 2*(1). Retrieved November 28, 2012 from htt://www.nova.edu/ssss/QR/Backissues/QR2-1/cole.html

Connelly, M. F., & Clandinin, D. J. (1990). Stories of experience and narrative inquiry. *Educational Researcher, 19*(5), 2-14.

Creswell, J. W. (2008). *Narrative design in educational research: Planning, conducting and evaluating quantitative and qualitative research* (3rd ed.). Upper Saddle River, NI: Pearson Education Inc.

Cuevas, G. J. (1984). Mathematics learning in English as a second language. *Journal for Research in Mathematics Education, 15*(2), 134-144.

D'Ambrosio, U. (1985). Ethnomathematics and its place in the history and pedagogy of mathematics. *For the Learning of Mathematics, 5*(1), 44-48.

D'Ambrosio, U. (1999). Literacy, matheracy, and technoracy: A trivium for today. *Mathematical Thinking and Learning, 1*(2), 131-153.

de Abreu, G., Bishop, A. J., & Presmeg, N. (2002). Mathematics learners in transition. In G. de Abreu, A. Bishop, & N. Presmeg (Eds.), *Transitions between contexts of mathematical practices* (pp. 7-21). Dordrecht: Kluwer Academic Publications.

Devlin, K. (1994). *Mathematics: The science of patterns*. New York: Scientific American Library.

Dewey, J. (1933). *How we think*. Boston, MA: D. C. Heath.

Dick, B. (1992). *You want to do an action research thesis?* Interchange document, University of Queensland.

Dooley, L. M. (2002). Case study research and theory building. *Advances in Developing Human Resources, 4*(3), 3335-354.

Durkin, K., & Shire, B. (1991). Lexical ambiguity in mathematical contexts. In K. Durkin & B. Shire (Eds.), *Language in mathematical education: Research and practice* (pp. 71-84). Buckingham: Open University Press.

Dutcher, N. (2001). *Expanding educational opportunities in linguistically diverse societies*. Washington, DC: Center for Applied Linguistics.

Ellis, C. (1995). *Final negotiations: A story of love, loss and chronic illness*. Philadelphia: Temple University Press.

Ernst-Slavit, G., & Slavit, D. (2007a). Educational reform, mathematics, and English language learners: Meeting the needs of all students. *Multicultural Education, 14*(4), 20-27.

Ernst-Slavit, G., & Slavit, D. (2007b). Teaching mathematics and English to English learners simultaneously. *Middle School Journal, 39*(2), 4-11.

Eshun, B. A. (2000).Mathematics education today. *Mathematics Connection, 1*(1), 12-17.

Eubanks, P. (1991). Clinicians: Manage your move to manager. *Hospitals, 65*(5), 60.

Fennema, E., & Franke, M. (1992). Teachers' knowledge and its impact. In D. A. Grouws (Ed.), *Handbook of research in mathematics teaching and learning*. New York: Macmillan Publishing.

Fenstermacher, G. D. (1994). The knower and the known: The nature of knowledge on teaching. *Review of Research in Education, 20*, 3-56.

Ferreira, J.G (2011). Teaching life sciences to English second language learners: What do teachers do? *South African Journal of Education, 31*, 102-113.

Feza-Piyose, N. (2012). Language: A cultural capital for conceptualizing mathematics knowledge. *International Electronic Journal of Mathematics Education, 7*(2), 61-79.

Fleer, M., & Robins, J. (2005). "There is much more to this literacy and numeracy than you realise ...": Family enactment of literacy and numeracy versus educators' construction of learning in home contexts. *Journal of Australian Research in Early Childhood Education, 12*(1), 23-41.

Flores, A. (1997). "Si se puede," it can be done: Quality mathematics in more than one language. In J. Trentacosta & M. J. Kenney (Eds.), *Multicultural and gender equity in mathematics classrooms: The gift of diversity* (pp. 81-91). Reston: National Council of Teachers of Mathematics.

Fredua-Kwarteng, E., & Ahia, F. (2005). Ghana flunks at math and science: Analysis (2). Feature article. *Ghana News*, 23 February.

Gardner, I. (2001). *Non-traditional management education: The academic experience*. EdD Thesis. Melbourne. Australia: Monash University.

Garrison, L., & Mora, J. K. (1999). Adapting mathematics instruction for English language learners: The language-concept connections. In L. Ortiz-Franco, N. G. Hernandez, & Y. de la Cruz (Eds.), *Perspectives on Latinos (Changing the faces of mathematics)* (pp. 35-48). Reston, VA: National Council of Teachers.

Gerdes, P. (2003). *Awakening of geometrical thought in early culture*. Minneapolis: MEP Publications.

Gerdes, P. (2008). *Exploration of technologies, emerging from African cultural practices in mathematics education*. Centre for Mozambican Studies and Enoscience, Maputo, Mozambique: Universidade Pedagogica.

Greenwood, D., & Levin, M. (1998). *Introduction to action research: Social research for social change*. Thousand Oaks, CA: Sage.

Greenwood, J. (1994). Action research and action researchers: Some introductory considerations. *Contemporary Nurse, 3*, 84-92.

Gollnick, D., & Chinn, P. C. (2006). *Multicultural education in a pluralistic society*. Upper Saddle River, NJ: Pearson.

Gove, A., & P. Cvelich (2010). *Early reading: Igniting education for all*. A report by the Early Grade Learning Community of Practice. Research Triangle Park, NC: Research Triangle Institute.

Gutierrez, R. (2002). Enabling the practice of mathematics teachers in context: Toward a new equity research agenda. *Mathematics Thinking and Learning, 4*, 145-187.

Halmos, P. (1980). The heart of mathematics. *American Mathematical Monthly, 87*(7), 519-524.

Hammond, T. (2000). *Ethnomathematics: Concept definition and research perspectives*. Unpublished Master's Thesis. New York: Columbia University.

Hannabuss, S. (2000). Being there: Ethnographic research and autobiography. *Library Management, 21*(2), 99-106.

Hansen-Thomas, H. (2009). Reform-oriented mathematics in three 6th grade classes: How teachers draw in ELLs to academic discourse. *Journal of Language, Identity & Education, 8*(2), 88-106.

Izmirli, I. M (2011). Pedagogy on the ethnomathematics-epistemology nexus: A manifesto. *Journal of Humanistic Mathematics, 1*(2), 27-50.

Janzen, J. (2008). Teaching English language learners in the content areas. *Review of Educational Research, 78*(4), 1010-1038.

Jaworski, B. (1998). Mathematics teacher research: Process, practice and development of teaching. *Journal of Mathematics Teacher, 1*(1), 3-31.

Kennedy, P. (2002). Learning cultures and learning styles: myth-understandings about adult (HongKong) Chinese learners. *International Journal of Lifelong Education, 21*, 430-445.

Khisty, L. L. (2006). Language and mathematics: Toward social justice for linguistically diverse students. In J. Novotná, H. Moraová, M. Krátká, & N. Stehlíková (Eds.), *Proceedings of the 30th Conference of the International Group for the Psychology of Mathematics Education* (Vol. 3, pp. 433-440). Prague, CR: Charles University.

Khisty, L. L., & Chval, K. (2002). Pedagogic discourse and equity in mathematics: When teachers' talk matters. *Mathematics Education Research Journal, 14*, 154-168.

Kilpatrick, J., Swafford, J., & Findell, B. (2001). *Adding it up: Helping children learn mathematics*. Washington, D. C.: National Academy Press.

Knight, G. (1997). *I do and I understand, and then I forget. The role of memory in mathematics education*. Keynote address, Mathematics Education Research Group of Australasia (MERGA), New Zealand.

Lager, C. A. (2006). Types of mathematics-language reading interactions that unnecessarily hinder algebra learning and assessment. *Reading Psychology, 27*, 165-204.

Lan, O. S., & Tan, M. (2008). Mathematics and science in English: Teachers' experience inside the classroom. *Jurnal Pendidk dan Pendidkan Jil, 23*, 141-150.

Langa, M. (2006). *An investigation of learners' home language as a support for learning mathematics*. Unpublished Master's Dissertation. Johannesburg, South Africa: University of the Witwatersrand.

Larwin, K. H. (2010). Reading is fundamental in predicting math achievement in 10th graders. *International Electronic Journal of Mathematics Education, 5*(3), 131-145.

Lesh, R., & Zawojewski, J. (2007). Problem-solving and modeling. In F. Lester (Ed.), *Second handbook of research on mathematics teaching and learning* (pp. 763-804). Reston, VA: NCTM.

Leung, F., & Park, K. (2002). Competent students, competent teachers? *International Journal of Educational Research, 37*, 113-129.

Manu, S. S. (2005). Language switching and mathematical understanding in Tongan classrooms: An investigation. *Direction: Journal of Educational Studies, 27*(2), 47-70.

Martin, D. (2007). Beyond missionaries or cannibals: Who should teach mathematics to African American children? *The High School Journal, 91*(1), 5-28.

Mason, J. (2002). *Researching your own practice: The discipline of noticing*. New York: Falmer.

Matang, R. A. (2006). *Linking ethnomathematics, situated cognition, social constructivism and mathematics education: An example from Papua New Guinea*. ICME-3 Conference Paper, New Zealand.

Mayers, C. (1994). Mathematics and mathematics teaching: Changes in pre-service student teachers' beliefs and attitudes. In G. Bell, B. Wright, N. Leeson, & J. Geake (Eds.), Challenges in mathematics education: Constraints on construction (Vol. 2, pp. 419-428). Lismore: Mathematics Education Research Group of Australasia.

Mereku, K. (2003). Methods in Ghanaian primary mathematics textbooks and teachers' classroom practice. *Proceedings of the British Society for Research into Learning Mathematics, 23*(2), June, 61-66.

Mereku, K. D., Amedahe, F. K., & Etsey, K. (2005). *Opportunity to learn: English and mathematics.* Report of a study conducted on behalf of Ghana Education Service, Curriculum Research and Development Division (CRDD) to facilitate the Basic Education Comprehensive Assessment System (BECAS). June 27. Accessible at http:// http://www.equip123.net/docs/e2-OTL.pdf

Merriam, S. B. (2001). Andragogy and self-directed learning: Pillar of adult learning theory. *Directions for Adult and Continuing Education, 2*(89), 3-13.

Mestre, J. P. (1988). The role of language comprehension in mathematics and problem-solving. In R. R. Cocking & J. P. Mestre (Eds.), *Linguistic and cultural influences on learning mathematics: The psychology of education and instruction* (pp. 201-220). Hillsdale, NJ: Lawrence and Erlbaum Associates Inc.

Miles, M. B., & Huberman, A. M. (1994). *Qualitative data analysis: An expanded sourcebook.* Thousand Oak, CA: Sage.

Ministry of Education, Youth & Sports. (2004). *Ghana's performance in TIMSS 2003.* Accra, Ghana: Ghana Education Service.

Ministry of Education, Science and Sports. (2007a). Teaching syllabus for mathematics (primary school 1-6). Accra, Ghana: Curriculum Research and Development Division.

Ministry of Education, Science and Sports. (2007b). Teaching syllabus for mathematics (junior high school, 1-3). Accra, Ghana: Curriculum Research and Development Division.

Moschkovich, J. (1999). Understanding the needs of Latino students in reform-oriented mathematics classrooms. In L. Ortiz-Franco, N. G. Hernandez, & Y. De La Cruz (Eds.), *Perspectives on Latinos (Changing the faces of mathematics)* (pp. 5-12). Reston, VA: National Council of Teachers of Mathematics.

Moschkovich, J. N. (2002). A situated and sociocultural perspective on bilingual mathematics learners. *Mathematical Thinking and Learning, 4*(2&3), 189-212.

Moschkovich, J. (2007). Using two languages while learning mathematics. *Educational Studies in Mathematics, 64*(2).

Mullis, I. V. S., Martin, M. O., & Foy, P. (2008). *International mathematics report: Findings from IEA's trends in international mathematics and science study at the fourth and eighth grades.* Chestnut Hill: TIMSS & PIRLS International Study Center, Boston College.

Naroth, C. (2010). *Constructive teacher feedback for enhancing learner performance in mathematics.* Unpublished Master's Thesis. Bloemfontein, South Africa: University of Free State.

National Council of Teachers of Mathematics. (1991). *Professional standards for teaching mathematics.* Reston, VA: Author.

Nicol, C. (2005). Exploring mathematics in imaginative places: Rethinking what counts as meaningful contents for learning mathematics. *School Science and Mathematics, 105*(5), 240.

Nordin, A. B. (2005). *Students' perceptions on teaching and learning mathematics in English.* Accessible from http://www.eprints.utm.mg/1507/1KERTASINT.pdf

Obanya, P. (1980). Research on alternative teaching in Africa. In E. A Yoloye & K. H. Flechsig (Eds.), *Educational research for development* (pp. 67-112). Bonn, Germany: Deutsche Stiftung für Internationale Entwicklung.

Okpoti, C.A. (2001). Ethnomathematics: What is it? *Mathematics Connection, 2,* 57-60.

Ottevanger, W., van den Akker, J. J. H., & de Feiter, L. (2007). *Developing science, mathematics and ICT education in sub-Saharan Africa (SMICT): Patterns and promising practices.* Paper presented at the World Bank Working Paper.

Owu-Ewie, C. (2006). The language policy of education in Ghana: A critical look at English-only language policy of education. In J. Magame, J. P. Hutchison, & D. A. Worman (Eds.), *Selected*

Proceedings of the 35th Annual Conference on African Linguistics: African languages and linguistics in broad perspectives (pp. 76-85). Somerville, MA: Cascadilla Project.

Parker, C. E., Louie, J., & O'Dwyer, L. (2009). *New measures of English language proficiency and their relationship to performance on large-scale assessments.* Issues & Answers Report, REL. 2009-No. 066. Washington, DC: U.S. Department of Education. Accessed on November 12, 2012 from http://ies.ed.gov/ncee/edlabs/projects/project.asp?projectID=172&productID=125

Pirie, S. (1998). Crossing the gulf between thought and symbol: Language as (slippery) stepping stones. In H. Steinbring, B. Buss, & A. Sierspienska (Eds.), *Language and communication in mathematics classroom* (pp. 7-29). Reston, VA: NCTM.

Polya, G. (1962). *Mathematical discovery* (Volume 2). New York: John Wiley & Sons.

Robinson, C. D. (1996). *Language use in rural development: An African perspective.* The Hague: Mounton de Gruyter.

Rollnick, M., & Manyatsi, S. (1997). Language, culture or disadvantage: What is at the heart of student adjustment to tertiary chemistry. In *Proceedings of the Fifth Annual Meeting of the Southern African Association for Research in Mathematics and Science Education.* Johannesburg: University of Witwatersrand.

Rowlands, S., & Carson, R. (2000). Ethnomathematics: A liberation from the yoke of Eurocentrism or the biggest disaster that could befall mathematics education. *Proceedings of the British Society for Research into Learning Mathematics, 20*(3), November, 85-90.

Salend, S., & Salinas, A. (2003). Language differences or learning difficulties? *Teaching Exceptional Children,* March/April, 36-43.

Scherting, D. (1988). Making the transition from staff nurse to nurse manager. *ANNA, 15*(6), 369.

Schleppegrell, M. J. (2007). The linguistic challenges of mathematics teaching and learning: A research review. *Reading and Writing Quarterly, 23,* 139-159.

Setati, M. (1998). Code-switching in senior primary class of second language learners. *For Learning of Mathematics, 18*(2), 114-160.

Setati, M. (2002). Researching mathematics education and language in multilingual South Africa. *The Mathematics Educator, 12*(2), 6-20.

Setati, M. (2005a). Teaching mathematics in a primary multilingual classroom. *Journal for Research in Mathematics Education, 36*(5), 447-488.

Setati, M. (2005b). Power and access in multilingual mathematics classrooms. In M. Goos, C. Kanes, & R. Brown (Eds.), *Proceedings of the Fourth International Mathematics Education and Society Conference* (pp. 7-18). Brisbane: Centre for Learning Research, Griffith University.

Setati, M., & Adler, J. (2001). Between languages and discourses: Language practices in primary multilingual mathematics classrooms in South Africa. *Educational Studies in Mathematics, 43,* 243-269.

Setati, M., & Barwell, R. (2006). Discursive practices in two multilingual mathematics classrooms: An international comparison. *African Journal for Research in Mathematics Science and Technology Education, 10*(2), 27-38.

Shakur, N. (2009). Perspectives on language and thought: A critique. *International Research Journal of Arts & Humanities, 37*(37), 49-61.

Shulman, L. (1986). Those who understand: Knowledge growth in teaching. *Educational Researcher, 15*(2), 414-422.

Slezak, P. (2002). Thinking about thinking: Language, thought and introspection. *Language and Communication, 22,* 353-373.

Steinberg, D. D. (1982). *Psycholinguistics: Language, mind and world.* New York: Longman.

Stoddart, K. (2001). People like us: Memories of marginality in high school and university. *Qualitative Inquiry, 7*(2), 171-191.

Sua, T. Y., & Raman, S. R. (2007). Problems and challenges of learning through a second language: The case of teaching science and mathematics in English in the Malaysian primary schools. *Kajian Malaysia Jid, XXV*(2), 129-154.

Tenni, C., Smyth, A., & Boucher, C. (2003, March). The researcher as autobiographer: Analysing data written about oneself. *The Qualitative Report, 8*(1). Retrieved October 11, 2012 from http://www.nova.edu/ssss/QR/QR8-1/.html

Thomas, N. J. T. (2004). *Imagination.* Retrieved May 22, 2007, from http://www.imagery-imagination.com/

Tood, L. (1988). Language options for education in a biligual society: Cameron. In C. Kennedy (Ed.), *Language planning and language education* (pp. 160-171). London: George Allen & Unwin.

Weissglass, J. (2002). Inequity in mathematics education: Questions for educators. *The Mathematics Educator, 12*(2), 34-39.

West African Examination Council (WAEC). (2006). *Chief examiners' report on basic examination certificate examination: 2006 mathematics.* Accra, Ghana: Author.

Whale, S. G. (2012). *Using language as a resource: Strategies to teach mathematics in multilingual classes.* Unpublished Master's Thesis. Port Elizabeth, South Africa: Nelson Mandela Metropolitan University

Wilcox, S., Lanier, P., Schram, P., & Lappan, G (1992). *Influencing beginning teachers' practice in mathematics education: Confronting constraints of knowledge, beliefs, and context.* Research report 92-1. East Lansing, MI: The National Center for Research on Teacher Learning, Michigan State University.

Williams, E. (1996). Reading in two languages at year 5 in African primary schools. *Applied Linguistics, 17*, 182-209.

Wilson, B. (1992). Mathematics education in Africa. In R. Morris & M. S. Arora (Eds.), *Studies in mathematics education: Moving into the twenty first century* (Vol. 8, pp. 125-147). Paris: UNESCO.

Wolf, E. (2011). Background and history-language politics and planning in Africa. In A. Ouane & C. Glanz (Eds.), *Optimizing learning: Education and publishing in Africa: The language factor* (pp. 49-102). Hamburg, Germany: UNESCO Institute of Lifelong Learning.

Yin, R. K. (2003). *Case study research: Design and methods.* Thousand, Oaks, CA: Sage.

Yost, D. S., Sentner, S. M., & Forlenza-Bailey, A. (2000). An examination of construct of critical reflection: Implications for teacher education programming in the twenty-first century. *Journal of Teacher Education, 5*(1), 39-48.

Yushau, B. (2004). *The role of language in teaching and learning of mathematics.* Technical Report Series (TR3181). Dhahran, Saudi Arabia: Department of Mathematical Sciences. King Fahd University of Petroleum and Minerals.

Yusuf, M. W., Saidu, I., & Halliru, A. (2010). Ethnomathematics: A mathematical game in Hausa culture. *Sutra: International Journal of Mathematical Science Education, 3*(1), 36-42.

Zevenbergen, R. (2001). Mathematics, social class and linguistic capital: An analysis of mathematics classroom interactions. In B. Atweh, H. Forgasz, & B. Nebres (Eds.), *Sociocultural research on mathematics education: An international research perspective* (pp. 201-216). Mahwah, NJ: Lawrence Erlbaum Associates.

Zevenbergen, R. (2008). The dilemmas of indigenous education: The passion for ignorance. In J. F Motos, P. Valero, & K. Yasukawa (Eds.), *Proceedings of the Fifth International Mathematics Education and Society Conference* (pp. 505-514). Albufeira, Portugal, February 16-21th.

GEORGE J. SEFA DEI

13. INDIGENIZING THE SCHOOL CURRICULUM

The Case of the African University

INTRODUCTION

This chapter might have been titled the "African academy" since the issues I speak
about could very well apply to schools, colleges, and universities in Africa. Let me
stick with the university, though it is important for the reader to work with the
interplay of the schools, colleges, and universities in thinking about what the
academy actually is. I also bring a broad view of education in terms of engaging
local, community, and off-school knowledges (which are rooted in the African
Indigeneity) in both formal and informal sites as part of the processes of a re-
reading the 'school curriculum.' Such Indigenous knowledges take the learner to
history, culture, tradition, past, and identity as both contested, concrete, and
meaningful to how we come to de-colonize the school/university curriculum and
create social and academic excellence. This chapter calls for an authentic African
education for the African learner. Authenticity should not be understood as
something pure and uncontaminated, but rather remaining true to ourselves as
African learners rooted in history, culture, past, tradition and with an African
identity/identities.

So I begin with a question: Has the African university lived up to the high
expectations as a centre of higher learning and excellence for the promotion of
African development? There is a reason for asking this simple question. Clearly,
among many there is some disquiet and disappointment with the African
university's role today. While excellence is considered to be a hallmark of the
university, there is some concern as to whether this excellence is really making an
impact on local communities. This leads us to an interrogation of what we mean by
excellence. No doubt, the African university is and should be a place of high
excellence. While the term "excellence" in teaching, research, and professional
development is contested, it cannot be denied there is a particular understanding of
excellence that reigns in the African university. With some exceptions, it is
excellence defined in terms of a validation with Western intellectual codes, norms,
and accreditation. How do we begin to think broadly about excellence in university
education that addresses foremost the needs, aspirations, and knowledge systems of
African peoples and, in particular, start from what African peoples and their
communities know? Notwithstanding the merits and benefits, the pursuit of the
internationalization of higher education has come with some negative results. And,
yet we hardly speak about this. Singh (2010) notes that among the effects and
consequences of internationalization, the potential for increasing the hegemony of

G. Emeagwali & G. J. S. Dei (eds.), African Indigenous Knowledge and the Disciplines, 165–180.
© *2014 Sense Publishers. All rights reserved.*

Western knowledge, cultural values, and languages at the expense of Indigenous knowledges and languages exists (Assie-Lumumba, 2006; Dei 2011a). Furthermore, a skepticism towards African cultural norms, identities, and local languages can develop (Brock-Tune, 2003; Barasa, 2009) as well as the trend towards cultural homogenisation (Knight, 2008), curriculum homogenization, standardization, and loss of cultural identity (Jowi, 2009) (see also Teferra & Altbach, 2004). In fact, a neo-liberal agenda of education has only intensified these costs. In rethinking the African university today and, specifically, Indigenizing the curriculum the question of how contemporary learners can be assisted in using African local and Indigenous knowledges to solve everyday problems is important. There are merits in working with and learning from knowledge one is most familiar with. Thus, I want us to bring an African-centred interpretation to excellence in terms of how the university prepares learners to be best able to help local communities solve pressing social issues using African knowledge and values. Notwithstanding the contestations and disagreements of scholarship/research/teaching and the ways university curriculum work with local and Indigenous knowledge, the critical role of the African university in leading the charge for development and social change in Africa cannot be underestimated. For many years now there has been scholarly treatise on how African universities have discharged, or failed to discharge, the enormous social and intellectual responsibilities placed on its shoulders. Perhaps much of the frustration in the critiques of the contemporary African university today can be summed up as a perceived failure to centre the African human condition in the intellectual and scholarly pursuits, whether through teaching, research, or dissemination of knowledge. This may stem from the fact that the university curriculum is by and large still caught in the tentacles of Eurocentric knowledge production. Some key questions have not received enough attention. For example, how do we [as African learners, scholars, and researchers] pioneer, cultivate, and sustain new analytical, conceptual, and methodological systems for understanding our Indigenous African communities (Yankah, 2004)? What do we see as the place and role of Indigenous and local knowledges in helping to Africanize the curriculum? What does it mean to Africanize the school curriculum? What are the implications for rethinking schooling and education in Africa?

And, how do we connect the pursuit of anti-colonial education with curriculum changes?

This chapter adopts a working definition of Indigenous knowledge as the knowledge of local African peoples rooted in our rich histories, cultures, and traditions through time. It is knowledge associated with "long-term occupancy" of the African land. Such knowledge is deeply rooted in the understanding of society, nature, and culture, as well as an experiencing of the social and natural worlds (see also Fals-Borda, 1991; Ermine, 1995; Kincheloe & Steinberg, 2008; Purcell, 1998; Semali & Kincheloe, 1999; Battiste & Youngblood Henderson, 2000; Dei, 2000). The "Indigenous" is about unbroken residence and the knowledge that comes with such a length of time. Indigenous is about land, place, body, and politics. While local knowledge addresses knowledge localized in a place, the question of land, connections with spirit and metaphysical realms of existence of a place, is central to a conception of Indigenous.

Africa had its Indigenous knowledge before the advent of colonialism. While colonialism and Euro-modernity have changed this body of knowledge, it has not been lost, but has been transformed to suit emerging contexts, situations, and challenges. Indigenous peoples possess Indigenous knowledges but one does not have to be Indigenous to work with such knowledge. In other words, in terms of the application, Indigenous knowledge is not for the sole use of Indigenous peoples.

African Indigenous knowledges speak to a local cultural resource knowledge base expressive of ideas, norms, cultural knowledges, and philosophies possessed by local peoples/communities concerning realities of everyday living and survival (e.g., oral histories, traditions, and proverbs, etc.). Borrowing from Castellano's (2000) categorization, I see such Indigenous knowledges as made up of traditional knowledge (i.e., inter-generational knowledge of communities); empirical knowledge (i.e., knowledge based on careful observations of their surrounding environments); and revealed knowledge (i.e., knowledges acquired through intuition, revelations, dreams, and visions). Such knowledge is also constitutive of land/earth teachings as well as spiritual knowings understood relationally in terms of the interface of self, personhood, and connections of the inner/outer space and environments. Such knowledge works with a cosmo-vision focusing on the inter-relationships and connectedness between physical and metaphysical realms of life. Such knowledge base recognizes emotions, spiritual essence, and intuition as a significant way of knowing and usually uses the personal histories, stories, and individual experiences/epiphanies as sources/entry points of teaching and knowing. It is called Indigenous because it is knowledge local to a place and to a given context through history and cultural memory and was developed in association with the land.

In this chapter, I envision a way of educating the African learner today where Indigenous knowledge will no longer be ignored, neglected, or misapplied. I place the discussion of African Indigenous knowledge in the broader challenge of Africanizing the 'school' (defined broadly to include schools, colleges, and universities) curriculum. This is an uphill intellectual task particularly given that Indigenous knowledges of Africa have hardly been emphasized in the conventional school curriculum. In order to bring the issues of local/traditional and Indigenous knowledges to the fore, this chapter will also highlight questions about de-coloniality, alternative forms of schooling and the necessity for African educators and learners to embrace a "political-epistemic potential" for educational change. How do we embrace a project of Africanizing the school curriculum through critical de-colonial pedagogies? The task requires the interpellation of educational domains grounded within a critique of the structures of schooling and educational delivery. This will include challenging the internalization of colonial difference and the 'banality of inclusion,' affirmations of de-colonial and anti-colonial pedagogies of African schooling and education, an understanding of the goals and objectives of education for young African learners, and an understanding of how culture and history can be fashioned to satisfy the interest of contemporary schooling. Africanizing the schooling curriculum also requires an interrogation of what constitutes Eurocentric understandings of history, modernity, and belonging.

INDIGINEITY AND AFRICAN EDUCATION

Among the philosophical principles for advocating Indigeneity in African education, specifically in the Africanization of school/university curriculum (for African youth education), one can point to ideas about voice affirmation, authenticity of selves, epistemic saliency of the African experience, recognition of the intellectual agency of African subjects, and the validity of learning beyond oneself and the self-referential. Indigenous knowledge is about representation of culture, history, local experience, and the teachings of land and socio-physical environments of communities. While conventional school curriculums purport to strive for the inclusion of different knowledges, experiences, and identities in the delivery of education, what we actually see is a banality of inclusion, including the institutionalization of [in]visibility of certain bodies and experiences, and a culture of hierarchies of people, knowledges, values, histories, and knowledges in the school curriculum (see also Da Costa, 2012).

Promoting Indigenous African languages in schools, colleges, and African universities is key to the success of a decolonized, inclusive education for all learners. Language is about the culture and identity as well as enhancing the self and collective esteem of African learners. Indigenous languages also become a site of resistance to the dominance of the colonial/imperial language, English. It is through language that African culture is learned and transmitted. There must be a family/community and school interface that will facilitate the introduction of local/indigenous knowledges in schools to create learning sites of different and multiple knowledges. There is a depth and wealth of family/community knowledge that schools can tap into. Given that Indigenous/traditional Africa has always been about "community," schools, colleges, and universities can work with an understanding of the African community as "communities of differences" with knowledge systems that can enhance learning for all. This is possible through a collective learning and the sharing of ideas and shared responsibilities, whereby learners have responsibilities to/for each other's learning. This is the only way to create collective success.

While Indigenous knowledge is context-specific, it seeks to promote holistic learning and education. By promoting Indigenous knowledges in the academy it becomes easier for schools, colleges, and universities to teach about African identity/identities in a way that is not constructed within a Euro-American hegemony, but as something rooted in the African sense of self, collective, culture, as well as the past, present, and the future. Such understanding of the African identity can be linked to knowledge production while simultaneously addressing such identities (ethnicity, gender, class, sexuality, [dis]ability, language, religion, spirituality) as sites of difference, power, and marginalization. The African identity/identities can also be conceptualized as a relationship to land, place, and spirit (i.e., concepts of self/personhood as relational and respectful of the relationship to a Creator, Mother Earth, Self/Other and the inner and outer connections), as well as claiming of an identity to have a sense of purpose and deeper meaning in life.

African Indigenous knowledges as educational philosophy are more complex than students are often taught to understand and appreciate. In fact we have a number of African scholars who will even dismiss such knowledges as authentic 'knowledge.' African students' flawed perceptions of such knowledges can be traced in large measure to the absence of critical thinking in schools (see also Letseka, 2012). But the introduction of African Indigenous knowledge systems in the university curriculum should be viewed as a project of the Africanisation of the academy. The African university is a colonial satellite of the Western academy. Working with Indigenous and local knowledges as a philosophy of education is a good basis for rethinking African schooling and education. It is important for critical African scholars to focus on the connections between African philosophies of education and Indigenous epistemologies. We need to address how we concretely present African philosophies of education using local and Indigenous knowledges (in terms of teaching, learning, and administration of education) as a decolonizing platform for students and educators. There is a lot to be learned from African ideas about connections with life systems.

Long ago, African learners raised the challenge for the African academy to "root their educational paradigms in Indigenous socio-cultural and epistemological framework" (van Wyk & Higgs, 2007, p. 62). African Indigenous philosophy must be re-visioned and rearticulated through the embodiment of different peoples and through different geographies. In Africanizing the university curriculum, educators must begin to conceptualize 'Indigenous' broadly – to implicate multiple bodies, spaces, and locations. I am aware of recent calls for the university to be rooted in the community and to have a community-based university, a sort of African multiversity (MPAMBO) (see Wangoola, 2000). The study of African Indigenous knowledge may call for bringing Elders, cultural custodians, parents, and Indigenous thinkers/sages into the university, to acknowledge and act on the central place of African spirituality in the schooling and education of the learner. African ways of knowing, systems of thought and/or life systems are more that concepts, idioms, and cultural expressions. Sages are informed by culture as a knowledge system. As Letseka (2012) argues, African systems of thought have their own internal logics, local sense-making and augmentation, innovation, Indigenous interpretations of evidence, rationality, reason, and criticality. These knowings are steeped in cultural-specific paradigms, including, but not limited to, community and communal interdependence conveyed through wisdom of sages as 'Indigenous thinkers,' and also laced in local parables, fables, folktales, proverbs, songs, cultural stories, myths, and mythologies.

DECOLONIZING EDUCATION AS A THEORY OF CHANGE
OF THE UNIVERSITY CURRICULUM

Given European colonialism, any attempt to Africanize the university curriculum must be through anti-colonial and decolonizing pedagogies. Such pedagogies are fraught with risks, entail claims of Indigeneity and the reclaiming of the spiritual, culture, and identity. Fanon (1963, 1967) reminded us long ago that the issues of decolonization have not yet been addressed because colonization is itself ongoing, and that the violence of the colonial encounter makes decolonization necessary. As decolonization emerges from colonization it must be rooted in a critical archeology and dialecticism of the past, culture, and history. It is the understanding of this dialecticism that fosters resistance. In this sense, resistance is about survival for the colonized body.

Just as decolonization can be discussed in its multifaceted forms given the tropes of colonialism, capitalism, and imperialism, there are many paths to decolonization. There is a dynamic of domination such that the colonized/oppressed abandon their culture, history, and past and further assume that of the colonizer/dominant. And yet through educational and political insurgency there is hope that the colonized will come to abandon the assumed dominant culture to embrace a new emancipatory culture (see Fanon 1963, 1967). I will argue that such political mobilization produced by colonization would emerge from critical learners and educators equipped to ask new and challenging questions of the status quo. I also agree with Ponniah (2012) that such mobilizations would not necessarily come from the most disadvantaged. They emerge from sectors with "collective institutions, a tradition of activism and … alternative symbolic order" whose resistance is "informed by an image of another, potentially more fulfilling world" (Ponniah, 2012). Decolonization should be about developing a critical consciousness of one self, place, history, identity, culture and politics, not about mainstreaming educational practices.

In rethinking schooling and education at the African university we must understand what is meant by the curriculum. The curriculum is not simply a given/mandated text for the educator to work with. The curriculum is a social construction of what skills, talents, knowledge, and capabilities the academy is supposed to bestow on the "educated learner." Given that the curriculum is constructed to be in line with the social values of the dominant in our communities, it becomes a site of resistance to produce educational change. In effect, educators and learners must begin to see and think of the curriculum in terms of the limitations and possibilities for change. Decolonization is only possible if the curriculum equips the learner to ask questions about omissions, negations, devaluations, and absences from texts, pedagogies, instruction, and the social and physical landscapes of the university. The school/university curriculum is broad, encompassing the hidden and tacit elements of the academy. Curriculum is about everything in the school system (e.g., a particular order of society; a path to follow, a course of action to take, etc.; Apple, 2004; Giroux, Penna, & Pinar, 1981) Curriculum includes the official written rules and regulations of the school, as well as the hidden norms and unwritten codes and stipulations. The 'Deep Curriculum' (Dei et al., 1997) includes culture, climate, environment, and the social organizational lives of schools, including the texts, instruction and pedagogies. The curriculum is power-saturated and involves the power to construct, validate, and legitimize knowledge, and what is acceptable and not. Furthermore, curriculum is about values, ideas, practices, as well as identities [race/ethnicity, class, gender, sexuality, disability etc.] and how knowledge production is linked to identities, power relations, and pedagogy. Curriculum and instruction go hand in hand. In fact they are interlocking and interdependent. One cannot and does not function in isolation. Curriculum speaks to the selection and engagement of texts, what mode of instruction and pedagogies are used to convey meanings of texts, and how experiences of students and teachers become central to knowledge production.

In another paper (Dei, 2013) I argue that fundamentally, 'decolonizing the curriculum' involves three central tenets – the idea of "Multi-centricity," "Indigeneity," and "Reflexivity." These tenets are appropriate and applicable across disciplines. A multi-centric approach is about cultivating multiple ways of knowing while working with the idea of multiple centres of scholarship. Regarding 'multi-centricity,' there is a need to fully recognize multiple civilizations as producers of knowledge systems of the world. Undertaking a multi-centric or polycentric approach to curriculum requires a critical review of university curricular in order to identify any universalizations of particular knowledges. For example, political science theory should not only explore Western democracy at the expense of excluding the ideas and practices of other civilizations like Chinese, Egyptian, Indian, and Mayan. Teaching political science in the African university will require that educators start from an understanding of Indigenous African political institutions and organization, and connecting the knowledge to the social theory of political studies. Furthermore, students should be encouraged to establish dialogic relations between these sets of ideas and practices of African peoples and other global communities in the realm of political studies. An important lesson from African systems of knowledges that is often omitted from Western political science theory is how politics is inseparable from economics, religion, spirituality, and the physical and metaphysical realms of life.

Indigeneity is both about identity and a process of coming to know. Consequently, Indigeneity is about Indigenous knowings. Indigeneity emphasizes students as active knowers and the relationship to land as an important source of teaching (i.e., land/earth teachings). Instead of perpetuating the lineage of European scholarship and practice, Indigenous education should reflect the lived experience and life situation of our students. It is almost impossible to capture and cover all ideas that have emerged from thousands years of human civilization in the past, nor is it conducive to students' intellectual development for the future. But by contextualizating education to land, the learner is offered a new understanding of what it means to become educated. The starting point and the finish line of education should be students' immediate life experience and local contexts. The African learner must first approach learning from his or her surrounding environments and contexts. Such context becomes a source of identity and a process of coming to know. Such education requires a problem- and contextual-based learning, as well as inquiry-based teaching for social action and practice. Education helps the learner deal with the challenges confronted as they experience life in their social contexts. We must recognize that education and the knowledge we have today, say in the field of engineering, might no longer be applicable and relevant in five years because of the rapid rate of technological advancements and innovation. The only way to equip the learners of tomorrow is to teach them how to problem-solve and develop the critical skills they require to adapt to rapid change.

Reflexivity means to reconnect individual and environment, self and society, identity and reality in social and scientific inquiry. Every discipline, be it humanities, pure science, medicine or professional training, should include the interrogation of interconnectivity of the self and the external world, and our responsibilities to our social, physical, and ecological environment. Reflection, particularly in the field of education, allows the African practitioner to think about what works, what does not work, what can be changed next time with this lesson plan/curricula, and how what the learner is doing is applicable to their daily practice. We need to ensure the theory and practice of reflexivity be included in the African school curricular. Practically, reflections could be completed by the means of reflective journal, creative group inquiry, or mentorship. Reflexivity in education helps to capture suppressed local cultures and the hidden rules, norms, and assumptions of schooling. Through reflexivity, educators bring integrity and a sense of purpose and meaning to their curricular and pedagogical practices.

RESEARCH AS AN AFRICANIZATION OF KNOWLEDGE

In Africanizing the university curriculum by centering African Indigenous knowledges, the question of research comes up. Research refers primarily to an approach to academic/scholarly inquiry. I take Indigenous research as the engagement of particular methodologies and methodological approaches that are African-centred in ensuring the particular aims, objectives, scope, and practices of what constitutes African scholarship. In viewing research as a way to produce, interrogate, validate, and disseminate knowledge there are clear differences as to what constitutes conventional 'academic'/Western research and Indigenous [African] research (see Dei, 2013b).

What then constitutes research in/on Indigenous African communities? The question is best answered by creating spaces for scholarly engagement and critical debate about teaching in Africa. There are some conceptual and practical grounds for developing a critical discursive approach that can under-gird the pursuit of Indigenous African research at the university. As Indigenous African scholars, researchers, and students, we need to establish new intellectual paradigms for the study of our communities. We must develop a critical research practice by first looking for and understanding local specificities of our knowledge systems. This sounds a caution against mainstreaming Indigenous African research and knowledges. While one may be interested in multiple approaches to research and knowledge production, I would also ask: How does a trans/multi-disciplinary approach to the co-evolution of knowledges and research methods truly rupture power relations of knowledge production in the academy? Is the approach to knowledge synthesis when it comes to research a necessary intellectual exercise for our decolonization as Indigenous African academics and students struggling to shed ourselves from the sway of Western humanist ideologies and research practices? If we are talking about parallel bodies of knowledges [not synthesis or integration], how do we challenge the dominance of Eurocentric knowledge and its tendency to devalue other bodies of thought and local communities (see also Dei, 2013)?

All knowledges borrow from each other. Cree scholar Margaret Kovach (2009) positions her work as being "premised on a belief that nested within any methodology is both a knowledge belief system (encompassing ontology and epistemology) and the actual methods" (p. 25). She also highlights that a significant site of struggle for Indigenous researchers will be at the level of epistemology, because Indigenous epistemologies challenge the very core of knowledge production and purpose (p. 29). As such, there also needs to be a recognition of the fact that there is the "incommensurability of certain knowledges." We must recognize that there exists some philosophical differences among knowledges and Indigenous research works with particular conceptual understandings that do not overlap or borrow from each other. This often presents a dilemma when we speak of Indigenous research in the context of Western science and knowledge production.

Eva Marie Garroutte (2003) presents an approach to American Indian scholarship that she has named "radical Indigenism." A she explains, "[i]t argues for the reassertion and rebuilding of traditional knowledge from its roots, its fundamental principles" (p. 101). From time immemorial Indigenous Peoples have always studied, analyzed, interpreted, and communicated their cultural and natural surroundings to themselves and to others. Their methods of knowledge production could only have been possible through a coherent research that in many cases was different from mainstream colonial research in terms of objectives. This has implications for research into Indigenous African knowledges. Indigenous African research should entail, and in fact, necessitates African scholars define our work so as to have community relevance and seek change. This is always difficult in the academy where we are constantly asked to separate our scholarship from political activism. As Indigenous African researchers, we do not stand apart from our local communities. After all, our communities help sustain us in the brutal world of the academy.

Indigenous African research must be a search for local/Indigenous/cultural knowledge production. Indigenous research requires a researcher to bring an embodied connection to the production of knowledges. Such embodied connection is more than a plea not to intellectually detach/distance ourselves from the knowledge we produce. It is about engaging in research that not only speaks of our experiential embodied knowledges and how these knowledges speak about our social realities, but that also helps address key questions of responsibility and ethics in the use and pursuit of knowledge.

[RE]SOURCING AFRICAN INDIGENOUS KNOWLEDGES

Indigenous African knowledges have for far too long been negated, ignored, and/or devalued in the academy. Promoting education about Indigenous people's ways of knowing is more than a challenge to the power of "modern science." Traditional lifestyles do not remain static or frozen in time and place, but are in continuous change to address contemporary challenges. Such knowledge forms can never be dismissed nor forgotten. The approach to Africanizing the university curriculum should work with the dynamism of all knowledges, while recognizing some uniqueness of locally contextualized knowledge and knowing. Such knowledge constitutes part of the Indigenous science, technology, and culture of African peoples. For example, there are Indigenous methods and systems of soil classification that point to types of soil and what they are used for. With a local nomenclature they can be taught to students as part of teaching geography, environmental studies, biological sciences, etc. Such local knowledge has been part of the cultural system from time immemorial and it has served local communities as they experience the vagaries of local environments. Local knowledge about the uses of soils and vegetation patterns have been helpful in farming and subsistence practices, as well as local architecture and housing. Embedded in such knowledge is an understanding that society, nature, and culture interface, and the particular responsibilities required of African peoples in maintaining and sustaining their local environments.

In the area of local plant pharmacology, a wide variety of plant species and their uses within local environments are well-known. Such knowledge can be documented and fed into the school curriculum to teach about Indigenous health and health prevention. Many of the bush plants have medicinal purposes and, in an era of rising costs for Western medicine, many communities have found it prudent to rely on local herbs for treatment of simple ailments and diseases. The study of local pharmacology is a study of Indigenous science. Integrating local knowledge about plants and herbs into the university curriculum can assist in the education of young learners who may not necessarily become medical doctors or health practitioners. But equipping learners with such knowledge goes a long way in promoting science education as well as offering preventive cure for community ailments. Learners are also able to learn more about their local environments/ ecology. This is a form of contextual learning that is very much needed within African schools, colleges, and universities in order to make education relevant to the needs of local communities. The delivery of such education can also be less expensive as it situates learners in their communities to pursue relevant knowledge. Indigenous knowledge of medicinal plants (which includes information of the different classifications and functions of plants) have been developed on the basis of careful observations and experimentation in local habitats. As noted in Dei (2011), these knowledges go way back to ancestral times and they are continually subjected to improvements and adaptations. Such a body of knowledge as traditional pharmacology is often contextualized in the community's historical experience with local health and illness situations and has been confirmed by their common usage and societal norms.

Taboos, religious rites, and cultural rituals offer another important entry point to engaging Indigenous knowledge in the school curriculum. They are encoded in the cultural system of local communities. They offer lessons in history, spirituality, sports, games, the environment and sustainable forest use, as well as political studies. Indigenous knowledge recognizes the important role of local peoples in preserving ecological balance and biodiversity. This is related to maintaining local health and well-being. There are customary laws, such as cultural taboos, rites, and rituals governing individual and community use of resources and land. These customary practices and belief systems form a built-in protection mechanism for over-exploitation of natural resources. Within local communities, certain forest areas are considered sacred (e.g., sacred groves), and individuals are either not permitted into them or are allowed to go into them on specified days. Similarly, there are restrictions on the use of some forest resources. Documentation of the knowledge base behind local taboos, rituals, resources and their usage, the history and traditions, social relations and details about who has access to what, and why, are all important information to teach not only about culture and history, but also Indigenous science, biology, arts, and technology. As noted in Dei (2011b), local ecological sustainability works when Indigenous peoples maintain ownership status of their resources, where they can freely adopt local strategies of conservation, regeneration and distribution and control of resources. A careful study of such knowledges in the school/university curriculum will point the learner to social integrity and communal ethics, as well as the sophistication, complexity, and intellectual resource knowledge of Indigenous African communities.

Notwithstanding their differences, the oral culture, proverbs, riddles, story forms, cultural songs and stories, myths and mythologies, folktales and other folkloric productions all constitute part of African Indigenous knowledge systems. African proverbs, riddles, and folktales help establish the basis of a peoples' cosmology/worldview, or 'worldsense' (Oyewumi, 1997), stressing the under-pinnings of a social value system. There is a method and methodology of coming to know, understand, and interpret such knowledges. Proverbs, riddles, and folktales reveal different levels of intellectual sophistication and depth and represent a philosophy of life. They are embedded in customary teachings and wise sayings about social action and daily practice. As everyday cultural knowings they point to the power and relevance of intercultural communication. The power of such cultural sayings and knowings is that they allow the learner to grow mentally, spiritually, and morally into adulthood.

As part of African philosophies, the body of epistemology espoused in proverbs, riddles, and folktales connect place, spirit, and body and relate to the concept of self and the community, responsibility, respect for oneself, peers, and authority, and mutual interdependence and community-building. Such teachings have a place in school curricular, as well as pedagogical and instructional initiatives to enhance youth learning. Introducing such Indigenous knowledge in the school curriculum will not only bring in Indigenous languages in the education of young learners, but will also convey teachings about the learners' social responsibility, respect for elders and authority, the importance of developing strong moral character, self-discipline and collective accountability. Given the intellectual sophistication that is needed to unravel the meanings of proverbs and particularly riddles, such knowledges have the potential to educate the youth about some of the complex challenges facing local communities today.

Traditional handicrafts are another area where educators can source Indigenous African knowledge and integrate it into classroom teaching for young learners. Local artisans are a source of Indigenous knowledge in many African communities. The study of local arts and crafts such as pot making, basket weaving, blacksmithing, woodworking, hunting, painting, stone quarrying, and children's games offer important knowledges around culture, politics, spirituality, social organizational life of local communities, local mathematics and science, geometry, and history. This can be documented, studied, and taught in schools, colleges, and universities. For example, architectural and artistic designs and symbols in local communities have local interpretations. When children play traditional games, their antics and the rules of the game have been taught to them by adults as part of the socialization process. There are important lessons about social and moral conduct, artistic expressions and traditional handicrafts conveyed in these games. The craftsperson's work is normally seen as sacred activity with ethical rules of conduct. There are rules of apprenticeship very much tied to the cultural, political, and social ecologies of communities. Geometric designs seen in basket weaving, pottery making, and other art works can be entry points to teaching Indigenous mathematics to young learners. Understanding how traditional handicrafts fit into the local culture and cultural systems and the deeply embedded meanings behind local artwork (such as figurines and bronze casting) can point to the interface between social and physical environments. Handicrafts and artworks are significant sources of information on social and political relations in communities. How and where are such knowledges transmitted among groups and across generations? How are apprenticeships developed? What are cultural custodians and what place do they occupy in the local culture and the community's history and traditions? These are among the questions that can be explored as educators seek to include such local knowledge into the educational curriculum. African education must be able to tap into such wealth of Indigenous knowledge in order to ground experiential learning for students.

CONCLUSION: PRACTICAL STRATEGIES FOR AFRICANIZING THE
SCHOOL/UNIVERSITY CURRICULUM

In the final section of this chapter I suggest some practical ways of infusing Indigenous knowledges into the school/university curriculum. I want us to move away from the idea that the academy as it is set up today is not conducive to teaching Indigenous knowledges given, in part, its hierarchical ordering of knowledge, bodies, experiences, and representations. While it is important for us to rethink the spaces and sites for Indigenous knowledge education, I maintain that this is not an either/or approach. We must remake and create our institutions anew. But there must also be a parallel response strategy/approach that speaks to ways of integrating different knowledges so that we have a synthesis or a co-existence of multiple bodies of knowledge circulating as part of the contestations of knowledge systems. While I am aware that it is problematic to simply graft Indigenous knowledges on to a dominant culture of science, such that the former merely becomes an appendage while the dominant structure and system maintains its place, I have always argued for a multi-centric learning space (see Dei, 1996). This idea of multi-centricity, at least theoretically, undoes the existence of one dominant or hegemonic centre.

African universities need concerted and systematic educational efforts to research and document our Indigenous knowledges from everyday local practices in order to develop curriculum units for the respective disciplines. This can be initiated through the establishment of Centres of Excellence in Indigenous knowledge and African Languages in African universities. However, the exercise to integrate Indigenous bodies of knowledge into the school curriculum cannot be left for the Centres of Excellence alone. It is important for all subject fields in the social and natural sciences, arts, and humanities to explore, research, and document ways of integrating African Indigenous knowledges into their respective course offerings and class teachings. In other words, Indigenous knowledge cannot be taught as a separate area of study. The field of Indigenous Studies is relevant in and of itself, but the scholarship of African Indigeneity must be integrated across all disciplines in the African academy.

Steps must be taken to train local educators/lecturers in teaching African Indigenous knowledges. Though part of the problem has always been the extent to which some African scholars go to dismiss their own Indigenous knowledges in the race for acceptance, validation, and legitimacy in the Western academy and their knowledge of Western science, the fact of the matter is there is a privilege that higher education affords. It is privilege doled out because of the proximity (or the perception of proximity) to Whiteness/Western science and the access that this proximity affords the scholar. This mindset and practice must be changed. To move ahead on this suggestion as a practical strategy, it is incumbent upon Universities of Education in Africa to train educators/lecturers about how to teach African Indigenous knowledges in schools, colleges, and universities. Local elders and cultural custodians from various communities can be employed/contracted by universities in this exercise. Furthermore, serious considerations must be given to teaching and promoting our Indigenous languages in schools, colleges, and universities. As already alluded, we cannot teach nor learn African Indigenous knowledges outside of an understanding and appreciation of Indigenous African languages (see Brock-Utne & Skattum, 2009; Prah, 2009).

In the bid to Africanize our universities, the integration of local communities and institutions of higher learning must be pursued to its fullest extent. Since our universities tend to be further apart from our local communities, we need practical ways to ensure our universities are in tune with our local communities. There must be room in our universities for local cultural custodians, artisans, crafts people, traditional herbal practitioners, and local elders and parents to come and teach students. These community educators bring with them local/Indigenous knowledges. They can be engaged either as guest lecturers, community speakers, or visiting professors/tutors etc. Clearly, this entails a rethinking of credentialism and how we accord the merit badge of intellectuality (scholars and researchers) very broadly. Local communities, parents, Chiefs and Elders can be an integral part of the academy and their participation in lectures, seminars, conferences and workshops must be welcomed, not as a token gesture of gracing university occasions, but as legitimate co-producers or co-creators of knowledge. These community educators do a fine job making use of teachable moments and scenarios in everyday life and community living to engage the young learner.

Bringing Indigenous knowledges into the African academy will also mean relying on educational outlets such as concerts, radio, and public forums as sites of education. Students must also be encouraged to use personal everyday experiences in their local communities as part of the exercise of intellectual exchange and the promotion of scholarship. In Dei (2013), I write about what it means to diversify the school curriculum through the infusion of multiple teaching methodologies, pedagogies, and courses. For these teaching strategies to be deemed different, they have to be Indigenously informed. In the aforementioned publication, I also call for a consideration of more dialogical curriculum co-creation involving students, educators, school administrators, and local communities. By engaging community-based people in the process of curriculum creation, it may help ensure that Indigenous and non-conventional ways of knowing can be taken up. Even the whole area of re-conceptualizing the evaluation of students' work is important to address. How do we assess the African learner using non-conventional approaches and Indigenous methods? In bringing Indigenous knowledge into the universities, we may have to consider orality as an equal medium to written text. For example, educators/lecturers can give students opportunity to submit assignments orally in both English and local Indigenous languages. This exercise would still involve articulating theory and praxis, and students must still be able to demonstrate integrating in-class materials and Indigenous resources. Community-based events have always constituted important sites of learning. Students participating in cultural festivals and durbars and other community social events (e.g., child naming and traditional marriage ceremonies, puberty and initiation rites, age sets associations, community cleansing/purification rites, and other aspects of rites of passage, etc.) and then coming back to write or present reflections on these are helpful. It serves as an opportunity to integrate traditional and Indigenous knowledge into what they are learning in schools. Local community events also bring students in more contact with Elders and other parents as "teachers" in communities. Learners must be able to connect community work to their learning for it to be meaningful.

To reiterate, infusing Indigenous knowledges into schools, colleges, and the university curriculum is not going to be easy. There will be resistance to changing the status quo. I have not even addressed some other pressing issues like the current state of local/Indigenous knowledge in the face of globalization and a capitalist modernity whose ideals and ideas run contrary to issues of the Indigenous and Indigeneity. There is also the question of the method and approach to studying such knowledges. But the enormity of the challenge for African institutions of higher learning lies in the fact that the academy itself has been part of a historical process of delegitimizing and invalidating Indigenous knowledges. To be African is not presumed to be Indigenous to a Land and place. It is as if Africa was robbed of its Indigeneity and Indigenousness simply because of colonization! Indigeneity is both about an identity and a process. African scholars and young learners of today have a particular responsibility to challenge this insulting idea. Perhaps it may start with decolonizing the school curriculum and subverting the idea that Western science knowledge is the only knowledge worth pursuing in the Western academy and its colonial satellites.

ACKNOWLEDGEMENT

I am grateful to Kate Partridge of the Department of Humanities, Social Sciences and Justice Education, at the University of Toronto, for reading through, commenting on, and strengthening this chapter.

REFERENCES

Apple, M. (2004). *Ideology and curriculum*. New York: Routledge Falmer.

Assie-Lumumba, N. (2006). *Higher education in Africa: Crisis, reforms and transformation*. CODESRIA Working Paper. Dakar, Senegal: Council for the Development of Social Science Research in Africa.

Barasa, S. (2009). *Accommodative education language policies as a driving force in the internationalisation of higher education*. PowerPoint presentation at the ANIE conference, September 3-4, in Nairobi, Kenya. http://www.anienetwork.org.

Battiste, M., & Youngblood Henderson, J. (2000). What is indigenous knowledge? In *Protecting Indigenous knowledge and Heritage* (pp. 35-56). Saskatoon: Purich.

Brock-Utne, B., & I. Skattum (Eds.). (2009). *Language and education in Africa: A comparative and transdisciplinary analysis*. Oxford: Cambridge University Press.

Castellano, M. B. (2000). Updating Aboriginal traditions of knowledge. In G. J. S. Dei et al. (Eds.), *Indigenous knowledges in global contexts* (pp. 21-36). Toronto: University of Toronto Press.

Da Costa, A. (2012). Contested inclusions: Education reforms and the hyperconsciousness/negation of race. Unpublished paper, Department of Humanities, Social Sciences and Social Justice Education, Ontario Institute for Studies in Education of the University of Toronto (OISE/UT).

Dei, G. J. S. (1996). *Anti-racism education: Theory and practice*. Halifax: Fernwood Publishing.

Dei, G. J. S. (2000). Rethinking the role of indigenous knowledges in the academy. *International Journal of Inclusive Education, 4*(2), 111-132.

Dei, G. J. S. (Ed.). (2011a). *Indigenous philosophies and critical education*. New York: Peter Lang.

Dei, G. J. S. (2011b). Indigenous philosophies and critical education: An introduction. In G. J. S. Dei (Ed.), *Indigenous philosophies and critical education* ((pp. 1-13). New York: Peter Lang.

Dei, G. J. S. (2013). *Critical perspectives on indigenous research*. Socialist Studies, 9 (1).

Dei, G. J. S., Mazzuca, J., McIsaac, E., & and Zine, J. (1997). *Reconstructing > dropout=*. Toronto: University of Toronto Press.

Ermine, W. (1995). Aboriginal epistemology. In M. Battiste & J. Barman (Eds.), *First nations education in Canada: The circle unfolds* (pp. 101-112). Vancouver: UBC Press.

Fals-Borda, O. (1991). Some basic ingredients. In O. Fals-orda & M. A. Rahman (Eds.), *Action and knowledge: Breaking the monopoly with participatory action-research* (pp. 3-12). New York: The Apex Press.

Fanon, F. (1963). *The wretched of the earth.* New York: Grove Press.

Fanon, F. (1967). *Black skin, white masks.* New York: Grove Press.

Garroutte, E. M. (2003). *Real Indians: Identity and the survival of Native America.* Berkeley, CA: University of California Press.

Giroux, H., Penna, A., & Pinar, W. (Eds.). (1981). *Curriculum and instruction: Alternatives in education.* California: McCutchan Publishing.

Jowi, J. O. (2009). Internationalization of higher education in Africa: Developments, emerging trends, issues and policy implications. *Higher Education Policy, 22*(3), 263-281.

Kincheloe, J., &. Steinberg, S. (2008). Indigenous knowledges in education: Complexities, dangers and profound benefits. In N. Y. Denzin & L. T. Smith (Eds.), *Handbook of critical and indigenous methodologies* (pp. 135-156). Los Angeles: Sage Publications.

Knight, J. (2008). The internationalisation of higher education: Complexities and realities. In D. Teferra & J. Knight (Eds.), *Higher education in Africa: The international dimension* (pp. 1-43). Accra: AAU.

Kovach, M. (2009). *Indigenous methodologies: Characteristics, conversations, and contexts.* Toronto: University of Toronto Press.

Letseka, M. M. (2012). *An analysis of undergraduate philosophy of education students' perception of African philosophy.* Unpublished DEd. dissertation, University of South Africa. UNISA.

Oyewumi, O. (1997). *The invention of women: The making an African sense of western gender discourses* (pp. 1-30). Minneapolis: University of Minnesota Press.

Ponniah, T. (2012, September 26). 'White skin, black masks': Rewriting Frantz Fanon's anti-colonial theory. *rabble.ca.* Retrieved from http://rabble.ca/columnists/2012/09/white-skin-black-masks-rewriting-frantz-fanons-anti-colonial-theory

Prah, K. K. (2009). Mother-tongue education in Africa for emancipation and development: Towards the intellectualization of African languages. In B. Brock-Utne & I Skattum (Eds.), *Language and Education in Africa: a comparative and transdisciplinary analysis* (pp. 83-104). Oxford: Cambridge University Press.

Purcell, T. W. (1998). Indigenous knowledge and applied anthropology: Question of definition and direction. *Human Organization, 57*(3), 258-272.

Semali, L., & Kincheloe, J. (Eds.). (1999). Preface and introduction. In *What is indigenous knowledge? Voices from the academy.* New York: Falmer Press.

Singh, M. (2004). Higher education in Africa, international co-operation and GATS. In AAU (Ed.), *The implications of WTO/GATS for higher education in Africa* (pp. 107-118). Accra: AAU.

Teferra, D., & Altbach, P. G. (Eds.). (2004). *African higher education: An international reference handbook.* Bloomington: Indiana University Press,

Van Wyk, B., & Higgs, P. (2007). The call for an African university: A critical reflection. *Higher Education Policy, 20*, 61-71.

Vargas, H. H. C. (2004). Hyperconsciousness of race and its negation: The dialectic of white supremacy in Brazil. *Identities, 11*, 443-470.

Wangoola, P. (2000). MPAMBO: The Africa multivarsity: A philosophy to rekindle the African spirit. In G. J. S. Dei et al. (Eds.), *Indigenous knowledge in global contexts* (pp. 265-277). Toronto: University of Toronto Press.

Yankah, K. (2004). *Globalization and the African scholar.*

CPSIA information can be obtained
at www.ICGtesting.com
Printed in the USA
LVOW10s0641270717
542811LV00005B/54/P

9 789462 097681